Mining and Financial Imperialism

Mining finance houses were substantial public corporations with access to the money market in the City of London, the world's leading capital market for mining. These institutions became dominant at the inception of colonial rule and, in varying forms, remained so throughout the twentieth century.

Drawing on a rich corpus of primary sources, this book analyses the Western colonial origins of the mining industry and its post-colonial legacies in the Central African Copperbelt. It provides insights into the operations of the global business of mining: in particular, how these processes took place, why they were considered desirable by various interest groups, and the impact that these processes continue to have on physical and human environments in parts of the world where they took place. It also turns its gaze to the City of London, looking at who the financiers were and the nature of the power which they wielded. A long-term perspective on mining finance reveals that thus far the colonial governments have been the main focus in the history of imperialism in Central Africa, with little focus in many instances on the mining finance houses which have outlived them.

The book is a significant contribution to the economic, financial and business history of mining and extractive industries, Central Africa, the City of London and early forms of financial capitalism.

Timo Särkkä is a Senior Researcher at the Department of History and Ethnology, University of Jyväskylä, Finland. He teaches and publishes in the fields of imperial and global history.

Routledge Explorations in Economic History

Edited by **Lars Magnusson**, *Uppsala University, Sweden*

The Sustainability and Development of Ancient Economies
Analysis and Examples
Clement A. Tisdell and Serge Svizzero

The Economy of Classical Athens
Organization, Institutions and Society
Emmanouil M. L. Economou

The Political Economy of Interwar Foreign Investment
Economic Nationalism and French Capital in Poland, 1918–1939
Jerzy Łazor

The Development of European Competition Policy:
Social Democracy and Regulation
Edited by Brian Shaev and Sigfrido Ramírez Pérez

Economic History of the European Energy Industry
Lighting up Western Europe, 19th to 21st centuries
Alberte Martínez-López, Jesús Mirás-Araujo and Nuria Rodríguez-Martín

Economy of Ancient Egypt
State, Administration, Institutions
Mahmoud Ezzamel

Networks in the Early History of Capitalism
Merchant Practices in Renaissance Venice
Stefania Montemezzo

Economic History of Living Standards in Brazil
Policy, Health and Environment, 1850-1950
Daniel W Franken

For more information about this series, please visit: www.routledge.com/Routledge-Explorations-in-Economic-History/book-series/SE0347

Mining and Financial Imperialism

The Central African Copper Bonanza, *c.* 1890–1970

Timo Särkkä

Routledge
Taylor & Francis Group
LONDON AND NEW YORK

First published 2025
by Routledge
4 Park Square, Milton Park, Abingdon, Oxon OX14 4RN

and by Routledge
605 Third Avenue, New York, NY 10158

Routledge is an imprint of the Taylor & Francis Group, an informa business

British Library Cataloguing-in-Publication Data
A catalogue record for this book is available from the British Library

Library of Congress Cataloging-in-Publication Data
A catalog record has been requested for this book

ISBN: 978-1-032-16176-1 (hbk)
ISBN: 978-1-032-16177-8 (pbk)
ISBN: 978-1-003-24737-1 (ebk)

DOI: 10.4324/9781003247371

Typeset in Times New Roman
by Taylor & Francis Books

Contents

Illustrations

Figures

Tables

Preface

This research monograph originates from a paper read at Baltic Connections: A (Hybrid) Conference of Social Science History organised by the University of Helsinki, Finland on 20–21 April 2021, but the research had already been developing over the years in workshops, seminars, informal exchanges of opinion and at previous conferences: the Business History Conference 'The Virtues and Vices of Business — A Historical Perspective', Frankfurt am Main, Germany, 13–15 March 2014; the Southern African Historical Society's 25th Biennial Conference at University of Stellenbosch, 1–3 July 2015; the 26th Biennial Conference at University of the Witwatersrand, Johannesburg, 21–23 June 2017; and 'A Global History of Copper', Norwegian University of Science and Technology, Trondheim, 15–16 August 2019. I would like to thank the organisers for accepting my papers for their programmes and the participants for the stimulating discussions.

During the research work the following archives and libraries in the United Kingdom, South Africa, Canada, Finland, Sweden and Japan were consulted: The National Archives, Kew; the London Metropolitan Archives; the British Library of Political and Economic Science; the Guildhall Library; the British Newspapers Archive; the British Library; Senate House Library; The University of Manchester Main Library; Palace Green Library, Durham University; the William Cullen Library, the University of the Witwatersrand; the J.N. Desmarais Library, Laurentian University, Sudbury, Ontario, Canada; The Nordic Africa Institute Library, Uppsala, Sweden; Jyväskylä University Library; the Central Archives for Finnish Business Records; Helsinki University Library; the Library of Parliament, Helsinki; the Picture Collections of the Finnish Heritage Agency; the Finnish Heritage Agency Library; Kyoto Sangyo University Library; and Osaka University Main Library. I am grateful to those archives and libraries for granting me access to their collections.

Much of the research was conducted during a period of one year as a visiting researcher in 2022 and 2023 at the Division of Global History Studies, Institute for Open and Transdisciplinary Research Initiatives, Osaka University, Japan. The visit was hosted by Professor Shigeru Akita, Head of the Division of Global History Studies, and funded by the Academy of Finland

(Grant Number 343605). There were several aims in this research period: to prepare the book manuscript, to strengthen research cooperation with the research collaborators based at Osaka University, to further the research of the author and the international collaborators both individually and collectively, to add a more international and critical element to the national research systems, and to provide new insights for the research. I hope that all of these aims will be realised through the quality of this study. The preliminary research results were read at the 113th Global History Seminar of the Division of Global History Studies, 25 November 2022. I would like to thank Professor Akita and his research group for their collaboration, support and strong commitment to developing the field of global history; the hosting institution for inviting me as Guest Associate Professor; and the funding body for the faith displayed in my work. Finally, I am grateful to the Faculty of Humanities and Social Sciences, University of Jyväskylä for its financial support for Open Access publication.

Timo Särkkä
Osaka and Jyväskylä

Acknowledgements

I am grateful to Taylor & Francis Group for their permission to repurpose copyright material that originally appeared at: Särkkä, Timo (2016) 'The Lure of Katanga Copper: Tanganyika Concessions Limited and the Anatomy of Mining and Mine Exploration 1899–1906', *South African Historical Journal*, 68:3, 318–341.

Abbreviations and acronyms

BRC	Benguela Railway Company
BSAC	British South Africa Company
BTK	Bourse du Travail du Katanga
CK	Compagnie du Katanga
CSK	Comité Spécial du Katanga
Gécomin	Société Générale Congolaise des Minérais
LME	London Metal Exchange
RHOKAT	Rhodesia-Katanga Junction Railway and Mineral Company
RST	Rhodesian Selection Trust of Companies
SGB	Société Générale de Belgique
SGM	Société Générale des Minerais
SGMH	Société Générale Métallurgique de Hoboken
Tanks	Tanganyika Concessions
UM	Union Minière, Société Anonyme Belge
UMHK	Union Minière du Haut-Katanga
ZE	The Zambesia Exploring Company

1 Introduction

This chapter introduces the research setting, methods and materials, and the longitudinal scope of the book. Venturesome mining finance houses have played a major role in exploiting Central African copper resources since the early 1890s, and their role in tapping these resources has continued to be a subject of considerable interest right up to the present day. The mining finance houses, similar in structure and function, were substantial public corporations with access to money markets in the City of London – the world's leading capital markets for mining – and attractive, therefore, to venture capital. The mining finance houses became dominant at the inception of colonial rule and, in varying forms, remained so throughout the twentieth century. Despite extensive literature, it is curious that relatively little is known of their financial operations. Who were these financiers? What was the nature of the power they wielded? This research monograph seeks to answer these questions in eight chapters by focusing on the Tanks Group of Companies, a London-based mining finance house that was responsible for the far-reaching effort to set up a European mining industry in that mineral-rich region that later became popularly and loosely known as the Central African Copperbelt. The book maintains that analysis of the mining finance houses engaged in overseas natural resources businesses in Central Africa can contribute to our understanding of the ambiguous relationship between the interests of the British Empire and those of the money markets, which were by no means always the same. This argument is in line with the theory of imperialism formulated by J.A. Hobson: Imperialism is constituted by the intersection of two forms of competition, financial and geopolitical, but this competition is disproportionately dominated by finance.

Central African copper in the pre-colonial-era economy and society

The mineral-rich belts of Central Africa occupy a vast geological formation called the Lufilian Arc – an area about 500 miles across at its widest part, extending from eastern Angola across the Lualaba and the adjacent Haut-Katanga provinces in the southmost part of the Democratic Republic of the Congo to the Copperbelt Province in the north-western part of neighbouring

DOI: 10.4324/9781003247371-1

Zambia. The Lufilian Arc hosts extensive high-grade copper–cobalt (Cu–Co) mineralisation in very large stratiform deposits, the like of which is not known elsewhere. Still waiting to be systematically charted, it contains approximately 10% of the world's copper reserves and one-half of known cobalt deposits.[1] Together with non-ferrous metallic minerals (*e.g.* zinc, tin and nickel), high concentrations of precious metallic minerals (*e.g.* gold, silver and platinum), as well as rare quantities of radium, uranium and several rare-earth elements with high industrial demand (also known as the 'Congo caviar'), there are enough mineral riches in the Central African Copperbelt to corner the global metal markets.

Gold, copper and tin are generally accepted to be the oldest metals known to man. Whilst Neolithic people held gold in high cultural regard for its golden colour and everlasting qualities,[2] copper and tin were not only beautiful but also versatile and useful metals. Alloyed together they were fashioned into some of man's first metal implements and so, as bronze, they gave their name to one of the earliest distinguishable stages of man's progress towards being a maker and user of tools.[3] Central Africa appeared to progress to the Iron Age some 3,000 years ago, but the archaeological evidence suggests that, unlike many other locations, it did so without passing through the intermediate bronze period. Copper extraction is thought to have taken place with the arrival of the Bantu-speakers but the precise origins of copper mining and smelting practices are obscured by time and remain under speculation today. The first miners used few implements apart from simple iron tools for prying chunks of native copper out of surface outcrops. In its rare, directly usable metallic state, native copper could be utilised without any metallurgical treatment (*i.e.* native copper is chemically uncombined 100% pure copper). Usually, however, copper contains many other chemical elements, forming copper ores, the smelting of which requires a developed understanding of certain metallurgical principles. Smelting of malachite ore, an opaque green semi-precious stone revered since ancient times, was an extremely significant milestone in the technological development of copper treatment. At the Kipushi mine in Katanga ingot moulds and furnaces from the ninth to the twelfth century have been unearthed.[4] Archaeological evidence from the Kansanshi mine in Northwestern Province of Zambia suggests that mining there may go back as far as 400 CE.[5]

Why, then, did people regard copper as special? Chemically copper did not have any intrinsic value for the pre-colonial African societies. Instead, the 'red gold' was held in high cultural regard for its aesthetic appearance: its scarlet colour and everlasting qualities that are thought to relate to ceremonial or ancestral purposes. While copper is relatively inert, it is also very malleable and has a relatively low melting point: 1,085°C. The latter two physical properties allowed the coppersmith to smelt copper into ingots of varying shapes with a basic knowledge of metallurgy. Only then were the more elaborate indigenous techniques employed in processing copper. These included hammering, drawing, annealing and embossing copper metal into ornaments such as bangles, beads, necklaces and bracelets. In hierarchical societies rich in copper, such decorative ornaments could be worn by the political and religious elites and royal ruling classes as symbols of their authority, wealth and power.[6]

The realisation that copper was not just a useful and beautiful metal, but also a versatile one, goes back to the earliest times of copper mining in Central Africa. Besides its aesthetic, ornamental and symbolic purposes, copper was valued as an article of trade, and copper ingots of various shapes and sizes were used as the primary medium of exchange across the South-Central African region.[7] The trading of mineral products in their most rudimentary stage (*i.e.* the export of untreated native copper or malachite ore) did not contribute as much to economic development. It was only in the seventeenth and eighteenth centuries when the trade of the more sophisticated forms of metal products (*i.e.* the export of smelted copper in the form of unmanufactured Katanga 'crosses', ingots and cakes made by the master-smelters) became a significant element in Afro-European exchange, presumably first in response to demand by Portuguese and Dutch merchants, who had established fortified settlements on the Atlantic Coast since the late sixteenth century. The copper trade provided a basis for the rise of major centralised societies of the Central African region, most notably the Luba and Lunda Kingdoms, which traded with copper, along with slaves and ivory.[8] Another demand for copper came from the East Coast, where Swahili-speaking Moslem merchants served as middlemen, exporting copper along with gold, salt, ivory and slaves from the interior in exchange for cloth, muzzle-loaders and gunpowder arriving through the Indian Ocean world trade network. These trading patterns led to the development of a considerable copper trade in Central Africa, with volume rising and falling as prices fluctuated in such remote centres of demand as London or Bombay.[9]

The first known European reference to copper being worked in Central Africa was made by the Portuguese Filippo Pigafetta in 1591.[10] Over 200 years later in 1802 two merchants in Portuguese employ, B.J. Baptista and Amaro José, on their way across equatorial Africa from Angola to Tete in Mozambique, mentioned 'green stones' (*i.e.* malachite) dug out from the summit of copper-bearing hills in Katanga.[11] In the latter part of the nineteenth century, cast copper ingots and ornaments piqued the curiosity not only of the merchants, but also of seemingly disinterested British explorers and missionaries, including Verney Lovett Cameron and David Livingstone, who mentions in his *Missionary Travels and Researches in South Africa* (1858) an 'Arab caravan travelling east from the Katanga, with slaves carrying five tons of copper'.[12]

For about a third of a century (1856–91), the Central African copper trade was controlled by the Yeke Kingdom under Msiri, a Nyamwezi copper, ivory, salt, beeswax and slave trader from Tabora (in present-day Tanzania), whose family had consolidated his power over the copper-bearing territory by arranging marriages between his own Nyamwezi (or Yeke) followers and the local Luba ruling house. In about 1879 Msiri established the Kingdom's new capital in the town of Bunkeya, near the Lufira River in Ka-Tanga, the 'Land of Smelted Copper', where his trade radiated east to Zanzibar and west to the Portuguese settlement of Benguela on the Atlantic Coast. The first Europeans to settle permanently in Katanga were Frederick Stanley Arnot, a Scottish warehouse clerk turned Plymouth Brethren missionary, and his companion Charles Albert Swan, who worked in the region of Bunkeya in 1886–7. Arnot remarks on Msiri's suzerainty over the Katanga copper-bearing territory and was unable to uphold the nascent British interests over the region.[13]

By the time the mining interests intensified around the prospects of Katanga copper at the close of the 1880s, Msiri's dominion over his kingdom was already on the wane. The techniques of the slave-traders included the incitement of intertribal warfare, the motive of which was the capture of prisoners for sale. This process resulted in the strengthening of a few ethnicities and the terrorisation and rapid depopulation of the rest of the Katanga. Hence the Yeke were unable to resist the subsequent British and Belgian military and mine exploring expeditions, which, turn by turn, traversed their way into Katanga.[14] On 15 April 1891 the Belgian *Compagnie du Katanga* (CK) was founded to create and administer economic infrastructure in Katanga, and subsequently, in 1891–2, CK sent a military expedition, led by British Army Captain W.G. Stairs, into Katanga to persuade Msiri to hand over the mineral rights to the concessionary company. The standoff between the expedition and the Yeke resulted in a conflict in which Msiri was shot dead.[15]

The first systematic geological information available concerning Katanga is written by René Jules Cornet, a geologist with CK's mineral-seeking expedition led by Lucien Bia and Émile Francqui in 1891–3.[16] The expedition charted much of Katanga and located a number of copper mines, including the Kambove mine famed for its rich copper resources. With limited time and equipment at his disposal, Cornet concluded, despite high concentration of copper in places, that the ores he assayed were not rich enough to justify the great expense of developing the lodes with the modern means of mining technologies.[17] It took five more years before a more fully equipped mine-seeking and mineral-exploring expedition into Katanga was organised by CK. However, the conclusion of Captain Charles Lemaire's expedition of 1898 was similar to that of Cornet's. It was deemed that the Katanga copper mines were not rich enough, bearing in mind the significant capital outlays needed to develop them with modern Western mining technology.[18] Although mining had undergone a technical revolution in the 1880s with the introduction of a range of new industrial processes and engineering techniques, the establishment of modern transport and telecommunication links remained crucially important in considering the opening up of Central African mineral resources to the world metal markets.

The ultimate impetus and much of the capital for the exploitation of the Central African copper wealth came from British mining interests that had been operating in Southern Africa since the late 1860s. British companies made good use of their experience in South African and Rhodesian gold mining, as well as their relative geographical proximity, to expand their operations to Katanga at the time when the Belgian financial circles showed little interest in developing its resources. As it transpired, the most successful of these British mining companies proved to be Tanganyika Concessions (commonly known as 'Tanks'), an offshoot of The Zambesia Exploring Company (ZE) which had been founded to prospect gold in Mashonaland in 1891 and subsequently received a concessionary right from the British South Africa Company (BSAC) to exploit mineral deposits in the adjoining North-Western Rhodesia.

A major part of Tanks' history is the compensation that was given in exchange for prospecting the mineral resources in Katanga. When Tanks launched its mine and mineral exploring project in Katanga in 1901 it predictably paid a payment for the privilege to the *Comité Spécial du Katanga* (CSK), a parastatal joint body which was founded in 1900 to merge the concessionary rights of the Congo Free State (*État Indepéndant du Congo*) and CK. No thought was given to compensating the African miners for allowing the company to profit from extracting their valuable minerals. Significantly, when Tanks, together with the *Société Générale de Belgique* (SGB), financed the formation of the *Union Minière du Haut-Katanga* (UMHK) in 1906, Tanks received the lion's share of this new company as compensation for its loss of concessionary rights. Thus began the interconnection between ZE, Tanks and UMHK, the most prized holdings of the Tanks Group of Companies that were together responsible for the far-reaching effort to set up a European mining industry in that mineral-rich region that later became popularly and loosely known as the 'Copperbelt'.

The research premise, aims and objectives

> And it is true that the motor-power of Imperialism is not chiefly financial: finance is rather the governor of the imperial engine, directing the energy and determining its work; it does not constitute the fuel of the engine, nor does it directly generate the power. Finance manipulates the patriotic forces which politicians, soldiers, philanthropists, and traders generate; the enthusiasm for expansion which issues from these sources, though strong and genuine, is irregular and blind; the financial interest has those qualities of concentration and clear-sighted calculation which are needed to set Imperialism to work.[19]

It is precisely these sentiments of J.A. Hobson, the most prominent theorist of financial imperialism, that have led me to ask why and how financiers have aggravated the growing gaps between people, their economies and geographies. Such questions have been of enormous importance to the mineral-rich regions of Central Africa since the 1890s, when its resources first raised the attention of the international capital market for mining, leading eventually to the birth of a technologically driven copper mining industry. A major aspect of this story was finance, which gave the original impetus for the exploitation of natural resources in Central Africa. Hobson argued that the growth of the 'new imperialism' from the 1870s had coincided with a remarkable growth in the income derived from external investments. Imperialism was 'a source of great gains to the investor who cannot find at home the profitable use he seeks for his capital and insists that his Government shall help him to find profitable and secure investments abroad'.[20] *Cui bono?* Who benefits? Hobson's argument runs thus: the investor. The argument formed the core of what Hobson termed the 'economic tap-root of imperialism', which meant, in short, that the economic basis of imperialism lay in capitalism. The surplus capital accumulated in a few hands sought investment in unstable colonial polities such as Katanga or North-Western Rhodesia of the early twentieth century. The surplus capital, Hobson further argued, called upon the state to protect its investments, even though these investments were made by private investors. Imperialism would, thus, always continue as long as this surplus capital went on accumulating in the hands of the few, the investing and speculative classes, who employed the resources of the state to protect their investments.[21]

Hobson's analysis was the first discussion of the topic of imperialism in modern times which developed the general structural analysis of capitalism and connected overseas investments with the 'Scramble for Africa'. A succession of economic and imperial historians has analysed Hobson's theory in detail and studied the role of the metropolitan economy in overseas expansion. In their seminal works, Cain and Hopkins (1994) in *British Imperialism*, Dumett (1999) in *Gentlemanly Capitalism and British Imperialism* and Akita (2002) in *Gentlemanly Capitalism, Imperialism and Global History* defined the nexus of economic, social and political power centring on the City of London as 'gentlemanly capitalism'. In the metropolitan sphere, this gentlemanly dimension in the connections between the London capital market and mining companies operating overseas reflected an important aspect of the social nature of the prevailing organisational structures.[22] Wider network links provided evidence of the combination of social, organisational and financial interests centred on the City that helped to support overseas mining operations.

British investments in colonial Africa were often by nature based on the trust of close business partners and shared financial assets.[23] In their analysis of these vested interests, Cain and Hopkins (2002) have described gentlemanly capitalism as a process where industrial interests were shunned as socially inferior to the more lucrative and prestigious business of exporting capital.[24] Following Hobson's formulations, many of the mining companies floated during the early colonial era came to be seen as vehicles for rampant 'concession-mongering' and 'stock-jobbing imperialism'. The pervasiveness of this view (both at the time and beyond) can perhaps most obviously be seen in the overemphasis of previous studies on the role of powerful capitalists in capital accumulation such as Cecil Rhodes, the 'arch-filibusterer', who in Hobson's analysis seemed to possess almost superhuman powers, and his fellow

'Rhodesites', who tried to not only govern the natural resources but colonise African land.[25]

Economic explanations of imperialism and Hobson's theory in particular have been criticised by researchers of colonialism who have regarded it as mono-causal.[26] In imperial historiography a belief in economic determinism in historical writing that emerged in the interwar period in the form of the so-called 'Hobson–Lenin theory' tended to overemphasise the role of the capitalist at the expense of the worker and the peasant in making their own history. By the 1980s, the concentration on the financial explanation of imperialism had fallen out of fashion, allowing for the worker making his own labour history to come into vogue.[27] Once one gets a chance to study the laws of motion of capital, the more durable features of Hobson's intellectual heritage become irresistibly convincing. The present critique of globalisation and colonialism has inherited much from Hobson's treatment of finance, development and underdevelopment, the themes to which the present study repeatedly returns. But the critique must go deeper than simply focusing on the pernicious social and political influences of Western colonialism. What follows, then, is a Hobsonian approach to mining, finance and imperialism in Central Africa which considers them in the context of the unevenness of capitalist development.

Research methods and materials

There probably has never been a clearer example in history of the curse of natural riches than Katanga, the heart of Central Africa's mining industry. The orthodox analyses of this 'natural resource curse' or the 'paradox of plenty' have universally been heavily critical of Katanga's natural resource governance. Studies of international political economy have often made only a cursory reference to the ills of the 'Scramble for Africa' that reached an apex during the Berlin Conference of 1884–5, in which the Congo was promulgated as a free state, under the sovereignty of the *Association Internationale du Congo*. In such studies, the roots of the socio-economic crisis of Katanga were to be found entirely in the geopolitical sphere, stemming from the disruptive influences of Western colonialism and especially from its main epitome, King Léopold II, under whose personal domain the Congo was placed a few months after it had been declared 'open to all'. In this state-centric orientation, it was the personal fiefdom of the Belgian demon king and his economic system of kleptocracy that pushed the Congo over a point of no return into seemingly perpetual turmoil. But as recent evidence suggests, such approaches are not only outmoded but also unhistorical and have further obfuscated the already complex modes of natural resource governance that have determined the management of Central Africa's mineral wealth.[28]

With respect to the history of the extractive industries in Central Africa, there is a notable lack of systematic, up-to-date research. The most comprehensive previous book-length studies are from the 1960s and the 1970s,[29] and like some of the more recent book-length contributions,[30] they have mainly focused only on the Northern Rhodesian (Zambian) Copperbelt. Initially exploitation of the underlying copper sulphides in Northern Rhodesia was neglected in favour of the much more valuable oxidised concentrations in Katanga. It was not until the early 1920s that the value of these sulphide deposits was established, and the possibilities of Northern Rhodesian mines became apparent. Industrial-scale copper mining began in earnest in Northern Rhodesia in 1928, and during the colonial era in the Northern Rhodesian Copperbelt there developed a mining industry distinct from that in Katanga.

The most comprehensive book-length work focusing on the development of the mining industry in Katanga is Katzenellenbogen's (1973) seminal *Railways and the Copper Mines of Katanga.* [31] It focuses on the business management of the Tanks Group, the operations at its headquarters and the connections between finance and high politics in Britain and Belgium. It is a well-established fact that the growth of the new imperialism from the 1870s coincided with a remarkable growth in the income derived from external investments. The most recent work is Rönnbäck and Broberg's (2019) *Capital and Colonialism*, which convincingly shows the average annual real return on investments for numerous British business ventures in colonial Africa, and also includes some relevant information on Tanks' business operations.[32] In turning to other existing business historical studies, they tend to lack consistency of method in investigating the history of the mining industry. The corporate history of UMHK, published by the company to celebrate its 50-year semicentennial in 1956, can be mentioned as an illustrative example of a state-centred narration which is made solely in the context of the history of Belgian colonialism in the Congo.[33] This absence of up-to-date research invites an in-depth study in book-length form.

The contention of the present study is different from the previous approaches in three respects. First, it shifts the focus from the colonial governments to the operations of mining companies – to the complex interplay between the Head Office (*i.e.* the manager and the directors, who often were also the major shareholders or investors) and the local management on the ground who ran the operations with the help of engineering firms, suppliers and service sector agencies. Second, it concentrates on the interconnectedness of Rhodesian and Katangese mining regimes. The focus is on the history of mining in Katanga, where the mineral wealth remained under the management authority of UMHK, without much state interference until the end of the colonial era. Finally, the book is concerned with a longer timeframe: its analysis of mining and finance extends from their Western colonial origins to their imperial legacies in the post-colonial era. There is another aspect which makes the present study an addition to the existing literature: the use of a wide range of available materials. The records of stock exchanges, company archives, trade and production returns, assay reports and mining journals as well as personal material (*e.g.* diaries and photographs) of many workers of European descent in the field offer a fuller picture of mining in the Central African Copperbelt than is available elsewhere. The heterogeneous sources also complement each other, allowing a fuller story to be told and a sounder case to be made.

The research is motivated by the realisation that analysing the evolution of the Central African mining industry by using longitudinal and global economic history methods is a very revealing way of illustrating the often troubled road mining has travelled in the past, of exposing the complexities it is facing today, and of analysing its future prospects. Until very recently producer goods such as copper have not featured much in global history research. But new works in the field such as Evans and Miskell's (2020) *Swansea Copper: A Global History* and Declercq, Money and Frøland's (2022) *Born with a Copper Spoon: A Global History of Copper, 1830–1980* have firmly rooted their analyses in the framework of global history.[34] They highlight that metals are highly connective: Humans have traded with copper over long distances for its high commercial and industrial value and because there is no reason why mineral lodes should coincide with human settlements. Mines are where the prospector finds them and not where the miner might wish them to be.

The same applies to the history of mining in the Central African Copperbelt. It may have initially been removed from the established economic heartlands, but its history spans long periods of time and embraces people from highly diverse cultural backgrounds. Clearly, then, the history of Central African copper is a contribution to global economic history, a field which is concerned with networks and the interconnectedness of capital, technologies, raw material commodities, people and ideas across wide areas of space and over long periods of time. Such a theoretical paradigm also invites a re-examination of the existing narratives of finance, development, underdevelopment, globalisation and colonialism in the Central African Copperbelt.

This study will follow the business history tradition of in-depth and rich historical accounts based on primary (mainly archival) sources. It will employ records of the London Stock Exchange, various government bodies, trade, and production returns as well as company archives. A study of mining finance should not necessarily be concerned, however, with economic activity alone. European involvement in mining in Central Africa ultimately stemmed from colonial developments. Mining companies were direct participants in the colonising process, and their activities had physical and societal consequences in wider regions in Central Africa and beyond. Business history resources together with various written and visual materials produced by many company employees can provide some insight into how these processes took place, why they were considered desirable by various interest groups, and what implications such processes had for both physical and human environments.

The research material is divided into the following (a–h) categories:

a The primary source for studying various aspects of capital exports overseas is the Records of the Stock Exchange (SE), London Metropolitan Archives (LMA), City of London. The records include both applications for authority to deal (from companies seeking only to have their shares traded on the Stock Exchange) and applications for listing (from companies wishing to have their share price quoted in the Stock Exchange official list). They are arranged in two chronological series: the years covering 1850–1938 and 1939–65. The requirement for companies to present a full history of their trading activities and evidence of their financial stability remained unchanged during the research period although the volume of information grew considerably.

b Business history records held at the Guildhall Library, City of London: Information on share prices was listed on a daily basis in *The Stock Exchange Daily Official List* (1899 to date). Of the various Directories, *The Stock Exchange Yearbook* (1876 onwards in hard copy; microfilm edition 1875–1945) is the most comprehensive. Prominent members of the business community can be traced using sources such as trade and residential directories, such as *Who Was Who* and the *Directory of Directors.*

c Business history records held in The National Archives of the UK (TNA), Kew: The main series to examine is that of the Board of Trade (BT) and related bodies concerning government responsibilities for trade and industry. The records of the Foreign Office (FO), the Foreign and Commonwealth Office (FCO), the Colonial Office (CO) and the Dominions Office (DO) illustrate the British Government's interests in mineral resources in Central Africa.

d Company records: The most relevant for the present purposes is the Archives of the Tanks Group of Companies (TANKS), in the Special Collections of the Main Library at The University of Manchester (MU). Papers include extensive files of correspondence, annual reports, minutes, accounts, contracts and legal documents as well as photographs of mining and railway operations. They are a major source for studies of mining, colonialism and development in Central Africa.

e Personal material: These include diaries, memoirs and photographs of many workers in the field. The photographs of Carl Theodor Eriksson, a Finnish-born employee of the Tanks, whose materials are deposited at The Finnish Heritage Agency (FHA), Picture Collections (PC), Helsinki, Finland, provide significant evidence relating to the world of mining in the Central African Copperbelt. These include a collection of glass plates taken in North-Western Rhodesia and adjoining Katanga between 1901 and 1906. There is a wide range of subject matter depicted in Eriksson's photographs, ranging from various aspects of the early colonial economy (including the organisation and processes of the early mining work, modes of communication and relations between the mining company's white management and the African labour) to scenes of daily life in the colony, documentation of 'natives', 'wildlife' and portraiture. The photographs selected for this study cannot represent the full range of the entire collection, but their particularity in style and subject matter, as well as the engagement with photographic practice that they demonstrate, nonetheless allow us to analyse theoretical and conceptual definitions of the categories of 'coloniser' and 'colonised' more generally.

f Mining engineers' and other expert reports: Grey Estate Records (GRE), Durham University (DU), Barker Research Library (BRL) consists of a valuable collection of reports by J.R. Farrell, Mining Engineer, Franz E. Studt, Mineralogist, and the Bulawayo Assay Office and Public Laboratory reports, which illustrate professionalisation and education of the mining and metallurgical elite.

g Journals and magazines: These include prestigious economic publications such as the *Financial Times* and *The Economist*, revered mining journals such as the American *Engineering and Mining Journal* and journals and magazines with special reference to mining in Central Africa such as *Horizon: The Magazine of the Rhodesian Selection of Trust Group of Companies* and *The Northern Rhodesia Journal, Bulawayo Chronicle* and *The African Review of Mining, Finance and Commerce*, which circulated market reports from the eminent mining finance houses in the trade. These can be consulted at The British Newspapers Archive, London.

h Africana collections with special reference to the mining industry in Central Africa: The most important consulted here are the Africana Collections of the William Cullen Library, University of the Witwatersrand, Johannesburg, South Africa and the collections of The Nordic Africa Institute Library, Uppsala, Sweden.

The historical sources consulted are intended to underpin theoretical findings on the relationship between mining and financial imperialism. As Porter (2008) has pointed out in the introduction to the second edition of his influential *Critics of Empire*, Hobson's theory of imperialism has its value today because even if the empires he discusses have died, imperialism did not die with them. The durability of Hobson's theory demonstrates how each generation has recycled his views and found them illuminating for their own time.

This research takes its inspiration from the changes in the mining industry's financial structure since the beginning of colonial rule and highlights the changing pattern of the copper trade during the post-colonial era. Whereas the quest for base metals such as copper was first fuelled by the rising tempo of Western electrical industrialisation, the issue of climate change has in recent years been the prime mover behind the ever-growing demand for metals of high industrial use such as copper and cobalt, so sorely needed for electric transport and communications. The extractive industries have been going through a fundamental reorientation over the last few decades. They have seen the industry undergo exponential growth in 'peripheral regions', principally in the global south but also in places in the global north, as evidenced in numerous projects of 'green mining'. The common denominator in these projects is the discourse of climate change mitigation the extractive industries have adopted, partly due to the diminishing space for action. The extractive industries lobby themselves as being in the service of the transition away from fossil fuels, claiming to be in the business of mining minerals necessary for the green transition. In addition to the discourse that the increasing consumption of minerals is essential to sustaining the modern lifestyle and industrial growth, accelerating climate change has touched off an increasingly urgent discourse of the generic, global ecological challenges. These changes in orientation have triggered a growing interest in documenting the extractive industry's history.

In the post-colonial era, Chinese investors have been the most noticeable stakeholders in the development of mines and related infrastructure in the Copperbelt. In the twenty-first century more capital has flowed into the Copperbelt than at any time since the 1960s.[35] Such a dramatic reorganisation of the industry poses an important research question: In hindsight, what we can learn from the history of mining in Central Africa? The increased presence of multiple actors has also constituted a challenge to codes of business prescribed in the colonial era by Western mining companies. While there is a long tradition of analysing the presence of Western mining companies in terms of finance and imperialism, there is no established body of literature that would provide an equivalent methodology for analysing the impetuses of post-colonial-era operators. The absence of such a body of literature highlights the importance of recognising the diversity of actors and impetuses in the history of mining in Central Africa.

The recent interest in the extractive industry's role in the fight against climate change tends to focus on gadgets and innovations – for example the electric vehicle, the smart phone or the high-capacity lithium-ion batteries for storing power generated by solar panels or windmills. But the recent focus has stepped away from the financial explanations of the change and has rarely issued from mineral extraction processes that were large in scale, often dangerous and sometimes toxic for both people and the environment. Yet this revived interest in the role of strategic metals offers a way for reconceptualising past industrial experiences as well. Although extensively mined for centuries, Katanga continues to be held in the grip of a copper and cobalt fever which is as dramatic in its social effects as the colonial-era scramble for land and mineral wealth. So fine was the purity of the colonial-era ore that slag heaps and tailings of concentrate can still yield very healthy percentages of metals. Even at the time of the collapse of the Central Government in the Congo in the late 1990s and early 2000s, when the mining industry operated in the midst of insurgents, and Katanga appeared to be completely cut off from the global economy, the extraction of minerals continued with what little colonial-era equipment remained, despite decades of neglect and mismanagement including a lack of investment.[36]

Today the most striking physical evidence of the mining industry is the slag heaps, opencasts and pits which scar the Copperbelt landscape. Although the products which Central African minerals can help to build are essential ingredients in almost every aspect of modern electric transport and communication, the label modern is difficult to apply to Central African mining of the twenty-first century, which still continues, side-by-side with industrial-scale mining, using the pre-colonial methods of wielding mining bars, hammers, picks and shovels. It is estimated that daily some 50,000–250,000 Africans work as 'artisanal' or 'craft' miners (*creuseurs*) in Katanga. The miners are mostly young men and children who make precarious livings by digging virgin soil or slag heaps and tailings of concentrate at abandoned mines with artisanal tools, methods and processes. Artisanal mining was boosted by a collapse in global commodity prices in the late 1980s coupled with gross mismanagement of the economy which led to dwindling revenues from mining. This resulted in the serious indebtedness of the state-run mining operations, which – together with the chaos created by the collapse of the Central Government at the end of the First Congo War in 1997 and the liberalisation of the mining sector in 2002 – commenced a process of making redundant more than half of the 24,000 workers of the company along with other public sector staff, and forcing the dependants of thousands of workers to swap the classroom for the artisanal mine (*carrière*) as *creuseurs*, ore sorters, transport providers or middlemen (*négociants*).[37]

Artisanal exploitation often denotes ore 'thieving' (*e.g.* in terms of violating the existing concessionary rights of the industrial-scale operators or the *Code Minier* of 2002) from the active or closed mines, increasing industry volatility and the risk of conflict.[38] The lack of regulation in mining in Katanga has recently attracted much scholarly attention. In his recent work Kara (2023) elucidates how the illegally mined material ends up in the global supply chain. After being extracted by the artisanal miners, the mined material is sold to the local middlemen who then resell it to the mostly Chinese and Lebanese buyers in buying houses (*maisons d'achat*). Next the mined material is taken down in lorries to the local processing plants for concentrating and then across the Tanzanian or Zambian border, where the customs officials are often bribed to allow it through without any record or any export tax being imposed on this illegally obtained material. There is no difficulty on the Tanzanian or Zambian side of the frontier; the traffickers merely pay the local customs duties, and the concentrate goes through without trouble. From the border it is transported to the ports of Dar es Salaam or Durban and shipped away to be conveyed further for smelters and refiners in China or in Europe.[39]

The main beneficiaries are investors, producers and consumers globally, while the main losers of the Katangese mining economy are those who are left with the very high socio-economic, health and environmental costs in Katanga. There is also of course the financial loss, which is no small matter for an underdeveloped economy such as Katanga which, as it happens, is also one of the most well-endowed corners of the earth in terms of natural riches. The history of mining in Central Africa is a story of fluctuating fortunes, which have enriched, but also corrupted, petty miners and major corporations alike. In this sense little has changed in Katanga from the mining of the colonial era which was fuelled by the quest for bonanzas and windfalls.

To understand the links between the post-colonial discourses, financial regimes and the history of mining, in the seven chapters that follow I will focus on the mining companies as actors of financial imperialism, and as chains of investment and profit flows. Mining companies have played a major role in tapping industrial mineral resources in Central Africa from the 1890s right up to the present day. Whilst originally established in colonial settings they now tend to operate globally. Historically, industrial-scale mining has been a driver for the introduction of more direct modes of controlling mineral wealth as the history of ZE, Tanks and UMHK clearly illuminates. This study seeks to explore the role of these non-state actors – mining companies, financiers, bankers, stockjobbers, metal merchants, directors and chairmen of the companies together with the prospectors, managers, consulting engineers and labour recruiters on the spot – in setting rules and regulations for extracting minerals. Furthermore, it seeks to explain why and how mining companies leveraged their authority and legitimacy to govern the development of the extractive industry: how the global mining business has operated in the context of the discourse of development. How did these processes take place, why were they considered desirable by various interest groups, and what was their impact on physical and human environments in parts of Central Africa? The analysis extends from the origins of the European mining industry there in the early 1890s to the post-colonial legacies of the late 1960s.

Notes

1 Lydall and Auchterlonie 2011, 28; Cobalt Facts 2023.
2 Green 1982.
3 For a literature review on the evolution of copper extraction, see Gibson-Jarvie 1976, 7; Davis 1924; Newton and Wilson 1942; Metcalfe 1944; Brown and Butler 1968; Burt 1972; Prain 1975; Schmitz 1979; Langley 1980; Metzger 1980; Evans and Miskell 2020; Declercq et al. 2022, 3–25.
4 Bisson et al. 2000, 97, 120; Bradley 1952, 29, 32.
5 Gann 1971, 38–40; Katzenellenbogen 1975, 360; Herbert 1984; Jaeger 1981, 57.
6 For further information, see Herbert 1984.
7 Coleman 1971, 172–173.
8 Reefe 1981; Allen 1923, 23; Larmer 2017, 3; Bustin 1973, 20–22; Roan Consolidated Mines Public Relations Department 1978, 14–16.
9 Rothman 2002, 84.
10 Coleman 1971, 170–172; Roan Consolidated Mines Public Relations Department 1978, 14.
11 Refer, for instance, to Burton 1873; Bradley 1952, 29.
12 Cameron 1877, I. 134, 319–320, 372; II. 149, 323–325, 329; Baker 1921, 181; Livingstone 1858, 329. Quotation from Bancroft 1961, 25.
13 Katzenellenbogen 1973, 17–18; Rotberg 1964, 285, 288–293; Higginson 1989, 6–7; Baker 1921, 181. See also Monteiro 1875.
14 Bradley 1952, 32–33.
15 Gordon 2001, 319–320; Katzenellenbogen 1973, 18–19; Rotberg 1964, 285, 288–293; Siegel 1988, 63–64. See also Moloney 2011.
16 Studt 1913, 44.
17 For further information, see Cornet 1946.
18 Katzenellenbogen 1973, 19–20; Lemaire 1901, 526–552.
19 Hobson 1901a, 246.
20 Hobson 1901b, 210–211.

21 Hobson 1902, 219–232.
22 Harvey and Press 1990, 5.
23 Wilkins 1989, 4–20; Newbury 2008, 87.
24 Cain and Hopkins 2002, 337–338. For earlier versions, see Cain and Hopkins 1980, 463–490; Cain and Hopkins 1987, 1–26; Cain and Hopkins 1994.
25 Quotations from *Derbyshire Advertiser* 2 May 1896; 22 May 1896; 2 October 1896; *Manchester Guardian* 15 November 1899.
26 Cannadine 1998, 144–146, 150–154.
27 On this concern, see Phimister 1988.
28 On these concerns, see Grant et al. 2015, 8–9.
29 Bancroft 1961; Coleman 1971; Gann 1964; Gelfand 1961.
30 Refer, for instance, to Butler 2007.
31 Katzenellenbogen 1973.
32 Rönnbäck and Broberg 2019, 215, 217.
33 UMHK 1956.
34 Evans and Miskell 2020; Declercq et al. 2022.
35 For further information, see Curtis 2008, 86–107; Daly 2008, 45–49; Gadzala 2015; Haglund 2009, 77–96; Monsoon 2008, 197–219; Ndulo 2008, 138–151; Rotberg 2008, 1–20.
36 Mazalto 2009, 208–210.
37 Ericsson et al. 2024.
38 Makori 2017, 781, 789, 794–795.
39 Kara 2023, 21–23.

References

Akita, S. (2002) 'Introduction: from Imperial History to Global History' in S. Akita ed. *Gentlemanly Capitalism, Imperialism and Global History*, Palgrave Macmillan, Houndmills, Basingstoke, 1–16.

Allen, R. (1923) *Copper Ores*, Imperial Institute, Monographs on Mineral Resources with Special Reference to the British Empire, John Murray, London.

Baker, E. (1921) *The Life and Explorations of Frederick Stanley Arnot*, Seeley, Service & Co., London.

Bancroft, J.A. (1961) *Mining in Northern Rhodesia: A Chronicle of Mineral Exploration and Mining Development*, British South Africa Company.

Bisson, M.S., Childs, T.S., de Barros, P. and Holl, A.F.C. (2000) *Ancient African Metallurgy: The Sociocultural Context*, Altamira Press, Lanham, MD.

Bradley, K. (1952) *Copper Venture: The Discovery and Development of Roan Antelope and Mufulira*, Mufulira Copper Mines Limited, Roan Antelope Copper Mines Limited, London.

Brown, M.S. and Butler, J. (1968) *The Production, Marketing and Consumption of Copper and Aluminium*, Frederick A. Praeger, New York.

Burt, O.W. (1972) *The First Book of Copper*, Franklin Watts, New York.

Burton, R.F. (1873) *The Lands of Cazembe: Lacerda's Journey to Cazembe in 1798*, John Murray, London.

Bustin, E. (1973) *Lunda under Belgian rule: The Politics of Ethnicity*, Harvard University Press, Cambridge, MA.

Butler, L. (2007) *Copper Empire: Mining and the Colonial State in Northern Rhodesia, c.1930–64*, Palgrave Macmillan, Houndmills, Basingstoke.

Cain, P.J. and Hopkins, A.G. (1980) 'The Political Economy of British Expansions Overseas, 1750–1914', *Economic History Review*, 33:4, 463–490.
Cain, P.J. and Hopkins, A.G. (1987) 'Gentlemanly Capitalism and British Expansion Overseas II: New Imperialism, 1850–1945', *Economic History Review*, New Series, 40:1, 1–26.
Cain, P.J. and Hopkins, A.G. (1994) *British Imperialism: Innovation and Expansion, 1688–1914*, Longman, London, New York.
Cain, P.J. and Hopkins, A.G. (2002) *British Imperialism, 1688–2000*, Longman, London.
Cameron, V.L. (1877) *Across Africa*, 2 vols., Isbister & Co., London.
Cannadine, D. (1998) *History in Our Time*, Yale University Press, New Haven, CT.
Cobalt Facts (2023) 'Cobalt Facts'. Retrieved 24 May 2024 from https://natural-resources.canada.ca/our-natural-resources/minerals-mining/mining-data-statistics-and-analysis/minerals-metals-facts/cobalt-facts/24981.
Coleman, F.L. (1971) *The Northern Rhodesia Copperbelt, 1899–1962: Technological Development Up to the End of the Central African Federation*, Manchester University Press, Manchester.
Cornet, R.J. (1946) *Katanga: Le Katanga avant les Belges, et l'Expédition Bia-Francqui-Cornet*, L. Cuypers, Bruxelles.
Curtis, D. (2008) 'Partner or Predator in the Heart of Africa? Chinese Engagement with the DRC' in K. Ampiah and S. Naidu eds. *Crouching Tiger, Hidden Dragon? Africa and China*, University of Kwa-Zulu Natal Press, Scottsville, 86–107.
Daly, J.C.K. (2008) 'Feeding the Dragon: China's Quest for African Minerals' in A. Waldron ed. *China in Africa*, The Jamestown Foundation, Washington, DC, 45–49.
Davis, W. (1924) *The Story of Copper*, The Century Co., New York and London.
Declercq, R., Frøland, H.O. and Money, D. (2022) 'Introduction: Worlds of Copper?' in R. Declercq, D. Money and H.O. Frøland eds. *Born with a Copper Spoon: A Global History of Copper, 1830–1980*, The Chicago University Press, Chicago, IL, 3–25.
Derbyshire Advertiser (2 May 1896); (22 May 1896); (2 October 1896).
Dumett, R.E. (1999) *Gentlemanly Capitalism and British Imperialism: The New Debate on Empire*, Routledge, London.
Ericsson, M., Löf, A., Löf, O. and Müller, D.B. (2024) 'Cobalt: Corporate Concentration 1975–2018', *Mineral Economics*, 37:2, 297–311.
Evans, C. and Miskell, L. (2020) *Swansea Copper: A Global History*, Johns Hopkins University Press, Baltimore, MD.
Gadzala, A.W. ed. (2015) *Africa and China: How Africans and Their Governments are Shaping Relations with China*, Rowman & Littlefield, Lanham, MD.
Gann, L.H. (1964) *A History of Northern Rhodesia: Early Days to 1953*, Chatto & Windus, London.
Gann, L.H. (1971) *Central Africa: The Former British States*, Prentice-Hall Inc., Englewood Cliffs, NJ.
Gelfand, M. (1961) *Northern Rhodesia in the Days of Charter: A Medical and Social Study, 1878–1924*, Blackwell, Oxford.
Gibson-Jarvie, R. (1976) *The London Metal Exchange. A Commodity Market*, Woodhead-Faulkner and Metallgesellschaft AG, Cambridge.
Gordon, D. (2001) 'Owners of the Land and Lunda Lords: Colonial Chiefs in the Borderlands of Northern Rhodesia and the Belgian Congo', *The International Journal of African Historical Studies*, 34:2, 315–338.
Grant, J.A., Nadège Compaoré, W.R., Mitchell, M.J. and Ingulstad, M. (2015) 'New Approaches to Africa's Natural Resource Governance' in J.A. Grant, W.R. Nadège

Compaoré and M.J. Mitchell eds. *New Approaches to the Governance of Natural Resources. Insights from Africa*, Palgrave Macmillan, Houndmills, Basingstoke, 3–24.

Green, T. (1982) *The New World of Gold: The Inside Story of the Mines, the Markets, the Politics, the Investors*, Weidenfeld & Nicolson, London.

Haglund, D. (2009) 'In it for the Long Term? Governance and Learning among Chinese Investors in Zambia's Copperbelt Sector' in J.C. Strauss and M. Saavedra eds. *China and Africa: Emerging Patterns in Globalization and Development*, The China Quarterly Special Issues, no. 9. Cambridge University Press, Cambridge, 77–96.

Harvey, C. and Press, J. (1990) 'Issues in the History of Mining and Metallurgy', *Business History*, 32:3, 1–14.

Herbert, E.W. (1984) *Red Gold of Africa: Copper in Precolonial History and Culture*, The University of Wisconsin Press, Madison, WI.

Higginson, J. (1989) *A Working Class in the Making: Belgian Colonial Labour Policy, Private Enterprise, and the African Mineworker, 1907–1951*, The Wisconsin University Press, Madison, WI.

Hobson, J.A. (1901a) 'The Financial Direction of Imperialism', *Speaker*, 5:113, 245–246.

Hobson, J.A. (1901b) 'Imperialism the Policy of Investors', *Speaker*, 5:112, 210–211.

Hobson, J.A. (1902) 'The Economic Taproot of Imperialism', *Contemporary Review*, LXXXII, 219–232.

Jaeger, D. (1981) *Settlement patterns and rural development: a human geographical study of the Kaonde, Kasempa District, Zambia*, PhD thesis, University of Amsterdam.

Kara, S. (2023) *Cobalt Red. How the Blood of the Congo Powers Our Lives*, St. Martin's Press, New York.

Katzenellenbogen, S.E. (1973) *Railways and the Copper Mines of Katanga*, Clarendon Press, Oxford.

Katzenellenbogen, S.E. (1975) 'The Miner's Frontier, Transport and General Economic Development' in P. Duignan and L.H. Gann eds. *Colonialism in Africa 1870–1960*, Vol. 4: *The Economics of Colonialism*, Cambridge University Press, Cambridge, 360–426.

Langley, A. (1980) *Copper*, Wayland, Hove.

Larmer, M. (2017) 'Permanent Precarity: Capital and Labour in the Central African Copperbelt', *Labor History*, 58:2, 170–184.

Lemaire, C. (1901) 'On the Congo: The Belgian Scientific Expedition to Ka-Tanga, Communication Made to the Geographical Section of the British Association for the Advancement of the Sciences', *Scottish Geographical Magazine*, XVII, 526–552.

Livingstone, D. (1858) *Missionary Travels and Researches in South Africa*, Harper & Brothers, New York.

Lydall, M.I. and Auchterlonie, A. (2011) *'The Democratic Republic of Congo and Zambia: A Growing Global "Hotspot" for Copper-Cobalt Mineral Investment and Exploration'*, The 6th Southern Africa Base Metals Conference, Phalaborwa, 18–21 July 2011, The Southern African Institute of Mining and Metallurgy, Johannesburg, 25–38.

Makori, T. (2017) 'Mobilizing the Past: *Creuseurs*, Precarity and the Colonizing Structure in the Congo Copperbelt', *Africa: Journal of the International African Institute*, 87:4, 780–805.

Manchester Guardian (15 November 1899).

Mazalto, M. (2009) 'Governance, Human Rights and Mining in the Democratic Republic of the Congo' in B. Campbell ed. *Mining in Africa: Regulation and Development*, Pluto Press, New York, 187–242.

Metcalfe, J.M. (1944) *Copper: The Red Metal*, Viking Press, New York.
Metzger, D. (1980) *Copper in the World Economy*, Monthly Review Press, New York.
Moloney, J.A. (2011) *With Captain Stairs to Katanga*, British Library, Historical Print Editions, London.
Monsoon, J. (2008) 'Liberating Labour? Constructing Anti-Hegemony on the TAZARA Railway in Tanzania, 1965–1976' in C. Alden, D. Large and R. Soares de Oliveira eds. *China Returns to Africa. A Rising Power and a Continent Embrace*, Hurst & Company, London, 197–219.
Monteiro, J.J. (1875) *Angola and the River Congo*, 2 vols., Macmillan, London.
Ndulo, M. (2008) 'Chinese Investments in Africa. A Case Study of Zambia' in K. Ampiah and S. Naidu eds. *Crouching Tiger, Hidden Dragon? Africa and China*, University of Kwa-Zulu Natal Press, Scottsville, 138–151.
Newbury, C. (2008) 'Rhodes, De Beers and the Mining Finance in South Africa: The Business of Entrepreneurship and Imperialism' in R.E. Dumett ed. *Mining Tycoons in the Age of Empire, 1870–1945: Entrepreneurship, High Finance, Politics and Territorial Expansion*, Routledge, London, 85–108.
Newton, J. and Wilson, C.L. (1942) *Metallurgy of Copper*, John Wiley & Sons, New York.
Phimister, I. (1988) *An Economic and Social History of Zimbabwe 1890–1948: Capital Accumulation and Class Struggle*, Longman, London.
Porter, B. (2008) *Critics of Empire: British Radicals and the Imperial Challenge*, 2nd ed, I.B. Tauris, London and New York.
Prain, Sir R. (1975) *Copper: The Anatomy of an Industry*, Mining Journal Books, London.
Reefe, T.Q. (1981) *The Rainbow and the Kings: A History of the Luba Empire to 1891*, University of California Press, Berkeley, CA.
Roan Consolidated Mines Public Relations Department (1978) *Zambia's Mining Industry: The First Fifty Years*, Roan Consolidated Mines Limited, Ndola.
Rotberg, R.I. (1964) 'Plymouth Brethren and the Occupation of Katanga', *Journal of African History*, 5:2, 285–297.
Rotberg, R.I. (2008) 'China's Quest for Resources, Opportunities, and Influence in Africa' in R.I. Rotberg ed. *China into Africa: Trade, Aid and Influence*, Brookings Institution Press, Baltimore, MD, 1–20.
Rothman, N.C. (2002) 'Indian Ocean Trading Links: The Swahili Experience', *Comparative Civilizations Review*, 46:6, 79–90.
Rönnbäck, K. and Broberg, O. (2019) *Capital and Colonialism: The Return on British Investments in Africa 1869–1969*, Palgrave Macmillan, Cham, Switzerland.
Schmitz, C.J. (1979) *World non-Ferrous Metal Production and Prices, 1700–1976*, Frank Cass, London.
Siegel, B. (1988) 'Bomas, Missions and Mines: The Making of Centres on the Zambian Copperbelt', *African Studies Review*, 31:3, 61–84.
Studt, F.E. (1913) 'The Geology of Katanga and Northern Rhodesia: An Outline of the Geology of South Central Africa (Read 30th June, 1913)', *Transactions of the Geological Society of South Africa*, 16, 44–102.
UMHK (1956) *Union Minière du Haut-Katanga 1906–1956*, L. Cuypers, Bruxelles.
Wilkins, M. (1989) 'The Impact of Multinational Corporations', *South African Journal of Economic History*, 4:1, 4–20.

2 Mining, gentlemanly capitalism and the business of imperialism

This chapter discusses the various areas of concern relating to the London capital market for copper mining. Mining depends on the support of capital, and prior to 1914 the London capital market was especially geared towards supporting the mineral development of the world. The mineral wealth may be there, and labour ready to work, but without capital both would remain idle. The chapter is organised in four sections. Before investigating the structure of the London capital market in the second section, the first briefly outlines the late-nineteenth-century technology transfer in the fields of transport and communication that drastically increased the world demand for copper. The third focuses on the central role played by the London Metal Exchange in the world's copper trade, whereas the fourth investigates business formulas adopted by London-based companies engaged in the overseas mining business before 1914. The chapter concludes that rather than being simply profit-making organisations, the mining companies were the prime movers in the processes of colonisation and development. The exploitation of overseas mining regions was a complex and extensive process, involving much more than just the extraction of the ore. In many parts of the world, remote from the established economic heartlands, the mining companies themselves had to raise capital and acquire the expertise needed before full-scale mining could start. Investment in mine exploring and prospecting was a capital-intensive and risky business and implied long cycles of returns and calls for further investment. As a result, the mining industry was structured as a vertically highly integrated oligopoly.

The expansion of transport and communications

The history of Victorian Britain is the history of a society which underwent a rapid technological transformation and had to respond to it. The initial cause of many of the changes was connected with the development of steam-driven machines. Until the early eighteenth century, machines were driven by human, animal or natural power (*e.g.* wind, water or tidal power), which had set natural limits on productivity. The evolutionary change of steam-powered technology had many effects on society. By the early Victorian era the

DOI: 10.4324/9781003247371-2

transfer to cheap and accessible coal together with craftsmanship within a relatively orderly society and an efficient canal transport system had created a stimulus that allowed British mills and other industries to produce a much higher output than ever before.[1]

The British mining industry was in the vanguard of this technology transfer, which facilitated British dominance over the world's mineral wealth. In the early modern era Cornish mines were one of the major sources of copper and tin for the rest of the world, but the use of human, animal or natural power had set natural limits on productivity. Metallic ores were now transported from Cornwall across the Bristol Channel to Swansea, where coal deposits powered reverberatory furnaces in South Wales as well as steam engines in Cornwall. The Welsh Process of smelting copper with coal in reverberatory furnaces rose to prominence first in virtue of Cornish ores, and then from the 1770s new deposits of copper ore started to be transported to South Wales from Devon, the island of Anglesey and Ireland, further facilitating the rise of the Swansea and Neath Smelters. By the 1830s ores were shipped to South Wales from sources as distant as Australia and Chile, making Britain the world's foremost smelting country. Between the 1770s and the 1840s, the Swansea district routinely produced one-third of the world's smelted copper, sometimes even more.[2]

At times of high prices and demand Welsh copper could be shipped as far eastward as the South East and East Asian markets by the East India Company.[3] With such vastly increased movement of merchandise, in which raw materials became finished goods and progressed from producer to processor to consumer, came buoyant growth in global shipping. This was the fundamental *raison d'être* for the development of the countless highly specialised commercial houses in the City of London. In Gibson-Jarvie's (1979) formulation, 'movement had to be executed, financed, insured and made as continuous as possible both as to the availability of goods, and as to their price, on the due date.'[4]

At first, unburdened with the tons of coal which steamers had to carry, the sailing ship remained economically a more viable vessel than the steamship for the haulage of freight, especially where it was a question of transporting relatively low-value bulk producer goods from distant sources to the centres of demand. From the perspective of the global transport network, however, it was the steamship that most effectively helped to shrink the world. The first ocean steamers fitted with screw propellers were built in Britain in the mid-1840s. By the mid-century, the major long-distance lines were operated by the great transatlantic ocean liners, which conducted the passenger and mail traffic from Britain to the North Atlantic, the West Indies and South America. The repercussions on global relationships were profound. The steamship reduced travelling times, facilitated the travel of colonial elites and the large masses of European emigrants alike, and gave to the West an impressive lead in military technology over the non-European empires. Steam technology also enabled the efficient and cost-effective transport of cargo to and from distant markets.[5] The main beneficiary of the steam technology was Britain, as the dominant economic, colonial and naval power. By the Great Exhibition of 1851 Britain had become 'The Workshop of the World', producing over 40% of the entire world output of traded manufactured goods, the prominent examples being Manchester piece goods and the metal goods of Birmingham and Sheffield. Respectively over one-third of raw material and foodstuff exports of all other countries went to Britain,[6] whose quest for raw materials for manufacturing knew no political boundaries.

Copper played a pivotal role in this growth of global transport. At first copper was consumed mainly in the sheathing of wooden ships by Muntz metal (a corrosion-resistant brass alloy to protect the hulls of the naval and merchant fleets), and, later on, in railways and other applications of steam power.[7] The most intensive development phase of the world's copper wealth took place, however, when modern technology had found that the traditional virtues of the malleability, ductility and reflectivity of copper were matched by its ability as a thermal and electrical conductor, the foundation stones of modern electrical industries. In the era of electricity, copper proved the most practical and economic medium, in the form of either rod, cable or wire, for the transmission of power over distances.

The development of the telegraph – the first invention to bring electricity to the service of people – gave new opportunities to bind the international capitalist economy together. The earliest overhead telegraph lines in Britain were established at the beginning of the 1840s. By the middle of the 1850s telegraphic communication was already relatively widely used in Britain, Europe, North America, Australia and India, and, at the very close of the decade, in December 1859, the first public telegraph was opened in Cape Town. Thus by 1860 there were several separate telegraph networks, but the system of international communication relied on postal traffic carried by steamship.[8]

Construction of overland and undersea cable networks gave governments and corporations alike the opportunity to improve the efficiency of the management of international organisations. The first cable under the Atlantic was laid as early as 1858, but it burnt out after only 730 messages had been transmitted.[9] The failure of this cable made it clear that the technical problems involved in telegraph communication technology had not been fully understood. The faults were due to the lack of technical experience in the manufacturing of undersea cables, which consisted of multiple-strand copper core, covered with several layers of gutta-percha, wrapped in tarred hemp and protected by steel wires. Even the smallest production defects had major consequences for communication. In virtue of the state of cable technology, there was the ever-looming possibility of a communication breakdown somewhere down the line. It was impossible to predict how long a message would take: Would it arrive in ten hours, in ten days, in a month – or never? The delays caused financial losses and meant that it was always advisable to confirm a message with a letter, which reached its destination in a steamship with greater certainty than in the form of a telegraph message.[10] The opening of the North Atlantic Cable Line between Britain and North America coincided with the peace negotiations of the United States Civil War, and one of the first messages announced that Lincoln had agreed to open peace negotiations with the South. The message created a panic in Liverpool and Manchester as peace in the United States would have serious economic consequences for merchants trading Indian cotton.[11] The telegraph bound the international capitalist economy together almost in real time, and there was no way of escaping this fact once established.

In 1858–9 British engineers had already tried to link Britain to India by way of a cable laid in the Red Sea, but the technology would not be ready for a successful undersea cable service until the opening on 25 March 1870 of the service for international correspondence. The cable ran from Porthcurno in Cornwall via Carcavelos (near Lisbon), Gibraltar, Malta and Aden to Bombay. This connection was especially important from the point of view of Indian correspondence. It meant that it was possible to send messages between Britain and India by using cables owned, operated and maintained by British companies.[12] Within a few years of its establishment, the telegraph had become so important for communication to India that breaks and other irregularities in the service led to loud criticism, as illustrated by a column in the *Bombay Gazette*: 'The interruption of a day is of serious consequence and people are disposed to commit themselves to transactions of any kind without the latest information being available.'[13] By 1876 the cables extended to Australia, New Zealand, China and Japan. New means of communication became a necessity not only for economic but also for political and military reasons. In the absence of the telegraph, it took three weeks before news of the British military defeat at the Battle of Isandhlwana during the Anglo-Zulu War in South Africa in January 1879 reached Whitehall.[14] This adverse situation led to the building of the East Coast submarine cable, which connected Durban to European cable networks in December 1879.

The near-global telegraph communications were transformed by the 1890s, and telegraph wires were manufactured in ever-growing quantities, as were electric trams. Simultaneously electric lightning installations replaced gas and oil, and electrical machinery began to take the place of steam-driven engines in factories. All these innovations in electrical industries needed copper, which became an indispensable natural resource for the Second Industrial Revolution. By the 1920s, the electrical industries absorbed two-thirds of the world's total production of copper.[15] Fuelled by the rising tempo of industrialisation in Britain, Continental Europe, North America and Japan, demand for new sources of ores increased, with profound repercussions on global relationships.[16]

Simultaneously British dominance over the world's copper trade had entered into definite decline. Following Britain's somewhat ill-advised 1842–8 copper tariff North American mining companies increasingly started to undertake the treatment of their own ores, and matte or metal was exported in place of raw ore. Britain's position as the world's biggest producer of smelted copper was first challenged by the rise of the North American smelters in Pittsburgh, Detroit and Cleveland which smelted copper from mines of the Upper Michigan Copper Country, Chile and Cuba. After 1860 smelting was established nearer the mines in the Copper Country proper, and then after 1883 mining companies in the North American interior, in the western states of Montana, Arizona and Utah, started to rise in prominence. Technological transformation of the industry followed. Copper was now being extracted from low-grade copper porphyry ore bodies in massive open-pit workings with steam shovels and processed by hydroelectric power.[17]

From 1901 to 1910 the world's average annual mine production of copper was 697.80 thousand tons, of which the United States produced 388.60 thousand tons (*i.e.* 55.7% of the world's total production capacity). Other significant copper-producing countries were Mexico (53.10 thousand tons); Spain (50.70); Japan (39.30); Australia (35.40); Chile (31.70); Canada (22.90); Germany (21.80); Russia (13.40); and Peru (11.90).[18] In the light of these figures, it was evident that Britain faced an ever-increasing dependence on imported copper metal and alloys. This dependency became acute during the First World War, when it was variously estimated that from 65% to 80% of the world's copper production was used for military purposes.[19] The munitions industry's ongoing demand for non-ferrous metals during the war and the resulting strategic importance of copper served to boost mechanisation in the industry after the war. The need for copper and the danger of dependence on the few producers and sellers stimulated production in other locations than the United States, the world's main producer, and contributed to opening up new overseas copper resources for the world's metal markets. Furthermore, it brought into being the British Metal Corporation, which was established in 1918 to act as a counterweight to the sales organisations abroad and to help the trade of the British Empire in non-ferrous metals.[20] Generally the expansion of British mining interests overseas was stimulated to some degree by the shortage of ores mined at home and their relatively high cost of extraction.[21] Yet it would be misleading to explain British involvement in copper mining overseas simply in terms of the scarcity of domestic resources.[22] The key for explaining this development is the prominence of the City financial institutions, which helped London to remain the chief capital market for mining in the world long after domestic production had all but ceased.

The London capital market for copper mining

Late-Victorian-era Britain was the world's largest mining creditor nation and the City of London was the uncontested centre of the world's financial market for mining, attracting funds from all around the world and then reinvesting them in different parts of it.[23] Crucial to the City's domination were its financial institutions, which had been developed over a number of decades: the Bank of England, the joint-stock banks, the Stock Exchange and the commodity markets.[24] The Bank Charter Act and the Joint Stock Banking Act of 1844 had laid the foundations for the banking system, with the functioning of the gold standard at its heart. Being promulgated in the aftermath of the Napoleonic Wars in the Coinage Act of 1816, almost every important economic power had adopted gold as the basis of its monetary system by the end of the century, and by the time the First World War broke out, 59 countries were on the gold or gold-exchange standard. For about two centuries the City was recognised as the world's main bullion market and the pound sterling was used as an international currency on par with gold. It was possible to convert sterling easily into gold and immediately establish its international exchange value, thus facilitating the rapid increase in the volume of global trade and exchange.[25]

As the leading metallurgical and financial centre, Britain secured an initial advantage in international investment and in the control of copper mining. Prior to the 1830s, capital for copper mining ventures had been for the most part devoted to mining within the British Isles, but the following decades saw significant expansion overseas. The oldest overseas working copper mine financed by British capital was the Copiapó mine in Chile, which was formed in 1836. With the benefit of shareholder participation and limited liability, the company was subsequently registered on the London Stock Exchange in 1861.[26] Then followed the flotation of Libiola Copper in 1867 in Italy,[27] and then the mines belonging to the Iberian Pyrites Belt: Tharsis Copper & Sulphur Company in 1866 and Rio Tinto Company in 1873 in Spain, and Mason & Barry in 1878 in Portugal.[28] The first London-registered copper company in the Southern Africa region was Cape Copper Company in O'Kiep, the Namaqualand district, South Africa. This company, a tributary of Swansea smelters, was established in 1863 and subsequently registered as Namaqua Copper Company on the Stock Exchange on 30 April 1888.[29]

By the late Victorian era the City had become the provider of mining finance for most of the rest of the world, and the centre for handling transactions in the one currency in which virtually all international obligations were discharged. Most of the capital for the development of mining and closely related railway infrastructure projects was raised through limited liability companies. They made up a large proportion of the £4,000 million that joint-stock companies had invested abroad by 1914.[30] Between 1880 and 1913, in all 8,408 companies involved in mining and mine exploration overseas were registered in Britain, with the vast majority on the London Stock Exchange.[31] The mining companies, under British management and control, traded on British markets with securities denominated in pounds sterling, and for the capital invested provided potentially profitable but also risky investment opportunities abroad.[32] The investment instrument was subject to British law, and thus it primarily encouraged the investment of British subjects, but could also lure foreign investors in London and beyond.

The first copper mining companies operating overseas registered in England as joint-stock companies were commencing their business operations under regulations of the Joint Stock Companies Act of 1856, the Act of 1862 and four amendments to it ending with that of 1879. The Companies Act of 1862 introduced a particularly significant addition in the interests of the investing public. The Act stipulated that the creditors and all other persons (and not only shareholders of the company) who contemplated dealing in some way with the company ought to be able – on payment of one shilling – to inspect the register of shareholders and satisfy themselves as to what extent they could safely trust the company.[33] After 1880 several other changes were made in joint-stock companies legislation in the presumed interest of the investing public, namely the Companies' Act of 1880; the Companies' Act of 1886; the Companies' (Memorandum of Association) Act of 1890; the Directors' Liability Act of 1890; the Companies' (Winding-up) Act of 1893; the Companies' Act of 1898; and the Companies Act of 1900. The legislation required that the registered companies operated under British management and control and traded on British markets with securities denominated in pounds sterling. It also required the business of the company to be managed by directors, the registration of shareholders and the payment of dividends out of the profits arising from the business of the company. A memorandum of association and articles of association defined company objectives and functions. For quotation and listing of companies on the Stock Exchange, formal application had to be made by a company before permission to deal in its securities was granted. The Share and Loan Department scrutinised a company's prospectus to ensure its compliance with company law and Stock Exchange rules, but the Quotations Department made the ultimate decision on the suitability of a company for its shares to be traded on the Stock Exchange. Victorian legal requirements governing managerial behaviour were however among the most liberal in Western Europe, ensuring that the directors remained in complete control of company assets.[34]

After passing the Act of 1900, the proliferation of different accounting methods contributed to the widespread incomprehensibility of balance sheets, accounts and prospectuses for investors.[35] As the venerable mining historian Ashmead (1909) has noted,

> Since 1900 a prospectus has become about the most confusing document legal ingenuity up to that time had devised. To trace a mining property through its complicated agreements, beginning, it may be, with some native chief, down to the company of the prospectus, requires an elaborate mental effort; while to get at the amount promoters and vendors, past and present, have got, or expect to get, under the many agreements is almost impossible to the average man; and when, as is too often the case, all this is printed in type almost invisible to the ordinary eye, confusing becomes worse confounded.[36]

To raise the money for large mining and railway infrastructure ventures it was essential to tap the resources of the public. The mining and railway endeavours were thereby playing an important role in the development of the characteristic forms of late Victorian public investments in ordinary shares; they were something of a 'lottery ticket', which nearly everybody with surplus funds would buy. A typical pre-1914 company floated for mining and mine exploration overseas was short-lived, speculative in nature and played a purely economic role in the development of its host country or countries. Even though most mining and mine exploration companies failed, they were not organisationally unsound per se. Limited companies were investment instruments, the floating of which was 'an easy matter, and a useful way of investigating a prospect without risking too much capital. Companies were formed and liquidated by collaborating groups of firms and individuals in the normal course of business.' With its 'propensity to create companies' the City proper – the Square Mile – was the focus of most of this financial activity. The registered firms had their premises and held their annual general meetings in the same small area where banking and other financial services, insurance, the Stock Exchange and the commodity markets were rubbing shoulders with each other.[37]

The financial market being well-developed and integrated does not suggest that all investments were sound ones and that there was no over-speculation. The investments were often by nature based on the trust of business acquaintances, who shared the risk by investing their financial assets in a promising venture.[38] As van Helten (1990) explains, 'social and business connections played a particularly important role in the mining market where "insider" information was at a premium and the key to short-term share speculation and long-term portfolio investment.'[39] The stockjobber, a wholesaler of stocks unique to London, acted as a useful and efficient buffer between the market and the investor. Trading as a principal on his account, the stockjobber held shares in more than one company and was prepared to sell from his own holding or to buy into it as appeared favourable. In this way it was the stockjobber who made a market in a share, but also ran enormous risks in terms of price movements amongst the shares he held. Despite the gradual improvement of the public image and development of stock-jobbing as a profession, in the late Victorian era the stockjobbers earned a rather notorious reputation in the 'Kaffir Circus', as the market for the Southern African mining shares was disrespectfully nicknamed. The stockjobbers were accused – sometimes no doubt with a measure of justification – of manipulating the market in making their quotations.[40]

Although the Stock Exchange rules stipulated that it was a *condicio sine qua non* that the public must subscribe no less than two-thirds of the capital,[41] the gradual increase in the cost of establishing a new mine made it impossible for ordinary shareholders to bear the brunt of the burden to muster both the capital and expertise essential in opening up new mining regions, often remote from modern means of transport and communication. This fact kept large numbers of nominally independent mining companies under the control of large mining finance houses and their major financial sponsors, acting individually or in concert. They provided the financial security, administrative experience and technical expertise that a single company could not hope to develop alone. The comforting knowledge that a mining finance house was administering a new mine was crucial in persuading investors to risk their money in a new venture, which often brought with it long cycles of calls for further investment and entailed a higher degree of risk than other businesses. There was usually a long period of time between flotation and production during which dramatic changes in the world demand for metals, political instability or shortages of labour could seriously affect the success of the venture. Technical hazards also affected mining operations, which might have shown promising assays during exploratory quarry operations but would later prove commercially unviable to mine at greater depths.[42]

The London Metal Exchange and the world's copper trade

Through the development of commodity markets London was also the main centre for the world's copper trade. Its international reputation as the thriving location for *entrepôt* business carried on at the docks and the efficient transfer of funds by documentary means took many years to develop, but in general it can be stated that the development of London terminal market trading owes much of its efficacy to the revolution of communications brought about by the invention of the telegraph. Before the electronic means of communication, Jerusalem Coffee House, off Cornhill, had proved both a convenient and congenial place for the business meetings of metal merchants and a necessary adjunct to their regular calls on each other in their own offices. After the introduction of the widespread use of the more or less instantaneous telegraph communication, it was vital for the metal merchants and others concerned with this particular trade to meet and exchange information promptly. For some time, this purpose was served by a 'walk' (*i.e.* a rendezvous concerned with metal trade) in the 1844-opened Royal Exchange building, where the metal merchants foregathered at certain regular times to exchange information and to do business.[43]

The great expansion of international trade handled and financed in London took place with the expansion of the undersea cable services in the late 1860s. It was becoming essential that London prices were representative of the situation day by day, and some sort of central forum was clearly needed for the purpose of exchanging intelligence and opinion. To this end, the establishment of a formally constituted body under centralised control, and governed by rules which were applicable to all, became a necessity. In 1869 the metal merchants established the London Metal Exchange Company, with its own premises in a room in Lombard Court. It provided telegraph facilities for gathering and disseminating information, and in 1880 the first telephone for the use of those present came into operation as well. LME was incorporated as a limited company on the Stock Exchange on 20 July 1881, and the 32 years which followed its first meeting on 18 September 1882 at Whittington Avenue, leading to the newly opened Leadenhall Market, up to the outbreak of the First World War, were the formative years in the development of LME. The market was formed to meet a need for facilities which had become increasingly felt by producers, merchants and consumers. As mining became more industrialised and output increased, producers wanted to be able to sell their products whenever they wished, in any quantity and for any delivery nearby or forward. Consumers required similar facilities to enable them to purchase their raw materials, whilst merchants were ready to buy and sell and maintain a balanced position between supply and demand.[44]

LME was not only the world's largest metal market, but also the world's most liberal, with almost no restrictions on import and export. It offered a forum for trading in physical copper which enabled daily prices to be generated which were widely held to reflect the current balance of supply and demand in the world market. At the outset, the metal was bought and sold on the basis of dock warrants, covering merchandise already landed and available for inspection and transfer. The next stage of development, assisted by the telegraph, was the offering for sale of goods 'on arrival of ship'. Such merchandise might either already be at sea *en route* from the original destination, or could still be pending embarkation from the country of origin. Either way, the goods were tangibly in existence at the time the offer was made. 'On arrival' was a convenient method for the producer to secure a price before the commencement of the voyage, which could well be lengthy and the whole market picture might alter during the course of it to the detriment of the producer.[45]

Initially the essential weakness of this arrivals market was that it was not standardised. These difficulties were overcome by the practice of trading in standard lots of a set quality (within the permissible variation laid down). The standardisation was embodied in the Standard Copper Contract of 1898, which provided standard terms for the delivery of all the major grades of copper of the time: Standard, Best Selected (B/S) and Electrolytic. For each of the three unmanufactured varieties of copper there was a special market price in pounds sterling per ton.[46] The standard LME contract was primarily drawn for hedging purposes as it gave an appreciable number of options to the seller as to the type of metal that could be delivered and the place of delivery in Britain. Standard terms were adopted to provide a hedging medium for importers and merchants to cover their commitments. This was a most important development since it introduced the concept of trading in perfectly standard goods, thus obviating the need for any bargaining over the quality or weight of a particular consignment.[47]

The final stage of metal trading in copper 'futures', dealings based purely on financial considerations or in promises to make or take delivery on a future date without the actual possession by the seller of documents to an existing parcel, was a natural step. By 1914, a distinction between a physical market, where specific lots of metal were bought and sold for delivery, and a market in arrivals where hedging and speculating with copper futures were complementary activities, was already emerging. The merchants needed a recognised forum where prices could be arrived at in public on the basis of worldwide supply and demand and, equally important, where they might cover their financial risk by hedging on the market. For copper and tin at least (the two major metals and those best suited to formal trading in standard lots and grades), the future triple role of LME was beginning to take shape and could be clearly identified: a hedging market, a clearing market for excess mine production and, most importantly, a price-making institution for large trade in physical metal that was handled outside London.[48]

The hedging facilities enabled consumers to protect themselves against increases in their raw material costs (insofar as these consisted of tin, copper, lead and zinc) and enabled producers to protect themselves against changes in the selling prices of these metals. These facilities also enabled producers and consumers to protect themselves against changes in the value of their stocks of these metals. The quotations were used not only to price transactions in refined metal, but also as an agreed and authoritative basis for pricing ores, concentrates, semi-manufactured and manufactured metals. With a market ethos founded on complete freedom to trade, based on mutual confidence amongst the members of the Exchange, the London metal market achieved a high degree of security combined with considerable – vital for its success – flexibility.[49]

The free market established on LME thus gained an unrivalled prestige in its special sphere. Its official quotations were recognised throughout the world as authoritative prices on standard articles. Whilst a very large degree of business was in fact conducted outside LME on long-term contracts between producers and consumers based on London quotations, LME provided a market where producers and consumers could sell their surpluses or make up deficiencies not covered by long-term contracts, and it also provided a market for buyers and sellers of copper who wished to hedge by means of forward sales and purchases.[50] The London price became effectively the world price – quite irrespective of the volume of physical metal in which it dealt – reflecting the complex variety of economic and social forces of the City termed by Cain and Hopkins (1994) as 'gentlemanly capitalism'.[51]

Brass nameplate companies in the Square Mile

The usual business formula adopted by a London-based firm engaged in overseas mining and mine exploration was to court investment, primarily from British individuals but also from foreign investors in London and elsewhere. Companies would seek to attract the attention of investors by circulating a favourable report from a mining expert. After this initial establishment period, it was usual for technical and production matters to be left in the hands of local managers, who ran operations in the host countries with the help of engineering firms, suppliers and service sector agencies. The board exercised financial power with the support of the corporate secretary and the financial and marketing services provided by commercial and financial City firms.

London-based mining and mine exploring companies making foreign direct investments encountered alien working environments and employed a special type of organisational structure to manage increased costs and risks. In business history theory a company form employed by British companies operating overseas has been termed by Wilkins (1988) 'free-standing', which is, by definition, a company which was registered in one country and had headquarters there to conduct business in another country. In contrast with a multinational enterprise a free-standing company did not grow out of the domestic business operations of existing enterprises but was organised for the specific purpose of undertaking business in another country or region.[52] Another defining factor of the free-standing companies was that they mostly operated in colonies as the company structure had no sustained advantage outside the British sphere of influence.[53] Beyond their small staff and seemingly limited managerial resources, companies operating overseas had little but the brass nameplate of their headquarters in the Square Mile.[54]

If the board of directors was to exercise control over business operations and monitor business activities overseas, some institutional apparatus was necessary. The required functions were undertaken by clusters consisting of numerous overlapping circles of individuals and enterprises. Such loose clusters were united by founders, directors, suppliers and service sector agencies, many of whom also were major shareholders of the companies and thus had vested interests in the return of their investments. As a result there were conflicts of interest, interdependences between companies reliant on one another and loyalties towards networks of trusted business partners.[55] As an alternative, and to compensate for their limited managerial resources, the free-standing companies could draw on the facilities provided by the City commercial and financial firms.[56] One of the main attractions of the metropolitan business community was that it could offer companies a bundle of competitively priced financial, marketing and consulting services. Together with well-established institutions like the Stock Exchange and the Metal Exchange there was a comprehensive range of financial and trading services specially tailored for overseas business ventures, including solicitors, auditors and merchant bankers, which were often specialised in doing business in a single country and in arranging the finance of long-term investments overseas.[57]

The free-standing companies either operated directly overseas or might be holding companies owning securities of a subsidiary or subsidiaries that operated overseas. If they were holding companies, they typically adopted 'double boards' (*i.e.* the board of the host company and that of its offshoot consisted of the same directors).[58] The investors in a company and the company itself could be one and the same, or the investor may have been strictly financial in character and appear only in the form of capital loans for firms operating overseas. However, often investors were interested in financial power retained to control and run the business overseas. Thus the relationship between the investor and the beneficiary tended to be close and quite often reinforced by vested interests. The managing director was expected to select the local manager, who reported to the Head Office and ensured prudent and efficient management of operations on the ground. The local manager, who was normally tied with shareholdings and other loyalties to the company, was given the responsibility of finding trusted individuals for the many operations on the ground.

The local manager of a mining company operating overseas faced the difficult task of handling the day-to-day business dealings of mining companies, which set out to prospect for, open, work, explore, develop and maintain mines, mineral and other rights, properties and works, and to carry out and to conduct the business of raising, crushing, washing, smelting, reducing and amalgamating ores, metals and minerals, and to render the same merchantable and fit for use. A typical mining company carried on, as well as mining, the business of farmers, graziers, planters, engineers, quarry owners, brickmakers, builders, contractors, merchants, dealers in metals and stones, importers and exporters, bankers, shipowners, wharfingers, hauliers, warehousemen, hotel keepers, storekeepers, publishers, printers, agents and general merchants. For these varied tasks, the managers needed to employ and pay mining experts, and to organise, equip and despatch expeditions for prospecting, exploring, reporting on, surveying, working and developing lands, farms and properties. In so doing they assisted in the colonisation of the said lands and properties and promoted settler colonialism for that purpose. They often became involved in administrative tasks and entered into agreements with territorial, district, municipal or local authorities, to obtain rights, privileges and concessions, which empowered them to carry out their multiple roles.

The management of the mining companies operating overseas was vested with directors with varied business acumen. Typically the directors consisted of men active in the same or in a closely associated economic sector and they often had some prior experience of the operations in the respective host countries in the form of prior business operations, experience in colonial administration or military service, for instance. The directorates were often by nature based on the trust of close friends or relatives who shared their financial assets.[59] The board of The Zambesia Exploring Company (ZE), the parent company of the Tanks Group, is illustrative in this respect. The long-time Managing Director of ZE, Sir Robert Williams (1860–1938), was born in Aberdeen, north-east Scotland. Williams had been an apprentice of the firm Blaikie Brothers, general engineers and ironfounders, which had connections to another Aberdeen-based engineering firm MacKenzie and Anderson, then operating in the South African diamond fields in Kimberley. The latter firm asked Blaikie Brothers to find an engineer able to take charge of their small Kimberley engineering works. The young Williams applied for the job and was subsequently sent to Kimberley in 1881. In the course of his work Williams met most of the mine owners and managers and later made good use of his networks in the Witwatersrand goldfields, where he became well-known as a mining consultant engineer in the late 1880s.[60] Familiarity and experience with the mining industry and the country enabled Williams to recognise a profitable opportunity when one was presented to him in 1891 by Cecil Rhodes, who proposed that Williams should form an exploring company to prospect the mining opportunities of Mashonaland, which was later to become a part of Southern Rhodesia. These two men in the same sector sought to be involved in ZE not only for financial gain but also to remain well informed and to influence the course of events by controlling, stabilising and neutralising the competition.[61]

Besides the men of the trade, the British aristocracy featured predominantly in the board of directors of ZE, as they often sought honourable and profitable employments for their sons. Tyndale White, a wealthy City businessman and a long-time (1898–1925) Chairman of Directors of ZE, and his son Captain Maurice White provide an example of such a lineage. After being discharged from active military service in 1918, Captain White, who had gained his rank in the Rifle Brigade, followed in his father's footsteps and became a director of the Rhodesia-Katanga Junction Railway and Mineral Company, an offshoot of the Tanks Group, incorporated in 1909 to link the Rhodesia Railway with the railway system in Katanga. There is no evidence to suggest that Captain White had any prior experience of mining before being nominated as a director of the said company, which he served until his death in 1925.[62]

Whilst women did not yet feature on boards of directors, they could own major shareholdings and wield their financial power through their husbands. Dolores Pauling, wife of George Pauling (1854–1919), a railway contractor and founder of Pauling & Co., a major British civil engineering company renowned chiefly for building the railways of South-Central Africa, is a rare example of a powerful woman in an otherwise very masculine world of mining. George Pauling, who had emigrated to South Africa in 1875, was a business acquaintance of both Rhodes and Williams, who leveraged his networks in securing railway contracts that linked the Central African Copperbelt to the world metal market. In this capacity Pauling was a director and a major shareholder in several business ventures belonging to the Tanks Group. After Pauling passed away, Dolores Pauling continued to control her late husband's shareholdings – a reminder that the seemingly masculine world of mining might have been more inclusive in its outlook than at first glance it appeared to be.[63]

Concluding discussion

Financial power is a central concept in the theory of imperialism.[64] Yet it remains elusive and, in general, it poses a challenge to any research trying to unravel the social nature of the London capital market and the prevailing organisational structures of the late nineteenth and early twentieth centuries. There is no unit of power *per se*, so it cannot be directly quantified in economic terms. We can speak of having less power or more power in terms of amounts invested but these are at best assessments, even guesses. When it comes to investigation of vested interests in the field of the mining industry, much of the wielding of financial power went on behind the scenes. It was often in the interests of powerholders not to allow how much power they possessed to be discovered. Some may even have appeared to hold power when they did not possess it. Previous analysis of the history of mining and colonialism in South-Central African regions has often had great difficulty in identifying who held ultimate responsibility for what happened. The usual culprits are held to be mining companies and their financial power holders, the likes of Rhodes, Williams and their fellow mining tycoons, but often without adequately explaining why they were responsible. But it is equally important to note that evaluating the amount of financial power is impossible unless one can attribute responsibility for outcomes.

An analysis of London-based mining companies can contribute to our understanding of the ambiguous relationship between the interests of the British Empire and those of the City. For Phimister (2000) it has enabled a 'better understanding of the peculiar nature of British overseas expansion and imperialism' and highlights the point that 'the concerns of the City, where these approximated to informal imperialism, were not always the same as the interests of formal empire'.[65] Similar conclusions were reached by Hobson in the context of South African mining finance.[66] While researchers have shown that the distribution of investments was extremely uneven, varying from colony to colony and district to district,[67] the broad point that British capital ultimately revolutionised the economy and society throughout colonial Africa has remained undisputed. In the Transvaal (the South African Republic) where British investments accounted for an estimated 70% of the total, the mining industry was dependent on the City for investments, loans and other financial services. In Rhodesia the relationship between financial imperialism and territorial expansion was less evident,[68] and even less so in Katanga which remained outside the formal British sphere of influence.

There is another aspect in this tendency to see capitalist exploitation in mining; it has deflected attention from the histories of mining companies. In fact, the nature of colonial business ventures is very difficult to appreciate without a company-level study aiming to research capital accumulation.[69] As the present study suggests, companies such as ZE were not simply a vehicle for market manipulation but instead established to explore, prospect and mine, and consequently were directly responsible for the dramatic impact on both human and physical environments in parts of South-Central Africa. What follows then in Chapter 3 is an analysis of the geographies of ZE's mining finance and its wider links to mine exploration and empire-building. The analysis provides evidence of the complex nexus of social, organisational and financial interests centring on the City that helped to support the development of mining operations in colonial-era South-Central Africa.

Notes

1 For further information, see Mokyr 1990.
2 Hamilton 1967, 2; Allen 1923, 2; Velanzuela 1990, 657–686; Evans and Saunders 2015, 3–26; Evans and Miskell 2020, 1–3.
3 Glamann 1953, 41–79; Evans and Miskell 2020, 10, 50, 55.
4 Gibson-Jarvie 1979, 2.
5 Kubicek 1999, 249.
6 Refer, for instance, to Hobsbawm 1999, 112–131.

7 Allen 1923, 1.
8 Ahvenainen 2011, 14–15.
9 Ahvenainen 1996, 10.
10 Ahvenainen 2011, 72, 81–82, 87.
11 *The Times* 6 April 1865.
12 Ahvenainen 2011, 157–158.
13 *Bombay Gazette* 17 December 1875.
14 Ahvenainen 1996, 60.
15 Allen 1923, 1.
16 For further information, see Declercq et al. 2022, 3–25.
17 Evans and Miskell 2020, 4; Schmitz 1979, 6–11; Leitner 2001, 401–411, 416–427.
18 Pascual and Nadal 2008, 18–19.
19 Allen 1923, 1.
20 Ball 2004, 451–489; Allen 1923, 25.
21 Harvey and Press 2000, 91.
22 Skelton 1937, 392.
23 Platt 1968, 3; Harvey and Press 1989, 64–86; van Helten 1990, 159–185.
24 McRae and Cairncross 2017; Kynaston 2012.
25 Ally 1994, 1–6; Green 1982, 21–22; Gibson-Jarvie 1979, 50.
26 *The Stock Exchange Year-book* 1874, 158–169; Mayo 2001, 392.
27 *The Stock Exchange Year-book* 1874, 158–169; *Journal of the Society of Arts* 4 December 1868, 45.
28 Harvey 1981; *Mineral Resources of the United States* 1886, *234–238.*
29 Evans and Miskell 2020, 12; Smalberger 1969, 117.
30 Refer, for instance, to Rönnbäck and Broberg 2019; Stone 1999.
31 van Helten 1990, 161–163.
32 Wilkins 1988, 263–264, 277–278; Wilkins 1998, 10–11. See also Hobson 1901, 210–211.
33 Companies Act 1862.
34 For further information, see Maltby 1998, 9–32; van Helten 1990, 165–166; LMA, SE, CLC/B/004/F/01/MS18000.
35 van Helten 1990, 165–166, notes 30, 36, 40.
36 Ashmead 1909, 155.
37 Harvey and Press 2000, 102.
38 Newbury 2009, 87.
39 van Helten 1990, 165.
40 Gibson-Jarvie 1979, 100–113.
41 *Cf.* Lukasiewitcz 2017, 723, 725.
42 Burt 1998, 717.
43 Gibson-Jarvie 1976, 9–10.
44 Gibson-Jarvie 1976, 9–10, 13.
45 Prain 1975, 86–88.
46 Prain 1975, 83–84; Allen 1923, 22.
47 Gibson-Jarvie 1976, 33–35, 37, 48; Gibson-Jarvie 1979, 62, 65–67.
48 Prain 1975, 88–91.
49 Gibson-Jarvie 1976, 23, 31, 42.
50 Schmitz 1986, 408–409.
51 Cain and Hopkins 1994.
52 Wilkins 1988, 261; Wilkins 1998, 3–64; Casson 1994, 95–108; Corley 1994, 71–88; Hennart 1994a, 51–70; Hennart 1994b, 118–131; Jones 2005, 20–21, 23–24.
53 Wilkins 1988, 276–277.
54 Harvey and Press 1989, 67, 69; van Helten 1990, 165–166; Wilkins 1988, 264.
55 Wilkins 1988, 265; Wilkins, 1998, 10.
56 For further information, see Michie 1992.
57 Dunning and Morgan 1971, 33–34; Jones 1993, 9–10.

58 Wilkins 1988, 262–263.
59 Newbury 2009, 87.
60 Katzenellenbogen 2004, 287–288; Hutchinson and Martelli 1971, 15–57.
61 Wilkins 1988, 259, 263–264, 267.
62 TNA, BT 31/32010/101258, RHOKANA, Prospectus, n.d.; Accounts, Balance Sheet, 30 September 1919.
63 TNA, BT 31/32010/101258, RHOKANA, Accounts, Balance Sheet, 30 September 1919; Pauling 1926.
64 Refer, for instance, to Arrighi 1983.
65 Phimister 2000, 38.
66 Hobson 1905, 117–118.
67 Duignan and Gann 1975, 19–23.
68 Phimister 2002, 74, 79.
69 Phimister 2003, 88–97.

References

Ahvenainen, J. (1996) *The History of the Caribbean Telegraphs before the First World War*, The Finnish Academy of Science and Letters, Helsinki.

Ahvenainen, J. (2011) *The History of the Near Eastern Telegraphs before the First World War*, The Finnish Academy of Science and Letters, Helsinki.

Allen, R. (1923) *Copper Ores*, Imperial Institute, Monographs on Mineral Resources with Special Reference to the British Empire, John Murray, London.

Ally, R. (1994) *Gold & Empire: The Bank of England and South Africa's Gold Producers 1886–1926*, Witwatersrand University Press, Johannesburg.

Arrighi, G. (1983) *The Geometry of Imperialism: The Limits of Hobson's Paradigm*, Verso, London.

Ashmead, E. (1909) *Twenty-Five Years of Mining. 1880–1904: A Retrospective Review with an Appendix Four Years Later, 1905–1908*, The Mining Journal, London.

Ball, S.S. (2004) 'The German Octopus: The British Metal Corporation and the Next War, 1914–1939', *Enterprise & Society*, 5:3, 451–489.

Bombay Gazette (17 December 1875).

Burt, R. (1998) 'Segmented Capital Markets and Patterns of Investment in Late Victorian Britain: Evidence from the Non-Ferrous Mining Industry', *The Economic History Review*, New Series, 51:4, 709–733.

Cain, P.J. and Hopkins, A.G. (1994) *British Imperialism: Innovation and Expansion, 1688–1914*, Longman, London, New York.

Casson, M. (1994) 'Institutional Diversity in Overseas Enterprise: Explaining the Free-Standing Company', *Business History*, 36:4, 95–108.

Companies Act (1862) Retrieved 24 May 2023 from commencement 7 Aug 1862. https://assets.publishing.service.gov.uk/media/5a7ec52de5274a2e8ab4817c/comm7Aug1862CoAct1862_P1.pdf.

Corley, T.A.B. (1994) 'Britain's Overseas Investments in 1914 Revisited', *Business History* 36:1, 71–88.

Declercq, R., Frøland, H.O. and Money, D. (2022) 'Introduction: Worlds of Copper?' in R. Declercq, D. Money and H.O. Frøland eds. *Born with a Copper Spoon: A Global History of Copper, 1830–1980*, The Chicago University Press, Chicago, IL, 3–25.

Duignan, P. and Gann, L.H. (1975) 'Introduction' in P. Duignan and L.H. Gann eds. *Colonialism in Africa 1870–1960*. Vol. 4: *The Economics of Colonialism*, Cambridge University Press, Cambridge, 1–30.

Dunning, J.H. and Morgan, E.V. (1971) *An Economic Study of the City of London*, George Allen & Unwin, London.

Evans, C. and Miskell, L. (2020) *Swansea Copper: A Global History*, Johns Hopkins University Press, Baltimore MD.

Evans, C. and Saunders, O. (2015) 'A World of Copper: Globalizing the Industrial Revolution, 1830–70', *Journal of Global History*, 10:1, 3–26.

Gibson-Jarvie, R. (1976) *The London Metal Exchange: A Commodity Market*, Woodhead-Faulkner and Metallgesellschaft AG, Cambridge.

Gibson-Jarvie, R. (1979) *The City of London: A Financial and Commercial History*, Woodhead-Faulkner, London.

Glamann, K. (1953) 'The Dutch East India Company's Trade with Japanese Copper, 1645–1736', *Scandinavian Economic History Review*, 1:1, 41–79.

Green, T. (1982) *The New World of Gold: The Inside Story of the Mines, the Markets, the Politics, the Investors*, Weidenfeld & Nicolson, London.

Hamilton, H. (1967) *The English Brass & Copper Industries to 1800*, Augustus M. Kelley, Bookseller, New York.

Harvey, C.E. (1981) *The Rio Tinto Company: An Economic History of a Leading Mining Concern 1873–1954*, Alison Hodge Publishers, Penzance, Cornwall.

Harvey, C. and Press, J. (1989) 'Overseas Investment and the Professional Advance of British Metal Mining Engineers, 1851–1914', *The Economic History Review*, New Series, 42:1, 64–86.

Harvey, C. and Press, J. (2000) 'The City of London and International Trade, 1850–1914' in R.C. Michie ed. *The Development of London as a Financial Centre*, Vol. 2: *1850–1914*, IB Tauris, London, 87–105.

Hennart, J.-F. (1994a) 'International Financial Capital Transfers: A Transaction Cost Framework', *Business History*, 36:1, 51–70.

Hennart, J.-F. (1994b) 'Free-Standing Firms and the Internalisation of Markets for Financial Capital: A Response to Casson', *Business History*, 36:4, 118–131.

Hobsbawm, E.J. (1999) *Industry and Empire*, Penguin Books, London.

Hobson, J.A. (23 November1901) 'Imperialism the Policy of Investors', *Speaker*, 5:112, 210–211.

Hobson, J.A. (29 April1905) 'The Structure of South African Finance', *Speaker*, 12:291, 117–118.

Hutchinson, R. and Martelli, G. (1971) *Robert's People: The Life of Sir Robert Williams Bart. 1860–1938*, Chatto & Windus, London.

Jones, G. (1993) *British Multinational Banking, 1830–1990*, Oxford University Press, Oxford.

Jones, G. (2005) *Multinationals and Global Capitalism: From the Nineteenth to the Twenty-First Century*, Oxford University Press, Oxford.

Journal of the Society of Arts (4 December1868) 'Commerce', 17:837, 44–45.

Katzenellenbogen, S. (2004) 'Williams, Sir Robert, Baronet (1860–1938)' in H.C.G. Matthew and B. Harrison eds. *Oxford Dictionary of National Biography*, 59, Oxford University Press, Oxford, 287–288.

Kubicek, R. (1999) 'British Empire, Expansion, and Technological Change' in A. Porter ed. *The Oxford History of the British Empire: The Nineteenth Century*, Oxford University Press, Oxford, 247–269.

Kynaston, D. (2012) *City of London: The History*, Vintage Books, London.

Leitner, J. (2001) 'Red Metal in the Age of Capital: The Political Ecology of Copper in the Nineteenth-Century World-Economy', *Review* (Fernand Braudel Center), 24:3, 373–437.

London Metropolitan Archives (LMA), Records of the Stock Exchange, London (SE), Quotation and Listing of Companies (CLC).

Lukasiewitcz, M. (2017) 'From Diamonds to Gold: The Making of the Johannesburg Stock Exchange, 1880–1890', *Journal of Southern African Studies*, 43:4, 715–732.

Maltby, J. (1998) 'UK Joint Stock Companies Legislation 1844–1900: Accounting Publicity and "Mercantile Caution"', *Accounting History*, 3:1, 9–32.

Mayo, J. (2001) 'The Development of British Interests in Chile's Norte Chico in the Early Nineteenth Century', *The Americas*, 57:3, 363–394.

McRae, H. and Cairncross, F. (2017) *Capital City: London as a Financial Centre*, Routledge, London.

Michie, R.C. (1992) *The City of London: Continuity and Change, 1850–1990*, Palgrave Macmillan, Houndmills, Basingstoke.

Mineral Resources of the United States (1886) *Calendar Year 1885*, Division of Mining Statistics and Technology, Government Printing Office, Washington, DC.

Mokyr, J. (1990) *The Lever of Riches. Technological Creativity and Economic Progress*, Oxford University Press, Oxford.

The National Archives of the UK (TNA), Kew, Board of Trade (BT).

Newbury, C. (2009) 'Rhodes, De Beers and the Mining Finance in South Africa: The Business of Entrepreneurship and Imperialism' in R.E. Dumett ed. *Mining Tycoons in the Age of Empire, 1870–1945: Entrepreneurship, High Finance, Politics and Territorial Expansion*, Routledge, London, 85–108.

Pascual, P. and Nadal, J. (2008) *El coure*, Vol. I: *Producció i consum a l'era industrial*, Eumo Editorial and La Farga Group, Vic.

Pauling, G. (1926) *The Chronicles of a Contractor: Being the Autobiography of the Late George Pauling*, D. Buchan ed. Constable, London.

Phimister, I. (2000) 'Corners and Company-Mongering: Nigerian Tin and the City of London, 1909–12', *The Journal of Imperial and Commonwealth History*, 28:2, 23–41.

Phimister, I. (2002) 'Empire, Imperialism and Partition of Africa' in S. Akita ed. *Gentlemanly Capitalism, Imperialism, and Global History*, Palgrave Macmillan, Houndmills, Basingstoke, 65–82.

Phimister, I. (2003) 'Speculation and Exploitation: The Southern Rhodesian Mining Industry in the Company Era', *Historia*, 48:2, 88–97.

Platt, D.C.M. (1968) *Finance, Trade and Politics in British Foreign Policy 1815–1914*, Clarendon Press, Oxford.

Prain, Sir R. (1975) *Copper: The Anatomy of an Industry*, Mining Journal Books, London.

Rönnbäck, K. and Broberg, O. (2019) *Capital and Colonialism: The Return on British Investments in Africa 1869–1969*, Palgrave Macmillan, Cham, Switzerland.

Schmitz, C.J. (1979) *World non-Ferrous Metal Production and Prices, 1700–1976*, Frank Cass, London.

Schmitz, C. (1986) 'The Rise of Big Business in the World Copper Industry 1870–1930', *The Economic History Review*, New Series, 39:3, 392–410.

Skelton, A. (1937) 'Copper' in W.Y. Elliott, E.S. May, J.W.F. Rowe, D.H. Wallace and A. Skelton eds. *International Control in the Non-Ferrous Metals*, Macmillan, New York, 363–536.

Smalberger, J.M. (1969) *Aspects of the history of copper mining in Namaqualand*, MA thesis, The University of Cape Town.

The Stock Exchange Year-book and Diary for 1875 Containing a Digest of Information Relating to the Joint Stock Companies and Public Securities Known to the Markets of the United Kingdom, and a Calendar and Diary, the Former Especially Adapted to

Persons Concerned in Stock Exchange Business (1874) T. Skinner ed. Cassell, Petter & Galpin, London, Paris and New York.

Stone, I. (1999) *The Global Export of Capital from Great Britain, 1865–1914: A Statistical Survey*, Palgrave Macmillan, Houndmills, Basingstoke.

The Times (6 April1865).

van Helten, J.-J. (1990) 'Mining, Share Manias and Speculation: British Investment in Overseas Mining' in J.-J. van Helten and Y. Cassis eds. *Capitalism in a Mature Economy: Financial Institutions, Capital Exports and British Industry, 1870–1939*, Edward Elgar, London, 159–185.

Velanzuela, L. (1990) 'Challenges to the British Copper Smelting Industry in the World Market, 1840–1860', *Journal of European Economic History*, 19:3, 657–686.

Wilkins, M. (1988) 'The Free-Standing Company, 1870–1914: An Important Type of British Foreign Direct Investment', *The Economic History Review*, 2nd series, 41:2, 259–282.

Wilkins, M. (1998) 'The Free-Standing Company Revisited' in M. Wilkins and H. Schröter eds. *The Free-Standing Company in the World Economy, 1830–1996*, Oxford University Press, Oxford, 3–64.

3 The geographies of mining finance

This chapter considers the geographies of The Zambesia Exploring Company's (ZE) mining finance and its wider links to mine exploration and empire-building in early colonial Southern Africa. The first section of the chapter deals with the Mineral Revolution in Southern Africa, which involved a tripartite increase in capital investments in gold, coal and diamond mining. Before discussing the varieties of concerns pertaining to the geographies of ZE's mining finance in early colonial Southern Rhodesia (Zimbabwe) in the third section, the second section provides the historical context in which mining took place, and especially notes the pivotal role played by gold in bringing the Mineral Revolution into being in Southern Africa. The fourth section focuses on the prospects for companies associated with mining in Southern Rhodesia in the early 1890s in the form of the promotion of the company and share speculation that coincided with the remarkable growth of investments by the City of London in mining and mine-exploring companies. The final section concludes that investments in gold mining gave the ultimate impetus for the exploitation of mineral resources in Northern Rhodesia and led to the subsequent developments in mining in Katanga.

The Mineral Revolution in Southern Africa

Enterprises began investing in Southern Africa on a new scale and level of durability as rapid increase in international trade and transformation of steam transport and telegraph communication technologies enabled companies to exploit the natural resources of the newly colonised lands. The discovery of what proved to be the largest source of diamonds in the world, on the banks of the Orange River in the northern frontier of the Cape Colony in 1869, opened a new phase of imperial expansion in Southern Africa. In 1873, ignoring the rival claims of the region's Tswana and the two Boer republics, the Transvaal (the South African Republic) and the Orange Free State, the British Government declared the diamond fields a Crown Colony, Griqualand West, which was eventually incorporated within the Cape Colony in 1880.[1]

Following the proclamation of a new colony open for claim-staking, tens of thousands of prospectors from South Africa and overseas rushed to the

DOI: 10.4324/9781003247371-3

diamond-bearing area, where the diamond city Kimberley was born. In the struggle for holdings that followed, a few young immigrants from Europe managed to overcome their competitors. The most successful of them all proved to be Cecil Rhodes, who had arrived in the Colony of Natal in 1869 in an attempt to stave off pulmonary tuberculosis in a country known as having a cure-all climate for pulmonary complaints.[2] By the late 1870s the Kimberley diamond fields had already been transformed from being simply an area of small claims dotted all over the land into a mineralisation zone run by joint-stock companies limited by shares. The final contest for control of the diamond fields and the ultimate monopolising of the diamond mines was between the De Beers mine, which was controlled by Rhodes and his business associate, Charles Dunell Rudd, and the Barnato Diamond Mining Company, controlled by the Barnato brothers, Harry and Barnett Isaacs (Barney) Barnato, who had managed to acquire by speculation a substantial share in several mining companies in Kimberley. In this struggle for holdings, Rhodes and Rudd secured financial backing from Rothschilds of London, and from Rhodes' two other important business associates, Lord Gifford, and George Cawston, a stockjobber and barrister-at-law who had been called to the bar in 1882,[3] and with their support Rhodes persuaded Barnato to collaborate with him. In 1888 was born De Beers Consolidated Mines, which became the largest South African mining company of the time traded on the London Stock Exchange.[4]

The discovery of hitherto-unknown gold-bearing reefs in the Witwatersrand in the Transvaal (commonly known as the 'Rand'), an area of high veldt forming a divide between the Orange and Limpopo rivers, was of profound importance, not least because it formed a decisive part of what has been termed the 'Mineral Revolution' in Southern Africa. Within a span of just a few years, from the discovery of payable gold on the Wilgespruit farm in the West Rand area (the Confidence Reef), where the brothers Fred and Harry Struben had started mine quartz intrusions in 1884, and the discovery of the main gold-bearing rocky conglomerate outcrop (the Main Reef Group) on the Langlaagte farm in February 1886, Johannesburg was born and became the centre of what was to become the largest and richest gold field in the world.[5] As Richardson and van Helten (1984) have explained, the Rand's gold discoveries, together with the consolidation of the Kimberley diamond industry and the discovery of large deposits of coal first in Natal and then in the neighbouring Transvaal, created 'a tripartite transformation in the productive capacity' of the region, which 'changed the whole political and economic constellation' of Southern Africa.[6]

In the previous major gold rushes, such as in 1848 along the Sacramento River in California, or a few years later along the Macquarie River not far from Bathurst in New South Wales, and in Ballarat in the Colony of Victoria, the main sources of gold were initially alluvial gold deposits that had been weathered from the parent rock and concentrated in sediments. Such placer deposits of gold could be separated with a few simple implements: a pick, shovel, sluice and pan. Only in virgin quartz intrusion lodes or in particularly rich veins in bedrock were tunnelling and consequently employment of substantial amounts of capital and labour necessary.[7] Unlike those earlier alluvial gold bonanzas, the main bulk of Rand gold was present in minute particles embedded in vast quantities of hard quartz rock. The visible outcrops were quickly exhausted and from the early 1890s the industry developed into deep-level mining of the gold-bearing reefs, which extended from the surface at an average angle of 25 degrees to depths of many thousands of feet.[8]

Due to its peculiar geological characteristics, the Rand's gold mining required substantial amounts of capital before it could evolve into a major mining industry. By and large, for highly organised industries of the late nineteenth century such as mining it had become increasingly difficult to raise capital locally, so the leading South African mining companies, Consolidated Goldfields, Crown Mines, DeBeers Consolidated and Rand Mines, were mostly capitalised in London, with many others double listed, being on both the London and Johannesburg stock exchanges.[9] Their penetration of the entire financial structure of South African business, mining, manufacture, commerce, transport and banking was, as Hobson (1905) put it, 'the strongest consolidation of economic power ever wielded by a single group over a large profitable area of the globe'.[10]

Besides capital, engineering skill was also needed. The Rand's gold could not have been extracted without blasting gelatin, which shattered the gold-bearing rock into pieces; heavy steam-driven stamp mills that crushed the ore; and the MacArthur Forrest cyanide process, invented in 1887 by John Stewart MacArthur, working in collaboration with the brothers Robert and William Forrest for the Tennant Company in Glasgow, with the ore being treated chemically before the gold could be separated from the rock. By 1894 there were 2,642 stampers crushing gold-bearing rock that was brought from the diggings, and the total would ultimately rise to 10,000. At the same time the use of coal for energy rose exponentially. The Middelburg Colliery in the Transvaal, which commenced its operations in about 1895, achieved an output of 500,000 tons by 1900 – in just five years.[11]

The Rand was not only the world's greatest single source of gold, but the biggest employer of labour in Southern Africa. In just eight years from the discovery of the Main Reef (in 1894), there were already as many as 42,500 Africans employed in the mines together with 5,500 white miners.[12] The first Census of Johannesburg was made in 1896 and it revealed that immigrants who had descended on the 'City of Gold' were young bachelors from Britain, with young men from Cornwall and from Scotland making up more numerous single groups than men from other parts of the UK, and from Germany, Denmark, Sweden, Norway, Austria, Switzerland, France, Belgium, Portugal, Italy, Greece and Romania. There were prominent numbers of Americans and also of Chinese, as well as of British 'colonials' from Australia, New Zealand and elsewhere. Those born in the Russian Empire formed a significant part of the total white workforce, 3,335 in total, including those who had emigrated from the Grand Duchy of Finland.[13]

As earlier in the Cape Colony, segregation between those who were identified as 'white' or 'coloured' (*i.e.* Afrikaans-speaking freed slaves, those of mixed-race culture and the indigenous San and Khoe groups) as distinct from Bantu-speaking 'black Africans' indicated a rigorous form of economic and social control that was in the process of developing.[14] While the discovery of gold brought new opportunities for labour of all colours and helped to create an African bourgeoisie in the long run, it was black Africans who faced the worst aspects of the mining work. Those drilling the rockface, to make the holes for the explosives used to break the gold-bearing reef, and those who hand-loaded the cocopans were on the lowest social stratum of the industry.[15] In a joint-stock company form it had become more and more difficult to locate satisfactorily the different kinds and degrees of moral responsibility. The directors were appointed by and derived their power from the shareholders, and, as Hobson put it, they 'had no right to indulge their private philanthropic predilections' at the expense of the owners,[16] who were primarily motivated by the desire to make profit and only secondarily by a desire to confer benefit on workers.

The flow of African labour was guaranteed with the forced introduction of a sterling-based cash economy in the form of the so-called 'hut tax' (*i.e.* a tax per household or per male resident). The pound sterling had been introduced into the Cape Colony in 1825, and over the course of the century it had become legal tender in the British and Boer territories. The urge to earn tax money persuaded African men to leave their families in rural homes to work on the mines for several months at a time and to live in male-only compounds (derived from the Malay *kampong*, village) owned by the company they worked for. The low cost of African labour was the major asset of mining in colonial-era South-Central Africa. African labour was kept in unskilled employment at a permanently low wage while being permanently denied access to any skills. This racial segregation encouraged mining companies to use African workers indiscriminately and wastefully,[17] a state of affairs which was to become the hallmark of the mining industry in Southern Africa and beyond it in the Rhodesias and Katanga.

The longevity of the Rand's gold mines was another factor that separated it from the earlier alluvial gold rushes, which were relatively short-lived and generally died quickly once the gold had been scooped out.[18] For about 35 years (1886–1919), the Rand's gold formed the pivot of the monetary system of the international capitalist community. Sold to London at a standard price of £3.17.10½ per standard ounce (*i.e.* 22 carat), gold was almost universally acknowledged as the only true measure of value, the main standard of price, and the dominant monetary form, with its basis lying in the Rand's mining industry. The pre-eminence of the London bullion market lay in the Rand's gold, which was crucial to sterling's international supremacy as a trustworthy currency. The sterling price of gold (£4.4.11½ per fine troy ounce) suffered only minor fluctuations over a period of over 200 years (from the beginning of the eighteenth century until 1931).[19] While race relations hardened with the rise of Afrikaner nationalism in South Africa after the Second World War, gold output soared. By 1970 South Africa accounted for 70% of the entire world's gold production, with the vast majority of it originating from the Witwatersrand.[20]

The gold of Ophir

> But where gold is concerned emotion, rather than logic, tends to prevail.[21]

Of all the metals mined throughout history gold has been given the most varied meanings. Gold has been regarded as a sacred metal by many societies, and it has been a symbol of wealth and power all over the world. The earliest meanings of gold are thought to relate to ceremonial or ancestral purposes. It was thought to represent the sun, with its gleaming colour and timeless durability. Yet we do not know precisely when or how we became familiar with the use of gold. Discoveries unearthed at Varna in Bulgaria suggest that a rich gold-working industry was established there sometime between 4500 and 4000 BCE. In Egypt the earliest gold ornaments – simple gold leaf-covered earthenware beads – were made between 4000 and 3500 BCE. In Western Europe the first gold objects known are from Spain during the late fourth and early third millennia BCE. By the end of the third millennium gold working was firmly established in Britain and Ireland, where goldsmiths developed to a very high degree the metallurgical skills necessary to make a range of ornaments, as uncovered hoards of metal objects in lakes, rivers and other waterlogged locations such as bogs testify.[22]

One of the longest and oldest mining traditions anywhere in the world is found to come from Zimbabwe, a landlocked country of 154,446 square miles, located in the interior of Southern Africa. True testimony to mining's importance to the country is the Great Zimbabwe, derived from *dzimba dza mabwe*, 'houses of stone', the outstanding achievement which the Shona constructed and inhabited between the eleventh and sixteenth centuries. The Shona undertook mining as a community enterprise of entire villages early in the wet season (November to January) when the rivers provided water for washing the ore and before a rising water table flooded the mines. Whilst the Shona used copper and gold for both internal consumption and export, from the twelfth to the nineteenth century it was gold which constituted the single most important export item from the Zimbabwe Plateau.[23]

In the field of indigenous gold metallurgy in Southern Africa, the pinnacle is generally regarded to be Mapungubwe, an Iron Age trading kingdom (*c.* 1220–1290) situated on the Limpopo, straddling the borders of the modern states of Botswana, Zimbabwe and South Africa. In Mapungubwe society, gold ornaments and artefacts – such as the world-famous gold rhinoceros recovered from the royal burial site on the Mapungubwe Hill in 1934 – were presumably symbols of the great power and wealth of the political, religious and royal ruling classes. The Mapungubwe society, adept at mining, smelting and smithing iron, copper and gold, traded with people as far away as Egypt, India, South-East Asia and China.[24]

Besides its aesthetic appearance, its golden colour and everlasting qualities, gold has long been valued as an article of trade. Gold's high specific gravity, representing considerable weight in a relatively small space, means that a small quantity expresses a high exchange value, making it the metal best qualified to perform the function of currency. Gold is virtually indestructible, as the various unearthed ancient artefacts in pristine condition testify, being a noble metal that does not tarnish like silver (*i.e.* gold never oxidises and stays shining bright forever) nor corrode like copper or lead. While gold is relatively inert, it is also very malleable and has a relatively low melting point (1,064°C). The latter two physical properties have allowed goldsmiths to smelt and to work gold into units of varying shapes and sizes with relative ease.[25]

While the mining of metals such as iron, copper and gold has been going on in Southern Africa for thousands of years, it was not until the discovery of Great Zimbabwe by the Portuguese in the earlier part of the sixteenth century that the Great Dyke's ancient rocks came to be known by the West to be rich in minerals. In the wake of colonialism, the origins of Great Zimbabwe became a subject of racialist mythology-building. Its ruins were considered to be the lost 'Havilah', the location of King Solomon's mines and the source of the gold of 'Ophir'.[26] In the late nineteenth century, Zimbabwe's golden lure was popularised in novels such as Rider Haggard's *King Solomon's Mines* (1885), replete with exciting romances. There was the romance of prospectors' and hunters' camps, the romance of the transport rider and of the trooper, the romance of gorgeous sunrises and sunsets, of cloudless skies and of vast expanses of the *veldt*. [27]

The arrival of the white settlers to the Highveld depended upon the expectation that gold lodes in the Zimbabwe Plateau could match the yields in the Rand goldfields. Combined with hopes and imprecise information, the gold fever contributed to expectations of a mining bonanza, and set on the move ever-growing numbers of settlers driven by popularised myths of exotic lands and easy riches. It is notable that in both East and West Africa the British government had attempted, as in the past, to rely on private trading companies to uphold its commercial and strategic interests, and that in both regions the government had finally been compelled to step in and take over colonial administration. Nonetheless in Southern Africa too, mineral resource governance was initially handed to a chartered company, the British South Africa Company (BSAC), which was incorporated on the London Stock Exchange by Royal Charter on 29 October 1889. The chartered company was an amalgamation of Rhodes' business group with a group controlled by his closest business associates from the Kimberley diamond business, Charles Dunell Rudd and Alfred Beit, and a London-based group headed by Lord Gifford on behalf of the Bechuanaland Exploration Company, George Cawston and Baron Nathan de Rothschild.[28]

The Charter did not grant any mining rights but empowered BSAC to acquire the rights by negotiating with local African rulers and entering into concessionary agreements, in order to gain full and exclusive access to the mineral resources of the territory and the right to exploit them in any manner it deemed fit.[29] First of these was the 'Rudd Concession', signed on 30 October 1888, in which the paramount ruler, Lobengula Khumalo of the Matabele Kingdom, granted the mineral rights to the chartered company, hoping to strengthen his rule against the Shona in the east and the Boers in the south. Having secured a territory embracing 750,000 square miles in total as its domain, BSAC acted as a parastatal hybrid, combining private, for-profit interests while at the same time being endowed with quasi-governmental powers and functions for the mining industry.[30] It aimed to provide administrative and transport infrastructure, including the railway and telegraph, but would otherwise take its profits through shareholdings in companies that were formed, with its consent, to promote trade and commerce and to develop minerals in the company territories.[31]

Besides being a skilful businessman as well as an apt politician, Rhodes, the Managing Director of BSAC, was also an imperial visionary, who dreamt of a railway stretching from the Cape to Cairo, ensuring British dominance over the African continent. In the late nineteenth century the railway featured dominantly in Southern Africa, where it empowered the imperial agents – prospectors, soldiers, big-game hunters, missionaries and district commissioners. Fuelled by railway imperialism and the general share mania associated with the prospects of finding a second Rand, in 1890, BSAC's expeditionary force Pioneer Column trekked beyond the Limpopo River, surveying seemingly empty lands of the Ndebele and the Shona for railways, mining and for the promotion of colonial settlement schemes.[32]

With the arrival of the settlers, and for the preservation of public peace in those then faraway regions, some arrangements had to be made to determine the area of ground on which a man was allowed to work, and the conditions under which he could hold and deal with it. Hence arose the right of the discoverer of workable gold, or other valuable ores or minerals, under certain specific restrictions, generally as to race and colour, to claim the ownership of a small plot of ground of limited area on which his discovery had been made. These plots of ground became known as the 'claims', and from there the term passed into common and also legal parlance.[33]

For BSAC the small-scale working of gold offered a way of making its claims over the country effective at a minimum cost by means of settler colonialism. In its way, and in direct competition with it, stood the Ndebele, whose simple forms of gold mining and crop farming provided them with an independent source of income and, therefore, effectively removed the incentive to enter into wage labour. Ultimately, the Ndebele resolved to oppose the emerging settler rule. On 16 October 1893, an Ndebele army of 3,000 and possibly even up to 5,000 combatants, equipped with assegais, muzzle-loaders, and some even with rifles, attacked the *laager* of the 700 BSAC troopers on the Shangani River. The day was won by the devastating new weapon with which the troopers were equipped: the repeater called the 'Maxim gun', invented by Sir Hiram Stevens Maxim in 1884, capable of firing 500 rounds a minute.[34] Thus, with the help of the new military technology, a new colonial polity came into being, and in 1895 the whole of Matabeleland and Mashonaland was renamed Rhodesia in honour of Rhodes.[35] At the same location where Lobengula's former *kraal* stood, the white settlement of Bulawayo was born. By March 1894 small plots of land or 'stands' had been auctioned, and on 1 June 1894 the new town was thrown open for settlers.[36] The growth of the new Bulawayo settler community was immediately apparent. Within the next seven years, Ndebele-style straw houses were replaced by the modern American- or ancient Roman-style regular oblong grid, on which stood both brick and timber buildings of mining, finance and land companies and the modest corrugated iron or tin shanties of the Chinese, 'Kaffir' and Indian shopkeepers.

The most prominent buildings included the Stock Exchange Buildings, Scott's Offices, Willoughby's Buildings, Albany Chambers, Messrs. Robert Williams & Co. Buildings and the Mashonaland Agency. Public and private services expanded too and included the Bulawayo High Court, the Gaol, the Club, several small churches (such as the Anglican church, the Wesleyan church and the Catholic church), the convent, the Public Library, the Grand Hotel and the Memorial Hospital among others. Economic life diversified, and besides mining, finance and land businesses, there were two sawmills, the Bulawayo Steam and Saw Mills and the BSA Mills, as well as Rhodesia Breweries, and a wide variety of shops such as ironmongers, engineers, blacksmiths, saddlers, drapers, hatters, hosiers, outfitters, chemists, watchmakers, jewellers, opticians, groceries and shops of general merchants of guns, ammunition, boots, sports goods, 'native curios' and taxidermy specimens.[37]

From its modest beginnings the number of settlers in Bulawayo increased rapidly. The first census of 1 March 1895 revealed that the population of Bulawayo was 1,537 (adult males 1,232; adult females 164; children 141). Those from the United Kingdom were by far the largest group (1,017), followed by various 'colonials' from not only South Africa, but also Australia, New Zealand and Canada (299). Settlers from Germany (108) and the USA (33) were considered sufficiently numerous to be counted separately. The remaining 79 settlers were designated bluntly as 'others', indicating the presence of even the more obscure European ethnicities in the colonial context, such as Finns for example.[38]

Because the provenance of Bulawayo's white population was so heterogeneous, the town strongly proclaimed and insisted on its British character. Though from a motley of nationalities, the settlers shared similar outlooks in many respects. Most were young bachelors, but beyond differences of age, marital status and gender it was the contrasts and interactions between blacks and whites that most defined them. These interactions were governed by strict social divisions derived not only from the conventional bourgeois taboos of race, class and gender which the settlers brought with them, but, perhaps even more importantly, from the Christian ethic according to which men should work to save money and improve themselves. It was perceived by the settlers that African men did neither but just basked themselves in the sun. So they were consequently criticised for being idlers who noble-mindedly lived off the labour of their dozens of exploited wives.[39]

Believing in the economic future of the country and in the prospects of gold mining, the settlers hoped that the mines would soon go into production and that the mining companies would already be able to pay dividends to their shareholders in 1896. The settlers thus became actively involved in building the economic foundation of the new colonial polity. During the dry season of 1896–7, a settler became a prospector, who, liberated by BSAC even from purchasing a prospecting licence, went off to where he pleased to peg his 10 claims (those who were Pioneers of the 1890 Column were each allowed to stake 15 claims).[40] They thought that they had only to peg claims and their fortune was made. They had not yet learnt that winning gold from a quartz lode is an expensive process, demanding a great deal of capital, and in consequence the work was for big corporations, not petty prospectors. Besides prospecting for gold, the most obvious way of making a living, cultivating the Nbedele and Shona land, was not seen as an attractive option for long. The settlers tended to be adventurous young men who lacked the mentality to be family men. It was easier to try to buy food from the local African population than to try to grow and sell cash crops.[41]

The structure of Rhodesian mining finance

Mining companies were not only instrumental in opening up Africa's mineral wealth to the world's metal markets, but they also played a significant part in the enforcement of colonial rule. In early 1891, when Rhodes was anxious to justify the expansion of BSAC further north, to Mashonaland, he sought the means to undertake the exploration work. To verify its mineral wealth and to ascertain if it could be made to support the extension of the railway from the south, Rhodes persuaded Robert Williams, then a well-known mining consultant in Johannesburg, to lead an expedition into Mashonaland in the spring of 1891. To finance the expedition, Williams registered ZE on the London Stock Exchange on 25 March 1891. The nominal capitalisation of ZE, a measly £20,000 divided into twenty thousand shares of one pound each,[42] gave little indication that the company would eventually emerge as the parent of the great Tanks Group, the registered capital of which would ultimately rise to tens of millions of pounds by the end of the colonial era.

Upon the company's registration Williams became African manager. His responsibility was to organise, equip and lead an expedition to Mashonaland as well as to carry out the initial mine exploration work. Williams' brother Oliver John Williams was appointed London manager and Tyndale White became the Chairman of the board of ZE. Initially Williams was entitled to receive 35% of all net profits made or realised whether in cash, shares, debentures or other securities.[43] Later, on 20 April 1898, this agreement was amended with Robert Williams replacing his brother as the Managing Director of ZE.[44]

Investors in ZE were part of an inter-organisational network, which was linked through managerial control and the interlocking directorates of several other companies, most notably BSAC. Subscribers for shares included South African mining tycoons such as Rhodes and Sigismund Neumann (1857–1916), as well as prominent figures from late-Victorian high society such as George Holford (1860–1926), a British Army officer and a wealthy landowner, and the 4th Earl Grey (Albert Grey, 1851–1917), who also served on the board of directors of BSAC.[45] From its modest beginnings, the capitalisation of ZE progressed with some rapidity, facilitated by the Rhodesian gold fever. By the end of 1897 investors had registered £145,000 worth of capital in ZE and the list of subscribers was 26 pages long, comprising mostly small-scale investors, whose shareholding varied from one up to about 1,000 shares.[46]

In the structure of Rhodesian mining finance, The Standard Bank of South Africa, based in Cape Town, but headquartered in the City, held a key position. A feature of the early finance markets in Rhodesia was a drastic scarcity of cash money, which was accelerated by the scarcity of commodities, and, before the arrival of the railway in Bulawayo in 1897, very heavy transport costs. To mitigate this problem, in July 1892, just five months after connecting Salisbury (Harare) with a telegraph from the south, Rhodes' business associate and Standard's General Manager, Lewis Michell, facilitated the opening of Standard's first branch in Rhodesia, in Salisbury. Standard offered an acceptable currency supply to replace BSAC's cheques, and it also enabled the money to be promptly transferred for the needs of the mining industry. By 1900 Standard held deposits of £2.5 million against advances of just £0.25 million in Rhodesia, a deficit which is partly attributable to the difficulty of assaying the value of the gold lodes and ultimately the land, and partly to Standard's control over gold assaying and purchasing in the Bulawayo Assay Office and Public Laboratory.[47]

Another significant feature of the early Rhodesian financial market was the availability of portfolio funding for its nascent stock market, which stemmed from a lengthy international depression in the 1880s and, in general, from the global financial hegemony enjoyed by the City. One of the symptoms of this dominance was a chronic excess of financial liquidity, or 'surplus capital' as defined by Hobson, in the London Stock Exchange in the 1890s.[48] Capitalisation was particularly intense in 1895, when 40% of the total of 369 mining companies, nicknamed as 'Rhodesians', with registered capital of £50.59 million, that were listed in a span of just 15 years (1889–1904) were underwritten.[49] In Rhodesia, the focal point of capital accumulation was the Bulawayo Stock Exchange and Transfer Agency, which in its first financial year of 1895 registered £15 million worth of shares[50] – an astonishing feat for any financial operator of the time, let alone for one that stood in the 'barren dreariness of the Highveld'.[51] From 1891 to 1904 cash investments in the BSAC territories accounted for another £10 million.[52]

In March 1896 the sudden and unexpected Ndebele and Shona uprisings halted prospecting and exploitation of mineral resources in Rhodesia. The Ndebele killed a number of settlers outside Bulawayo and besieged the town itself, bringing the settler community to the brink of destruction. During the siege Bulawayo's early hearty, devil-may-care attitude was replaced by a gloomy atmosphere and dead silence on the streets. Mining properties lost their value and commodity prices soared. As it turned out, Rhodesia had yielded more promises than gold, and in the aftermath of the war on the savannah the flow of capital evaporated along with the value of mining company shares. Following the early euphoria, which caused £1 shares in ZE to touch over £5 at the end of 1895, the shares fell below par on the market by early 1898.[53] The shareholders of the chartered company itself were among those who suffered most. Before the war in 1895 BSAC shares were quoted on the Bulawayo Stock Exchange at an average of £8.17.6, but after the war in 1898 they changed hands at an average of £2.15.0.[54] As Standard's Michell put it, 'the share markets were no longer in any mood to absorb fresh issues of speculative capital.'[55]

The vastly overestimated gold reserves were the single most important element determining the nature of the economic and political development of South-Central Africa.[56] As Phimister (1988) has put it:

> This collapse of the speculative bubble forced the B.S.A. Company to try, much more seriously this time, to foster genuine mining activity. In short, the time had come to curb what critics had slated as 'trading upon the unknown, this traffic in fairy tales, this capitalization of dreams'.
>
> The new situation was to be one in which the large capitalist 'should be encouraged, but only as a mining and industrial factor, not as a speculator pure and simple'.[57]

The outbreak of the South African War in 1899 (the Boer War, 1899–1902) dashed any further short-range speculative dreams, notwithstanding a major railway investment programme financed mainly by private investments in the late 1890s. After the war, as the regional economy began to pick up again, other major South African and British companies eventually followed, and became involved in mining and agriculture as well as land speculation. The subordination of production to speculation ceased, and efforts were directed at reducing costs in order to enhance the profitability of those enterprises which had survived the crisis.[58] Among the winners were Mashonaland Agency; Matabele Gold Reefs and Estates Company; Willoughby's Consolidated Company; Charterland Goldfields; Rhodesia Investment Company; Sebakwe & District Mines; Rhodesia Mining and Finance Company; Forbes' Rhodesia Syndicate; Rhodesia Exploration and Development Company; Bulawayo Estate and Trust Company; Rhodesia Goldfields; Bulawayo Market and

Offices Company; Consolidated Goldfields; Goldfields of Matabeleland; Matabele Mines; Matabele Gold Reefs and Estates Co.; Rhodesia Limited; and Messrs. Robert Williams & Co., Mining and Consulting Engineers.

The emphasis of capital accumulation shifted from pure mining extraction to a combination of mining and agriculture. BSAC transformed the territory's finances, mainly through marketing cut-rate land to settlers, in order to compensate for the sunk rail and land investment. But the subjugation of mining to speculation in gold mining stocks forced the new rulers to attract an agricultural bourgeoisie and to broaden the rest of the economy over the next three decades. As Bond (1998) has put it, 'of profound importance was the way in which control of economy passed from petty settlers into the hands of concessionary companies and their financiers in London.'[59]

Northern Rhodesian mineral rights

Unlike in Southern Rhodesia, where white settlers and the claim system offered a way of making the colonisation effective at a minimum cost, in Northern Rhodesia the mineral wealth lay in other articles of commerce than gold, mostly in the base metals and particularly in copper sulphide ores which could not be worked to any profitable scale by petty entrepreneurs. In Northern Rhodesia colonisation was enforced with the powers of the Mining Law of the British Empire, which regulated the acquisition and tenure of mining rights. The country was opened to employees of BSAC and to traders but remained closed to settlers, ensuring that right from the start the land beyond the Zambesi River would become the domain of concessionary companies whose responsibility was to arrange organised expeditions. Yet there were many connections between Southern Rhodesia and the mineralised north-western portions of the BSAC territory beyond the Zambesi River. Northern Rhodesia's copper mining was to some extent financed by gold mining interests in the south; many of its early 'pioneers' had previously worked there; and, ultimately, the whole economy of both Southern and Northern Rhodesia came to depend on the development of their premier industry, mining.[60]

BSAC obtained its mineral rights in the northern territory during the 1890s from the local African rulers for a negligible consideration. The first of these agreements was the 'Lochner Treaty of 1890' signed by the paramount ruler Lewanika of Barotseland, whose rule extended as far as the Kafue River in the east, and into Portuguese territory in the west (the Lozi Kingdom), with Frank Lochner acting on behalf of BSAC.[61] Lewanika, who was apprehensive about possible incursions by the Ndebele from the south, had already been influenced towards seeking British protection by François Coillard, a missionary of the Paris Missionary Society stationed then at Lealui, when he assigned the Lozi Kingdom to the chartered company's domains. In June 1898, Lewanika consented to grant BSAC further powers for administration and jurisdiction, with exclusive mining and commercial privileges within certain defined boundaries.[62] In contrast to Barotseland, no treaties regarding mineral rights were made in North-Western Rhodesia with the local Kaonde chiefs and village headmen. BSAC based their right to mineral exploitation in the area on a treaty made with Lewanika, presuming that the whole area to the north of Barotseland came under his sphere of influence.[63]

Regarding mining and commercial privileges in Northern Rhodesia as its legitimate prerogatives, BSAC leased the land at its discretion, reserving for itself a large interest in any future claims staked. At first BSAC levied 50% of all mineral ventures but reduced its claim to 30% in 1902.[64] In what can be designated as the concession system, mining was regarded as the exclusive privilege of BSAC. Only companies which received privileges from BSAC were entitled to prospect or carry out mining operations in Northern Rhodesia.[65] The disadvantages of the concession system were evident. It placed unduly large powers of the control of mining properties in the control of concessionary companies, or the holders of large prospecting concessions. By terminating competition over the claims, the concession system also placed in the hands of concessionary companies the power of capitalising the mining properties, and dealing with their finances as they pleased, and thus enabled them to make inordinate profits on the Stock Exchange.[66] Despite these concerns, the concession system appeared to host more advantages than the claim system. With very large areas still waiting to be explored, comprising thousands of square miles of often difficult and unhealthy country to traverse, prospecting was thought to be conducted more thoroughly and economically, and to produce mines of a far healthier state of finance, if the concessionary rights were handed over to a few strongly capitalised concessionary companies, rather than to a host of petty prospectors and undercapitalised exploring companies such as had overrun the Southern Rhodesian gold mining industry.

Initially there was only one beneficiary, Tyndale White, the Chairman of ZE, to whom BSAC granted a private 6,000-square-mile concession in early 1895.[67] The prospecting was delayed, however, by the Ndebele and Shona uprisings and the sunk gold mining investments. In the late 1890s the Rhodesian gold mining industry was experiencing a period of mergers, and ZE was one of the winners; it amalgamated several of the speculative, undercapitalised exploring companies that had mushroomed across Southern Rhodesia. The offshoots of ZE included the following companies limited by shares: Bembesi Syndicate; Central Monomotapa (previously the Bonaventure Association); Zambesia-Rand Investment Company, Buluwayo Syndicate; St. Helen's Buluwayo Association; Copenhagen (Mashonaland) Company; and Northumberland Mining Syndicate.[68] It also formed Gwanda Mines, but the most successful of them all proved to be Tanganyika Concessions, which was registered on the London Stock Exchange on 20 January 1899. The objectives for which the company was established were to prospect for, to open, work, explore, develop and maintain diamond, gold, silver, copper, coal and iron and other mines; to acquire mineral and other rights and concessions, grants, leases, claims, mines and mineral properties in

Southern Africa and beyond; and particularly to enter into and carry out into effect an agreement between White and ZE on the one hand and ZE and BSAC on the other,[69] with the intention of exploring in Northern Rhodesia, where BSAC had granted ZE a renewed mining concession on 26 May 1898. The Concession covered an area of over 2,000 square miles and gave exclusive surface rights for prospecting and locating 1,000 claims.[70] Later the agreement was amended in such a way that allowed the location of any part of the 1,000 claims outside the original 2,000 square miles, if necessary.[71]

The nominal capital of Tanks, £100,000 divided into a hundred thousand shares of one pound each, was allocated in such a way that ZE subscribed £25,500, whilst White personally controlled most of the rest of the capital.[72] In effect, the two companies had a double board of directors, making their role for small-scale investors obfuscatory to say the least. In the role of one of them, Mr Morris lamented at the ordinary general meeting of Tanks:

> [...] it is unfortunate that the Directors of one Company should be the Directors of the other. Mr. Tyndale White, the Chairman of both comes to the Tanganyika meeting and says 'Gentlemen, I strongly advise you to buy,' and then he appears at the Zambesia meeting and says: 'Gentlemen, I strongly advise you to sell.'[73]

Concluding discussion

There are two broadly defined explanations for investments in high-risk exploratory projects in colonial South-Central Africa. Taken together they highlight 'the difficulty of coupling theories of mineral discovery to patterns of mining development'.[74] Initially, a combination of hopes and imprecise information, promoted by popularised myths of exotic lands and easy riches, contributed to expectations of bonanza profits, first from alluvial gold extraction. Unsound expectations of windfalls were supported by the reports of the mining engineers, the prospectuses of the mining companies and the statements of their chairmen, creating the impression of a centralised, highly efficient and organised mining industry in complete charge of itself. This was useful for convincing investors but it often bore little relation to the actual state of affairs at mine level, where there was a desperate shortage of managerial personnel skilled in mining techniques and labour management.[75] The expectations of windfalls did not concern precious metals alone, however, but the extraction of metals with high industrial demand such as copper, zinc, tin and chrome could also catch investors up in a frenzy of speculation.[76] By the early 1900s straightforward market dynamics, in particular the demand for new sources of copper and the potentially high rewards associated with them, came to play a significant part in the provision of capital for the mining industry. Estimations of when this transition took place vary from the turn-of-the-century to the 1920s.[77]

Many of the mining companies floated in the pre-1920s period have been seen as vehicles for rampant 'concession-mongering' and 'stock-jobbing imperialism' as defined by Hobson.[78] The pervasiveness of this view (both at the time and beyond) can be perhaps most obviously seen in the overemphasis placed on the role of powerful capitalists such as Rhodes in capital accumulation. For instance, ZE has generally been analysed as 'Rhodes' company',[79] even though he controlled only 5% of the authorised capital (*i.e.* £500), did not make further investments in the company and was not involved in the management of the company.[80]

In the late nineteenth and early twentieth centuries the proliferation of different accounting methods contributed to the widespread incomprehensibility of balance sheets, accounts and prospectuses on the capital formation of overseas mining companies. There was little or no relationship between nominal capitalisation and the actual capital subscribed and invested abroad. While it is axiomatic that such disparities lie at the heart of the difficulties in assembling usable data on the actual capital formation of overseas mining companies and estimating the amount of capital invested, there is also the point that the tendency to see capitalist exploitation in mining shares has often deflected attention from the actual histories of exploring companies.

Exploring companies such as ZE were not simply a vehicle for market manipulation but were established to engage in exploring and prospecting. Even those companies which failed were not organisationally unsound *per se*. Rather, the principal reason for the failure of mining in Southern Rhodesia was deficient information on which initial investment decisions were based, and specifically an erroneous belief in the wealth of gold deposits and an incomplete understanding of the means with which the subsequently discovered copper deposits in Northern Rhodesia might be extracted. Mining companies raised modest amounts of authorised capital to support their exploratory business projects on the basis of this deficient information. The very deficiency of information for investors reduced the perception of risk, and thus made further investment decisions more likely. So while this lack of information explains the behaviour of investors who bought shares in overseas mining companies, it also explains why undercapitalised companies such as ZE ultimately rose in size and significance.

Venture capital played an important role in mining operations. The prospecting for mines, the extracting of ore and the setting up of smelting works involved considerable outlays which were not remunerative for a long time after the initial expenditure. The archetypical company venturing into mine exploration and prospecting was an undercapitalised exploration company that sought high-risk venture capital to fund its exploration in the hope of eventually selling valuable deposits to larger companies that would possess the resources for longer-term mining development. Because of their limited nominal capital and reliance on venture capital, exploring and prospecting companies played an important role in initiating exploration in lesser-known, and thus higher-risk, areas. Such a business pattern proved very durable, as is revealed by this study.

Notes

1 Thompson 1995, 115–117.
2 Thompson 1995, 115–117. See also Thomas 1997.
3 Foster 1885, 79.
4 For further information, see Roberts 1972.
5 Rosenthal 1970.
6 Richardson and van Helten 1984, 320–321.
7 Green 1982, 1, 8–11, 15–16, 18. See also Eklund 2018, 190–193.
8 Feinstein 2005, 100.
9 See also Lukasiewicz 2024.
10 Hobson 1905, 117–118.
11 MU, TANKS, TC/179, Mr Studt's reports, April 1926.
12 Allen 1992, 132.
13 Report of Director of Census 15 September 1896, VIII. See also Särkkä 2021, 311.
14 Bickford-Smith 1989, 48; Bickford-Smith 1995. See also Särkkä 2021, 309.
15 Rosenthal 1970; van Onselen 1982; Moodie 2005, 547–567.
16 Hobson 1899, 78–81, 71–94.
17 Allen 1992, 147. See also Särkkä 2021, 323.
18 Green 1982, 12.
19 Ally 1994, 1–6; Green 1982, 21–23.
20 Rosenthal 1970.
21 Green 1982, xiv.
22 For further information, see Green 1982.
23 Zvobgo 2009, 4–6.
24 UP, MA, MAD, 1933–99.
25 For further information, see Green 1982.
26 Hall and Neal 1904, x, 3.
27 Haggard 1994.
28 Bancroft 1961, 45; Phimister 1988, 6–7; Robinson and Gallagher 1961, Chap. VII; Rotberg and Shore 1988, 252.
29 Slinn 1972, 23–24; Gann 1964, 101.
30 Hönke 2009, 279.
31 Galbraith 1974, 122.
32 Phimister 1988; Chikuhwa 1998, 43–45, 123–144; Zvobgo 2009, 11–32; Mlambo 2014.
33 Charles 1906, 1–4.
34 Ferguson 2004, 224.
35 Following common usage, 'Rhodesia' refers here to the territories administrated by BSAC in the interior of South-Central Africa, initially called 'South Zambesia' and 'North Zambesia' (until the name Rhodesia came into use in 1895). Rhodesia was formally divided into the protectorates of Southern Rhodesia and Northern Rhodesia in 1911.
36 *Bulawayo Chronicle* 1901, 3–7; Ranger 2010, 14–17.
37 *Bulawayo Chronicle* 1901, 3–7.
38 The BSAC Report 1894–1895, 71, 78. See also Keppel-Jones 1983, 379; Särkkä 2015, 83–84.
39 Särkkä 2015, 84–85; Ranger 2010, 23; 'Progress of Rhodesia' 1901, 3–7.
40 Phimister 1977, 188.
41 Keppel-Jones 1983, 370–371; Särkkä 2015, 83.
42 LMA, SE, CLC, B/004/F/01/MS18000/49B/603, Agreement for the Allotment of Shares, no date.
43 LMA, SE, CLC, B/004/F/01/MS18000/49B/603, Agreement between Robert Williams and The Zambesia Exploring Company Limited, 5 March 1891.

44 LMA, SE, CLC, B/004/F/01/MS18000/54B/321, Memorandum of Agreement, 8 October 1898; *Mining World and Engineering Record* 30 April 1898.
45 LMA, SE, CLC, B/004/F/01/MS18000/49B/603, List of Subscribers for Shares, no date; MU, TANKS, ZE, Board Minutes 1891–1893, List of Subscribers for Shares.
46 LMA, SE, CLC, B/004/F/01/MS18000/54B/321, List of Subscribers for Shares; Notice of Meeting, Report of the Directors, and Statement of Accounts, 31 December 1897.
47 Bond 1998, 43.
48 Hobson 1902a, 219–232.
49 Harvey and Press 2000, 95; Ashmead 1909, 53.
50 van Onselen, 1976, 14.
51 Quoted in Ranger 2010, 14–17.
52 Frankel 1938, 150–157.
53 LMA, SE, CLC, B/004/F/01/MS18000/54B/321, The Ordinary General Meeting of The Zambesia Exploring Company, 30 April 1898.
54 *Bulawayo Chronicle* 1901, 3–7; van Onselen 1976, 15; Särkkä 2015, 86.
55 Quoted in Bond 1998, 46.
56 Arrighi and Saul 1973, 336.
57 Phimister 1988, 21–22.
58 Arrighi and Saul 1973, 184; Bond 1998, 46.
59 Bond 1998, 40, 46.
60 Gelfand 1961, 35, 43; Gann 1958, 117.
61 Report of the Commission 1938, 79; Verrier 1986, 16.
62 Gann 1958, 1–7; Gelfand 1961, 33–35; Etherington 2004, 439–441; Mackintosh 1907, 380–395.
63 Jaeger 1981, 71–72.
64 van Onselen 1976, 14, 17. *Cf.* Slinn 1972, 28; Gann 1964, 101.
65 Gelfand 1961, 117.
66 Charles 1906, 1–3.
67 MU, TANKS, ZE/1–2, Land Concessions. See also Hutchinson and Martelli 1971, 79–81.
68 *Buluwayo Chronicle* 9 November 1894.
69 LMA, SE, CLC, B/004/F/01/MS18000/62B/419, Certificate of Incorporation, 1 May 1899.
70 MU, TANKS, ZE/4, Herbert Canning for BSAC to Robert Williams, 26 May 1898.
71 MU, TANKS, ZE/4, Robert Williams to ZE, 29 November 1898. This concession replaced an earlier concession given to ZE in 1895 (Katzenellenbogen 1973, 23–24).
72 Hutchinson and Martelli 1971, 100–101.
73 LMA, SE, CLC, B/004/F/01/MS18000/129B/277, Tanganyika Concessions, Ltd., the Ordinary General Meeting of, Winchester House, Old Broad Street, London, 18 Dec. 1908.
74 Phimister 2000, 38.
75 Mollan 2009, 230–232, 234, 243.
76 For a case study on chrome, refer to Phimister 1996, 77–89. For tin, refer to Phimister 2000, 23–41.
77 Phimister 2000, 23.
78 *Derbyshire Advertiser* 2 May 1896; 22 May 1896; 2 October 1896; Hobson 1902b, 80.
79 Katzenellenbogen 1973, 21–22; *cf.* Dietz 2021, 106–107.
80 LMA, SE, CLC, B/004/F/01/MS18000/49B/603, List of Subscribers for Shares, no date.

References

Allen, V.L. (1992) *Mining in South Africa and the Genesis of Apartheid: The History of Black Mineworkers in South Africa*, Vol. I: *1871–1948*, The Moor Press and Merlin, Keighley and London.

Ally, R. (1994) *Gold & Empire: The Bank of England and South Africa's Gold Producers 1886–1926*, Witwatersrand University Press, Johannesburg.

Arrighi, G. and Saul, J.S. (1973) *Essays on the Political Economy of Africa*, Monthly Review Press, New York.

Ashmead, E. (1909) *Twenty-Five Years of Mining. 1880–1904: A Retrospective Review with an Appendix Four Years Later, 1905–1908*, The Mining Journal, London.

Bancroft, J.A. (1961) *Mining in Northern Rhodesia: A Chronicle of Mineral Exploration and Mining Development*, British South Africa Company.

Bickford-Smith, V. (1989) 'A "Special Tradition of Multi-Racialism"? Segregation in Cape Town in the Late 19th and Early 20th Centuries' in W.G. James and M. Simons eds. *The Angry Divide: Social and Economic History of the Western Cape*, David Philip, Cape Town, 47–62.

Bickford-Smith, V. (1995) *Ethnic Pride and Racial Prejudice in Victorian Cape Town: Group Identity and Social Practice, 1875–1902*, Cambridge University Press, Cambridge.

Bond, P. (1998) *Uneven Zimbabwe: A Study of Finance, Development and Underdevelopment*, Africa World Press, Inc., Trenton, NJ and Asmara, Eritrea.

The British South Africa Company: Report on the Company's proceedings and the condition of the Territories within the sphere of its operations (The BSAC Report) (1894–1895).

Bulawayo Chronicle (1901), Christmas number of 1901, 'Progress of Rhodesia', 3–7.

Buluwayo Chronicle [later *Bulawayo Chronicle*] (9 November 1894).

Charles, J.A. (1906) *Mining Law of the British Empire*, Charles Griffin & Company, London.

Chikuhwa, J.W. (1998) *Zimbabwe: The Rise to Nationhood*, AuthorHouse, Bloomington, IN.

Derbyshire Advertiser (2 May 1896); (22 May 1896); (2 October 1896).

Dietz, S. (2021) *Entrepreneurship in the Age of Empire: Colonialism, Collaboration and Exploitation*, Routledge, London.

Eklund, E. (2018) 'Creating a Global Industry? Geology, Capital, and Company Formation on the Goldfields of the Industrial Age' in B. Mountford and S. Tuffnell eds. *A Global History of Gold Rushes*, University of California Press, Oakland, CA, 184–205.

Etherington, N. (2004) 'Coillard, François (1834–1904)' in H.C.G. Matthew and B. Harrison eds. *Oxford Dictionary of National Biography*, 12. Oxford University Press, Oxford, 439–441.

Feinstein, C.H. (2005) *An Economic History of South Africa. Conquest, Discrimination and Development*, Cambridge University Press, Cambridge.

Ferguson, N. (2004) *Empire: How Britain Made the Modern World*, Penguin, London.

Foster, J. (1885) *Men-at-the-Bar: A Biographical Hand-List of the Various Inns of Court, Including Her Majesty's Judges, etc*, 2nd ed, Hazeli, Watson, and Viney, London and Aylesbury.

Frankel, S.H. (1938) *Capital Investment in Africa: Its Course and Effects*, Oxford University Press, Oxford.

Galbraith, J.S. (1974) *Crown and Charter: The Early Years of the British South Africa Company*, University of California Press, Berkeley.

Gann, L.H. (1958) *The Birth of the Plural Society: The Development of Northern Rhodesia under the British South Africa Company, 1894–1914*, Manchester University Press, Manchester.

Gann, L.H. (1964) *A History of Northern Rhodesia: Early Days to 1953*, Chatto & Windus, London.

Gelfand, M. (1961) *Northern Rhodesia in the Days of Charter: A Medical and Social Study 1878–1924*, Basil Blackwell, Oxford.

Green, T. (1982) *The New World of Gold: The Inside Story of the Mines, the Markets, the Politics, the Investors*, Weidenfeld & Nicolson, London.

Haggard, H.R. (1994) *King Solomon's Mines*, Penguin Popular Classics, Penguin, London.

Hall, R.N. and Neal, W.G. (1904) *The Ancient Ruins of Rhodesia (Monomotapæ Imperium)*, Methuen, London.

Harvey, C. and Press, J. (2000) 'The City of London and International Trade, 1850–1914' in R.C. Michie ed. *The Development of London as a Financial Centre*, Vol. 2: *1850–1914*, IB Tauris, London, 87–105.

Hobson, J.A. (1899) 'On Capital' in J.E. Hand ed. *Good Citizenship: A Book of Twenty-Three Essays by Various Authors on Social, Personal, and Economic Problems and Obligations*, George Allen, London, 71–94.

Hobson, J.A. (August 1902a) 'The Economic Taproot of Imperialism', *Contemporary Review*, LXXXII, 219–232.

Hobson, J.A. (April 1902b) 'Imperialism and the Lower Races. II', *British Friend*, New Series, XI:4, 80–83.

Hobson, J.A. (29 April1905) 'The Structure of South African Finance', *Speaker*, 12:291, 117–118.

Hutchinson, R. and Martelli, G. (1971) *Robert's People: The Life of Sir Robert Williams Bart. 1860–1938*, Chatto & Windus, London.

Hönke, J. (2009) 'Extractive Orders. Transnational Mining Companies in the Nineteenth and Twenty-First Centuries in the Central African Copperbelt' in R. Southall and H. Melber eds. *A New Scramble for Africa? Imperialism, Investment and Development*, University of KwaZulu-Natal Press, Scotsville, South Africa, 274–298.

Jaeger, D. (1981) *Settlement patterns and rural development: a human geographical study of the Kaonde, Kasempa District, Zambia*, PhD thesis, University of Amsterdam.

Katzenellenbogen, S.E. (1973) *Railways and the Copper Mines of Katanga*, Clarendon Press, Oxford.

Keppel-Jones, A. (1983) *Rhodes and Rhodesia: The White Conquest of Zimbabwe, 1884–1902*, University of Natal Press, Pietermaritzburg.

London Metropolitan Archives (LMA), Records of the Stock Exchange (SE), Applications for authority to deal and applications for listing (CLC).

Lukasiewicz, M. (2024) *Gold, Finance and Imperialism in South Africa, 1887–1902: A View from the Stock Exchange*, Palgrave Macmillan, Cham, Switzerland.

Mackintosh, C.W. (1907) *Coillard of the Zambesi: The Lives of François and Christina Coillard, of the Paris Missionary Society, in South and Central Africa (1858–1904)*, T. Fisher Unwin, London.

Mining World and Engineering Record (30 April 1898).

Mlambo, A.S. (2014) *A History of Zimbabwe*, Cambridge University Press, Cambridge.

Mollan, S.M. (2009) 'Business Failure, Capital Investment and Information: Mining Companies in Anglo-Egyptian Sudan, 1900–13', *The Journal of Imperial and Commonwealth History*, 37:2, 229–248.

Moodie, T.D. (2005) 'Maximum Average Violence: Underground Assaults on the South African Gold Mines, 1913–1965', *Journal of Southern African Studies*, 31:3, 547–567.

Phimister, I. (1977) 'White Miners in Historical Perspective: Southern Rhodesia, 1890–1953', *Journal of Southern African Studies*, 3:2, 187–206.

Phimister, I. (1988) *An Economic and Social History of Zimbabwe 1890–1948: Capital Accumulation and Class Struggle*, Longman, London.

Phimister, I.R. (1996) 'The Chrome Trust: The Creation of an International Cartel, 1908–38', *Business History*, 38:1, 77–89.

Phimister, I. (2000) 'Corners and Company-Mongering: Nigerian Tin and the City of London, 1909–12', *The Journal of Imperial and Commonwealth History*, 28:2, 23–41.

Ranger, T. (2010) *Bulawayo Burning: The Social History of a Southern African City 1893–1960*, James Currey, Harare.

Report of Director of Census (15 September1896) Sanitary Department, Johannesburg.

Report of the Commission Appointed to Enquire into the Financial and Economic Position of Northern Rhodesia (Report of the Commission) (1938) 145, His Majesty's Stationery Office, London.

Richardson, P. and van Helten, J.-J. (1984) 'The Development of the South African Gold-Mining Industry, 1895–1918', *The Economic History Review*, 2nd series, XXXVII:3, 319–340.

Roberts, B. (1972) *The Diamond Magnates*, Hamilton, London.

Robinson, R. and Gallagher, J. (1961) *Africa and Victorians: The Official Mind of Imperialism*, Macmillan, Basingstoke.

Rosenthal, E. (1970) *Gold! Gold! Gold! The Johannesburg Gold Rush*, Macmillan, New York.

Rotberg, I. and Shore, M.F. (1988) *The Founder: Cecil Rhodes and the Pursuit of Power*, Oxford University Press, Oxford.

Slinn, P. (1972) 'The Legacy of the British South Africa Company: The Historical Background' in M. Bostock and C. Harvey eds. *Economic Independence and Zambian Copper: A Case Study of Foreign Investment*, Praeger, New York and London, 23–52.

Särkkä, T. (2015) 'Imperialists Without an Empire? Finnish Settlers in Late Nineteenth- and Early Twentieth-Century Rhodesia', *Journal of Migration History*, 1:1, 75–99.

Särkkä, T. (2021) 'The "Pioneer Men": Making of Finnish Settler Identity in Southern Africa Pre-1914' in R. Merivirta, L. Koivunen and T. Särkkä, eds. *Finnish Colonial Encounters: From Anti-Imperialism to Cultural Colonialism and Complicity*, Palgrave Macmillan, Cham, Switzerland, 303–329.

Thomas, A. (1997) *Rhodes: The Race for Africa*, Penguin Books, Harmondsworth.

Thompson, L. (1995) *A History of South Africa*, Revised ed. Yale University Press, New Haven, CT and London.

The University of Manchester (MU), Tanks Group Archive (TANKS), Zambesia Exploring Company (ZE), Tanganyika Concessions (TC).

The University of Pretoria (UP), Mapungubwe Archive (MA), Mapungubwe Archive Document (MAD).

van Onselen, C. (1976) *Chibaro: African Mine Labour in Southern Rhodesia 1900–1933*, Pluto Press, London.

van Onselen, C. (1982) *Studies in the Social and Economic History of the Witwatersrand, 1886–1914: 1 New Babylon, 2 New Nineveh*, Longman, London.

Verrier, A. (1986) *The Road to Zimbabwe 1890–1980*, Jonathan Cape, London.

Zvobgo, C.J.M. (2009) *A History of Zimbabwe, 1890–2000 and Postscript, Zimbabwe, 2001–2008*, Cambridge Scholars Publishing, Newcastle upon Tyne.

4 The anatomy of mining and the mine exploration business

Although mining in Northern Rhodesia and Katanga has been analysed both by economic historians and by researchers of colonialism, very little is known of individual mining companies' operations. This chapter concentrates on the inception of mining by, and the mine exploration economy of, Tanganyika Concessions (Tanks), which undertook the first successful effort to set up a mining industry in the mineral-rich region that later became popularly and loosely known as the Central African Copperbelt. The chapter draws on company records as well as the personal records of the early company employees who worked in Northern Rhodesia and Katanga until 1906. The most thought-provoking documents analysed include travelogues, diaries and photographs depicting the organisation and processes of early mining work, modes of mine exploration, and relations between white management and African labour. The wide range of available materials offers a fuller picture of the inception of European mining and mine exploration in Northern Rhodesia and Katanga than is available elsewhere. Taken as a whole, they provide insight into the operation of colonising processes and in particular how these processes took place, why they were considered desirable by various interest groups, and the impact that these processes had on physical and human environments in parts of Northern Rhodesia and Katanga.

The age of the prospector

For a short span of the late nineteenth and early twentieth centuries, it was the prospector – with much the same companions as mine seekers for centuries past: the horse, the mule, the carrier and the scout – who took charge in the quest for metals and minerals in South-Central Africa. The prospector of the age of exploration and empire-building has been mythologised in much of the colonial era and beyond. He had an almost uncanny ability to locate minerals by the very appearance of terrain, the varied colours of the rocks, the kind of vegetation and its characteristics, or even by the taste and odour of the water. While plants do alter their colour and adjust their characteristics in accordance with their surroundings and their growth in different types of soil,[1] in Northern Rhodesia and Katanga prospecting was mostly reduced to locating previously known ore bodies and workings of African miners.

DOI: 10.4324/9781003247371-4

By 1906 the period of experimental mining and smelting was over, and once the industry entered the era of production on a commercial scale, this fairly haphazard business of mine seekers generally fell within the franchise of the mining engineers who had the necessary knowledge to develop more scientific methods of exploring. Although many important mines were located by tenacity, pure luck or the guesswork of prospectors, the scientific techniques and instruments for locating deposits of ore or entire mineralisation zones gradually replaced the imaginative appeal of the prospectors' methods. Whilst the age of mine exploration and claim-staking of outcropping deposits did not last long, the prospector – with his crumpled clothes, battered hat with a wide brim and a sturdy pair of *veldt* boots – has ever since managed to capture our fascination and continues to fire our imagination of those halcyon days of exploring, pioneering and empire-building, when truly one carried one's life in one's hands.[2]

A study of a London-based mining and mine exploration company should not necessarily be concerned, however, with economic activity alone. British involvement in mining in parts of South-Central Africa ultimately stemmed from colonial developments. Tanks was also a direct participant in the colonising process, and its activities had physical and societal consequences in parts of Northern Rhodesia and Katanga. Business history resources together with various written and visual materials produced by many company employees can provide some insight into how these processes took place, why they were considered desirable by various interest groups, and what implications such processes had for both physical and human environments. In order to analyse these issues, the chapter draws on personal records of some of the first European employees in North-Western Rhodesia and Katanga. The labels 'white' and 'European' workers are commonly used as blanket terms to emphasise the stark contrasts between white and black labour relations. The difficulty is that the use of generic terms tends to obscure the extent of ethnic diversity on the ground. From its very inception, the Central African mining industry attracted a coterie of nationalities and ethnicities from diverse social and professional backgrounds. The early mining communities were highly cosmopolitan in nature: White workers would be defined as being 'Finnish-born', 'Transvaaler' and 'Portuguese', for example. Consequently some of the sources consulted in this chapter have been written in languages that have hitherto rarely been heard in accounts of the colonial experience.

Those Europeans who settled in the colonial world had multiple, often overlapping identities based on factors such as gender, race, language and profession, besides nationality. Besides, in different colonial settings, the same individuals may have had numerous, often conflicting identity labels.[3] For the present purposes, a settler is defined as being someone who migrated with the intention of establishing a permanent home in a new environment. Thus, a settler was also someone who was in the process of acquiring a new identity, at least to some extent. The term 'pioneer', on the other hand, is used to refer to the settlers in colonial Southern Africa's age of pioneering, exploration and adventure (*c.* 1870–1914). It can still be seen in use in museums and exhibitions in South Africa and beyond but rarely in rigorous academic research,[4] which is why I have chosen to put it in quotation marks.

Besides written records produced by European employees, the question of Tanks' impact on physical and human environments is approached through photography. The camera, 'a triumph of Western technology', played many roles in early colonial societies. Colonial photography has been analysed from the perspective of early photographers (imperial othering, intrusive colonial gazing as well as capturing and rearranging colonial subjects) and, conversely, the ways in which colonial subjects were able to use photography for their own ends (through poses and other choices relating to self-representation).[5] The photographs in question come from the picture collections of Carl Theodor Eriksson, a Tanks prospector from 1901 to 1906, whose life and times in colonial Southern Africa are exceptionally well documented thanks to his surviving diaries and photographs. His collection of photographs includes numerous original glass plate negatives taken during the five years of his employment with Tanks in North-Western Rhodesia and Katanga (between April 1901 and 31 May 1906). Some photographs from this collection have previously been reproduced in older Rhodesiana. However, none of this older material includes a photographer's credit, let alone a critical discussion of Eriksson's photography.[6] The selected pictures depict various aspects of the early colonial economy, including the organisation and processes of the early mining work, modes of communication and relations between Tanks' employees and the local population. The actual manual mining work undertaken by African labourers – such as the sinking of shafts and extraction of ore using only axes, picks and shovels – can hardly be appreciated without illustrations. Given our purpose of viewing depictions of scenes and people otherwise known to us only through the written word, it is nevertheless important to remember that photographs can also provide a means by which to analyse theoretical and conceptual definitions of the categories 'coloniser' and 'colonised' and to discuss their complex interplay.

The lure of Katanga copper

It was with the objective of prospecting for every kind of valuable mineral and metalliferous ore that Tanks organised its first mineral-seeking expedition to its concession in Northern Rhodesia during the dry season of 1899. In charge of the expedition was Captain George Grey (1868–1911), younger brother of Sir Edward Grey, the future British Secretary of State for Foreign Affairs (1905–16). Williams met Grey in 1891 at Fort Victoria (Masvingo) in Mashonaland, where Grey oversaw the operations of the Northumberland Mining Syndicate, which represented the interests of wealthy Northumberland landowners. Williams was captivated by Grey's aptitude and, undoubtedly, his family connection with the prominent and politically influential Grey family, with its estates in the northern part of Northumberland. Unlike Williams, Grey was not a trained mining engineer, but, as Williams put it, Grey was 'just a fine, plucky young Englishman full of refreshing honesty'.[7] Before transferring to the service of Tanks, Grey worked for Williams' Bulawayo-based Consolidated Buildings, fought in the First Matabele War and led the infamous Grey's Scouts in the Second.[8]

Grey believed that mineral deposits would be found on a plateau between the Kafue River and the Zambesi River, and to the north of the Kafue River. Owing to its elevation, the climate of the region was subtropical, with high temperature and great humidity present in the river valleys. A relatively long dry season, lasting roughly from April to November, was followed by the rainy season, when malaria and blackwater fever were severe and often of epidemic proportions. Although the relationship of the two was not yet universally recognised at the time,[9] Grey introduced quinine to his expedition as a preventive against malaria, which had caused high morbidity and mortality rates among the first Europeans in the region.

Grey's original plan had been to undertake an expedition lasting between six and nine months that would comprise 'myself and one other white man, twenty donkeys, two or four salted horses [*i.e.* horses who had recovered from horse-sickness], ten natives (Zulus, Basutos, or the best class of Matabele) who would be armed, a light wagon to be left on the South side of the river [Zambesi]'. He asserted that 'the most of the higher country to the North can be explored without encountering fly, thus rendering the possibility of travelling with horses and donkeys possible'. Grey based his estimations on information provided by Frederick Crewe, 'an accomplished native linguist' who had been engaged in the labour recruiting business to the north of the Zambesi River.[10] Ultimately, however, the expedition included five Europeans: Grey, Crewe (second in command), James Norval Justice (a geologist), Paul MacDonald (a prospector of many years' experience in South Africa) and Mowbray Gore Farquhar (who accompanied the expedition 'for the sake of sport'). It was also reported that 'the party takes with it thirty-five picked natives, Zulus, Fingoes, Mqousas, and Matabele, amongst whom is the well-known scout John Grootboom'. Accompanying the men were 67 donkeys, nine dogs, six oxen, seven horses and two mules.[11] Each white member of the expedition had an option on 200 Tanganyika shares for one year at two pounds each.[12] Later, Grey, Farquhar, Justice and MacDonald were given an extension for a further period of one year on account of the South African War.[13]

Grey's expedition set off from Bulawayo for the Congo–Zambesi watershed on 5 April 1899. The transport was very difficult as the railhead was still in Bulawayo. All goods had to come by ox-wagon and pack animals from Bulawayo to the Old Drift on the Zambesi River, a distance of 295 miles, where the provisions were taken across. It took five more weeks to reach Kalomo and four more weeks to get to Nkala, after which it was still necessary to trek hundreds of miles in the bush, relying on their scout and local assistance, before the concession was reached.[14] The expedition travelled along the east side of the Kafue River, with instructions to prospect the Rhodesian side of the Congo border. Roughly 135 miles west of the well-known Nchanga mine and less than 10 miles south of the Congo Free State (CFS) border, the party's attention was drawn to the extensive ancient workings, a series of approximately parallel crosscuts and pits, which traversed along an elliptical hill devoid of bush in a north–south direction. Named the Kansanshi after a river nearby – or, according to another version of the story, a nearby village of a chief named 'Kansanshi' – the expedition pegged off 30 claims on this ancient mine on behalf of Tanks on 6 September 1899.[15] After over six months of silence, Grey returned to Bulawayo and cabled his findings to Williams on 24 November[16] – to Williams' astonishment as in the press there had been rumours that the expedition had perished.[17]

Grey's report indicated that the main body of ore was situated in Katanga, known for its ancient copper mines worked by African miners for centuries, but now formally under the *Compagnie du Katanga*'s (CK) domain. Discouraged by CK's mining reports and hindered by limited transport and communications as well as tropical diseases, the British South Africa Company (BSAC) had been unable to exercise direct authority in the region, and in an Anglo-Belgian agreement signed on 12 May 1894 Britain had formally recognised that Katanga belonged within the boundaries of CFS. The frontier between CFS and BSAC territories had thus been set, and the initial concession granted to Tanks did not go beyond the exploration rights in North-Western Rhodesia.[18]

New negotiations over concessionary rights with the *Comité Spécial du Katanga* (CSK), a parastatal joint body founded in 1900, which merged the concessionary rights of CFS and CK, were now necessary. According to an indenture, reached on 8 December 1900, Tanks was granted exclusive prospecting rights in Katanga within an area of 60,000 square miles adjoining North-Western Rhodesia for five years and the right to work any discovered mine for a period of 99 years.[19] This agreement gave Tanks the freedom to prospect the Katanga mineral deposits. Together with its earlier 2,000-square-mile concession in North-Western Rhodesia, the whole formed a concession that was 185 miles wide east–west, and 45 miles long north–south, and which, significantly, was located within the territories of two very different colonial polities, Northern Rhodesia and CFS. This feature came to dominate the Central African mining industry until the early 1970s.

Mineral-seeking and empire-building

> [...] travelling through the bush [...] carrying his life in his hands from day to day, sleeping under the open sky at night. Surely this type of man is the true empire-builder.[20]

After a considerable delay caused by the ongoing South African War, on 15 April 1901 a second, much larger, expedition set out in small parties for the Kansanshi mine, some 850 miles north of Bulawayo. Such a large expedition required 200 oxen, the same number of donkeys and a few horses and mules, as well as the many dogs that were brought along for tracking and companionship. During the rainy season of 1900–1 a further six spans of Barotse oxen (some 120 animals) had been trained for transport purposes at Kalomo, 100 miles north of the Zambesi River, where they joined the main party.[21] It was estimated that no fewer than 1,000 porters had been hired by the expedition by the time they reached their base at Kansanshi in October 1901.[22]

In its account of the upcoming expedition the *Bulawayo Chronicle* reported:

> The white members of the expedition which leaves here [Bulawayo] are George Grey, Wynn, Jocks, Robinson, Ericson [Eriksson], Boijer, Whitton, Studt, and Dr. Middleton. Messrs Holland and Farrell will start from Abercorn, on Lake Tanganyika, and join the main body of the expedition in North-Western Rhodesia.[23]

Precious little is known of the expedition's wagon drivers and *voorloopers*, 'twenty-two Zulus armed with Martini-Henry rifles', personal servants, 'boys', porters or other casual labourers who accompanied the expedition to the north. Figure 4.1 depicts a party included in the Bulawayo section of the expedition ready to commence, in April 1901. Of the Europeans, standing, second left, is Dr Middleton; on horseback, first left, is W. Robinson, the Bulawayo section leader. In the front are a group of armed, barefoot African escorts, who were classified as being either 'Zulus, Fingoes, Mqousas, or Matabele'. This photograph was later reproduced in Middleton's published diary, but the photographer is not credited.[24]

We have much more information about the expedition's white members. From its very inception, the mining industry in Central Africa attracted a motley of nationalities and ethnicities from diverse social and professional

Figure 4.1 A party included in the Bulawayo section of the expedition, Bulawayo, April 1901
Source: FHA, PC, VKK871:62.

backgrounds which determined their positions in the mining industry hierarchy. Franz Edward Studt (Stüdt, 1873–1953), a London-born geologist,[25] whose work was used as the basis for the first systematic geological map of the concession,[26] was a recent graduate of the Royal School of Mines, established in Jermyn Street, London in 1851. An educated and professional mining and metallurgical elite of British origin emerged in the latter half of the nineteenth century.[27] The school was subsequently placed under the administration of the Imperial College of Science and Technology in 1907.[28] Mining engineers formed their own professional association in 1892, the Institution of Mining and Metallurgy, which by 1914 had 2,310 members employed in all parts of the world.[29]

Of the other members of the Bulawayo section, Dr Richard W. Middleton (1868–1913), from Leeds, had qualified as a medical doctor in 1898, and he had been working as a house surgeon at Grey's Hospital in Pietermaritzburg prior to joining the expedition. He continued to work as the company's medical doctor, based in Kalomo, until July 1905.[30] William Whitton, corporate secretary of the Bulawayo-based Williams' Consolidated Buildings, joined the party in his capacity as an accountant.[31]

Thirty-one-year-old Oscar Boijer (1868–1943) and twenty-six-year-old Carl Eriksson (1874–1940), a keen amateur photographer, joined the expedition as prospectors. Boijer and Eriksson had emigrated to South Africa from the Grand Duchy of Finland in a wave of migration that took place between the Witwatersrand gold rush in 1886 and the occupation of Rhodesia.[32] By 1901, Boijer's and Eriksson's outlook and experiences had already become largely indistinguishable from those of other white settlers. The merits of Boijer, an experienced bush prospector in the Gwai River District who could make himself understood by 'natives' and who had received schooling as a Civil Engineer, included service in Gifford's Horse during the Ndebele and Shona uprisings of 1896–7, whereas Eriksson had previously worked as an Electrical Engineer with the Bulawayo Electric Light Works. In August 1899, at the height of the rising tensions between the Boer Republics and the British South African colonies, Eriksson enlisted in the Rhodesia Regiment, and on the outbreak of the South African War, he served and fought under Major Duly in the Cycle Corps, which took part in the Relief of Mafeking in May 1900.[33] Eriksson's decision to align with the Rhodesian forces – unlike the majority of the Finnish-born volunteers in the South African War, who enlisted in the Scandinavian Corps, a voluntary enlistment fighting in the Boer ranks – suggests that the white settler identity quickly tended to blur existing national identities in Rhodesia.[34]

Other than being fit young bachelors, many of the prospectors had little in common. Charles J. Jocks, 'one of the best type of Dutchmen', was a Transvaaler. Six years later, Jocks became the first white settler to settle permanently with a white woman in country free from tsetse fly near the Kansanshi mine.[35] On the surface, the ethnicity and provenance of the prospectors seemed to matter little. One prospector called John was said to be 'a

Portuguese and no one appears to know his proper name, Portuguese John being all that he goes by. He [John] is a good hunter and prospector and a good comrade, which is quite sufficient.'[36] In reality, however, a strict ethnic division was a feature of relations between not only the local population and the class- and race-conscious Europeans, but also various interest groups in the service of the company. Ethnic definitions such as 'Finn' or 'Portuguese' often carried pejorative connotations.[37]

The Abercorn section leader was Michael J. Holland, who as the nephew of the former colonial secretary Lord Knutsford had:

> just the kind of influence what is wanted. He had been out in Mexico, and had lot of to do with the organizing of the expedition to Kumassi [the Gold Coast], and generally has had the sort of experience that is required for business of this kind.[38]

Durand, a representative of the African Transcontinental Telegraph Company, surveyed their routes.[39] John R. Farrell, newly appointed chief engineer of Williams' Bulawayo-based mine engineering company, was a graduate of the University of California's Department of Civil Engineering and had worked for 20 years as a mining engineer and mining superintendent in western American copper mines.[40] Farrell was contracted to assay the most important deposits and to present a report of his findings to Williams. It was the norm of the day that the expertise of consulting engineers was called upon to allay the fears of investors. The fact that the majority of consulting engineers had only limited experience of local conditions did not deter them from issuing glowing mine reports and estimates of the profits waiting to be won.[41] From the reports of the mining engineers, the prospectuses of the mining companies and the statements of their chairmen, the impression was created of a centralised, highly efficient and organised mining industry, in complete charge of itself. This was useful for convincing investors to invest in mining, yet it often bore little relation to the actual state of affairs at mine level, where there was a desperate shortage of managerial personnel skilled in mining techniques.

After spending 32 days out in the open, the Bulawayo section of the expedition arrived at Victoria Falls on 17 May and spent the next three weeks ferrying wagons and animals across the river at 'Sekuti's Drift' (*i.e.* the Old Drift, which was controlled by a chief called Sekuti), three miles above Victoria Falls. Figure 4.2 records their accomplishment. Eriksson (first left) has either entrusted his camera to an unknown assistant or used a shutter-releasing device to take a group photograph.

On 10 June, the expedition divided itself into five groups, one of which was composed of Eriksson, Boijer and 12 porters with 18 pack-donkeys and two mules for riding. The parties set out on a north-west course for Nkala, where there was a Methodist mission. During the 300-mile stretch from Nkala to Kansanshi the prospectors first encountered 'the fly'. After the first attack all the oxen were useless and had to be shot within a few days. Once almost all

Figure 4.2 The Bulawayo section of the expedition, Victoria Falls, 17 May 1901
Source: FHA, PC, VKK871:47.

the oxen and donkeys had died, the party was left virtually without any means of transport. The only real option was to induce the local population to carry the party's goods north. Encounters with the local population were not as a rule hostile, but nevertheless they were rather unwilling to offer their labour. Local quarrels, slave traders' raids and lack of previous encounters with prospecting parties made the local people suspicious of attempts to draft porters.

In his diary Eriksson (1932) details an incident with the Ba-Ila, who refused to carry loads on their tall head-dress, *impande*. The problem was resolved with the stereotypical calm, rational superiority of the 'pioneer': the perceived excuse for laziness, *impande*, was cut off.[42] Figure 4.3 titled 'Some of the forced Ba-Ila carriers whose hair-dresses were cut off' records the incident. The photograph depicts a group of Ila carriers, whose loads are put on the ground. The Ba-Ila who wears *impande* and the birds' feathers is easily recognisable. These features are perceived as what make him a representative 'type' of the Ila man. The photograph does not document the ethnographic type as such, however, but the photograph presents the carriers as self-conscious individuals. Eriksson does not discuss under what circumstances he came to photograph the Ba-Ila carriers. We therefore cannot determine whether he asked them to be in his photographs or they asked him to photograph them. This raises important questions about issues of representation in Eriksson's photography.[43]

Figure 4.3 Ba-Ila carriers, 1901
Source: FHA, PC, VKK871:176.

Like many other amateur photographers, Eriksson seems to have preferred to take photographs that were meaningful to him rather than adopting a more systematic approach.[44] Despite their historical value, the use of photographs as source material also presents various challenges: in many cases we have no information about the date, place, subjects or even identity of the photographer. Furthermore, it is important to remember that even those images that appear to be candid may in fact have been posed and selected by a photographer, subject or client (in this context the company).[45]

Figure 4.4 depicts Eriksson himself in Kasempa, North-Western Rhodesia in 1901. It has not been possible to identify the photographer by direct evidence. The photograph may have been taken by Eriksson himself using a shutter-releasing device or by an unknown assistant. Instead of facing the camera in a carefully composed formal pose wearing gentleman-like clothing, Eriksson seems to have chosen to present himself as a paragon of the turn-of-the-century Southern African pioneer-settler. He takes an informal seated pose on a folding camp chair, has a serious-minded look and wears a battered prospector's hat with a wide brim and a sturdy pair of *veldt* boots. Despite having immigrated only in the mid-1890s, he anchors himself to a much longer line of European settlers that had been subsumed into South-Central Africa since the late seventeenth century.

In 1932, the same image took on another documentary function in Eriksson's published travelogue, where it was reproduced as the frontispiece and

Figure 4.4 C.T. Eriksson, Kasempa, North-Western Rhodesia, 1901
Source: FHA, PC, VKK871:48.

titled: 'He who commands with a firm hand' (*Fundi-Wa-Kali*).[46] The caption provides us with further indication of the audience for which the travelogue was intended. References to behaving like masters and frustration with African workmen and personal servants are to be found in a wide range of travelogues situated in early colonial Rhodesia.[47] In this respect Eriksson's travelogue aligns well with this narration: it was aimed at gratifying audiences fantasising of halcyon days of exploring, pioneering and empire-building.[48]

The village of Kapile M'Panga, near Kansanshi, had been agreed on as a general rendezvous where all parties of prospectors should meet in October, the last month of the dry season. During November and December, mining huts and storehouses were built at Kansanshi Camp, and most of the supplies that the prospectors had been forced to leave behind were retrieved and transported. Everything had to be carried on the human back – tents, beds, furniture, cooking utensils, provisions, hunting rifles, ammunition and the prospecting and mining equipment.[49] Figure 4.5 depicts Kansanshi Camp in 1901.

At the same time, a separate section of the expedition had been despatched to Abercorn with instructions to locate the township, open a trading store

Figure 4.5 Kansanshi Camp, 1901
Source: FHA, PC, VKK542:17.

and make preparations for the launch of the *S.S. Cecil Rhodes* on Lake Tanganyika. The party included four Europeans and 'the requisite native escort'. In total some 200 carriers were employed to transport goods, while donkeys conveyed the whites. The Abercorn section of the expedition left for Katanga on 15 May and proceeded to Lufaku (Lufoi) in CFS territory; from Lufaku they travelled to Katanga, arriving on 22 June. The Abercorn party became the nucleus of the Katanga section of the expedition and established a permanent camp at Kambove,[50] and in this way, the expedition also operated as an unofficial settlement scheme in CFS territory.

The discovery of the copper mines of Katanga

> The discovery of many of the great copper mines of the world was made by prospectors, working on their own or as small companies with the minimum of equipment and the maximum of enterprise, patience and resolution – and often with a great deal of courage.[51]

The original plan of the Tanks prospectors had been to undertake mining development during the rainy season of 1901–2. There were serious challenges to overcome, however, in both Kansanshi and Kambove. Since only a limited amount of equipment could be taken, the early mining operations were similar to the traditional African mining, supplemented with technological knowledge the settlers brought with them. The first shafts were sunk with windlasses made of branch trees and with a natural double crook to serve as a handle, with ropes made from local fibres, and with buckets fashioned from zebra hide[52] (Figure 4.6). Without water pumps, all operations had to be stopped at the onset of the rains: 'B shaft, in which about eight feet of timbering gave in yesterday [8 February 1902] owing to the rain, still continues to collapse; to-night the rest of the timber and the windlass collapsed and are now at the bottom of the shaft' (which was 87 feet deep).[53] Figure 4.7 depicts shaft sinking, possibly at Kansanshi, in 1901–2.

On top of these technical troubles, the onset of the rainy season saw many men fall ill with high fever.[54] Prospecting and labour recruitment were difficult undertakings under these conditions. When Boijer returned to Kansanshi Camp on 21 February 1902 after several weeks without contact, Dr Middleton, who had begun to fear the worst, noted: 'Yesterday Boyer [*sic*] arrived from Kasempa. He looks very pale and ill and somewhat thinner than when we last saw him. He says he has had fever since early in December, off and on the whole time.'[55]

The self-assured portrait depicting Boijer himself in Figure 4.8 is entitled 'It is Christmas Day, 1901, and Boijer, a member of the expedition, is dressed up for the occasion. He stands at the now-completed shaft-head at Kansanshi.' The photograph was intended as a record of Boijer's existence, accomplishments and survival. In retrospect the expedition was lauded for having

Figure 4.6 Shaft sinking with a windlass, 1901–6
Source: FHA, PC, VKK871:133.

Figure 4.7 Shaft sinking, Kansanshi, 1901–2
Source: FHA, PC, VKK871:7.

survived the first rainy season without a single death. That is, of course, to say without a single European death, for right from the beginning of European mining in the Central African Copperbelt, mining work made the African labourers liable to injury, sickness and death.[56] In 1961 the photograph took on another documentary role when it was reproduced in a magazine article covering the early days of pioneering in the Copperbelt.[57]

The images created by Eriksson capture the spirit of the age of copper mining and mine exploring in the Central African Copperbelt. For the employees of European descent, his photographs depicted their much-venerated colleagues doing an important job for the company and the British Empire in one of the remotest parts of the world, though the degree of a sense of imperial duty varied. The directors looked to their own social class for managers who were all British, albeit sometimes in a modified form. Colonial military identity and rank was another important determining factor of rank in the Copperbelt. The expedition leader, Captain Grey, with his colonial military posture, embodied the authority vested in him by Head Office. His senior staff, called officers, Mr Studt, Mr Farrell, Mr Whitton, Mr Holland and Dr Middleton, were bound to Grey by ties of camaraderie, loyalty and

Figure 4.8 Oscar Boijer, Kansanshi, Christmas Day, 1901
Source: FHA, PC, VKK871:26.

mutual respect. The country's newcomers were predominantly young bachelors, who made precarious livings from prospecting. Beyond any major differences between them in age, marital status and gender, it was the contrast between black and white interactions that most defined them. These interactions were governed by the Christian ethic and vocation as well as the conventional bourgeois taboos about race, class and gender that Europeans brought with them.[58]

The first prospectors in Northern Rhodesia and Katanga worked in relative solitude in remote lands and amidst alien peoples. These circumstances, coupled with a strict racial division and the absence of labour regulations, often led to a situation in which the employees of African descent were governed through blows, shouts, insults and by jeering at their presumed laziness.[59] The job of compound managers and the mine supervisors (foremen) was to impose strict discipline on the constantly changing and mostly unskilled labour force, who invariably occupied the lowest rank in the hierarchy. Their work included the sinking of simple shafts, extracting the ore with picks, sledgehammers and mining bars, clearing the bush or carrying materials. The day-to-day lives of both white and African workers were a far cry from those who occupied the boardroom in the City. In general, the work was hard and characterised by scant use of machinery and frequent stoppages caused by accidents, weather or disease.

During the dry season of 1902 Tanks prospectors staked 52 mining areas in Katanga. They were located on a high plateau, whose surface was broken by rounded hills and deep valleys. A dominant feature of the geology was old red sandstone containing layers of shale and beds of limestone. The main ore body was a 45-mile-wide vein, on the side of which there were deposits filled with high-grade oxidized ores, with an assayed copper content of 10%–20% or more. The copper ores consisted of either malachite – the most important oxidised ore of copper – or chrysocolla of the copper silicate family. These ores were so ubiquitous – with the combined ore reserves amounting to approximately 75 million tons – as to justify being referred to as a 'geological scandal' in a telegraph message which was sent via a Morse Receiver by a trained African telegraph operator in service of the African Transcontinental Telegraph Company at Fort Johnston (Mangochi).[60]

Figure 4.9 depicts a runner with a cleft stick in his hand in which a written message was attached (messages were carried in a stick, fixed in a split at one end). His Majesty's mails were brought up by runners until the arrival of the telegraph to the Copperbelt. The mails used to arrive at Kambove once a week and were carried by relays of runners from Livingstone or Fort Johnston.[61]

The most significant mine commercially was believed to be some three-quarters of a mile long and 600–1,000 feet wide, an ancient working called 'Karukaruko',

Figure 4.9 A runner with a cleft stick, 1901–6
Source: FHA, PC, VKK871:166.

which was given a grand name, The Star of the Congo (*L'Étoile du Congo*). The story of how 'Karukaruko' came to be called The Star of the Congo is told by J.B. Thornhill, a sometime worker for Tanks who in 1906 applied to be Vice Consul in Katanga District of CFS,[62] who gives Eriksson credit for the find.[63] According to Harold Cookson, a sometime Tanks prospector, The Star was:

> a fine big mine with extensive native workings on it. It is the ordinary type of mine, laminated sandstone impregnated with malachite between walls of porous quartzite. The sandstone dips about 70 degrees to the south-west and the mine runs north-west and south-east. There is also a good deal of manganese about.[64]

The discovery of The Star was not the plucky event that it may have appeared to have been in retrospect. Prospecting in Katanga was reduced to locating ancient workings rather than using scientific exploration methods to discover previously unknown ore bodies.[65] Eriksson outlined the strategy his party employed: 'We just asked if the natives knew where we could find *makuba* [copper] and in exchange for the information we gave the negroes a few metres of cotton-textile [calico] or a cheap blanket, and the deal was done.' Hence the retrospective use of the term 'blanket' prospector.[66] Figure 4.10 depicts Boijer exchanging calico for information.

Figure 4.10 Oscar Boijer exchanging calico for information, 1901–2
Source: FHA, PC, VKK871:165.

After the necessary information was dispensed, pegging was a simple process. First a tree was felled and stripped of bark, after which an aniline pen was used to mark the local name of the mine or, if there was no mine, the local name of a nearby river or hill, the prospector and the date of the find. This was done solely for the purpose of informing other Tanks prospectors and to verify who had staked the claim: concessionary rights kept other mine exploration companies out of the concession. Then, a discovery beacon was erected, and finally the find was photographed.[67] Figure 4.11 depicts a native working on the Kipushi mine. Photographing the old workings and discovery beacons was part of prospectors' regular duties in Katanga, and some of these photographs were later reproduced in the reports of the discoveries made by Grey's second expedition.[68]

During the dry season of 1902, Farrell 'personally examined' Kambove No. 2, Chituru, Likasye, Kamatanda, Msesa No. 2, Kankeru, Karoanso, Kabalela, Kalabe, Karawano, Luushia, Kapushi and Lupota mines, and presented his detailed expert opinion on these mines to Williams.[69] There are indications, however, that Farrell was more or less incapable of carrying out his inspection work in the concession, which raises questions about the integrity of his report. At some point between November 1901 and May 1902, he became 'mentally affected', according to one of the prospectors, William Robert White.[70] On Farrell's arrival at the Kansanshi Camp, Dr Middleton noted his condition.

Figure 4.11 A native working, Kipushi, 1902
Source: FHA, PC, VKK871:108.

> Yesterday [8 May 1902] Farrell arrived on the mine [Kansanshi], accompanied by Durand (or in his charge would be more correct). Since coming up he has been living quite alone. He cannot speak any Native language and none of his boys speak English, his isolation therefore being complete. The result is that he has completely broken down mentally. He is rather difficult to manage; it is impossible to get him to take sufficient food or necessary medicine. He holds intercourse with the deity, who arranges all his affairs to him, telling him that he must not eat or take medicine. He appears to have been affected this way for some time.[71]

A month later, on 18 June, a decision had been taken to transport Farrell to Bulawayo.

> Mr. Farrell continues to improve in health and condition, but mentally there is none; in fact, the last day or two he has grown worse, so Mr. Grey has decided to send him down to Bulawayo in my charge, and we are now on the road, having left Kansanshi yesterday noon. White and John are with us and we travel with carriers, Farrell in a *machilla* [a hammock slung on poles and carried by Africans].[72]

In his report Farrell gives us a somewhat more polished version of his first trip to Africa, a reminder that one man's truth may be another man's fiction.

> From the time I crossed the Zambesi, going north, until I re-crossed it in October, the representatives of the British South Africa Company, in North-Eastern Rhodesia, made every effort to facilitate my journey. To their kindness, courtesy and organization I am indebted for much of the comfort and rapidity with which I made a trip unmarred by mishap or accident.[73]

It has been said that 'a general willingness to travel was matched by the emergence of a fresh sense of confidence and professionalism among leading mining sector engineers.'[74] However, whether consulting mining engineers' reports circulated disinterested expert opinion and consequently contributed to more sound investment decisions or whether they produced information which was difficult for non-professionals to evaluate or, worse still, whether they were in some cases even made by fraudsters, has been the subject of some debate among scholars. The probability that Farrell did not have particular expertise in Katanga copper deposits or their commercial possibilities illustrates the speculative aspect of mining. Investors were presented with his apparently disinterested expert opinion, the integrity of which was indeed difficult for non-professionals to evaluate.[75] Nevertheless, complicated and confusing expert reports reduced the perception of risk, and thus made investment more likely.[76]

The inception of the wage labour system

From the perspective of the Head Office, mine development in Central Africa required a unique set of skills. Success meant an ability to manage both labour and the investments required to develop the necessary infrastructure. This gave rise to two important economic processes during the pre-1906 era of mining: the first was the forced introduction of a sterling-based cash economy in the form of the so-called hut or head tax. Like earlier in South Africa and Southern Rhodesia, the hut tax persuaded African men to leave their families in rural homes to earn tax money on the mines for several months at a time and to live in male-only compounds owned by the company they worked for. The second economic process was massive investment in infrastructure, mainly railways, which would open up access between the Copperbelt and coastal ports. Initially the lack of rail transport was the main obstacle to more intensive development. During the first years of the 1900s the mining economy was still in its infancy in Northern Rhodesia and Katanga, and in its early operations Tanks was heavily reliant on African manual labour. An operational mining business required considerable infrastructure including roads and railways, which, like the site installation itself, were largely constructed by African workers wielding axes, picks and shovels. As a consequence, there was a massive, indiscriminate mobilisation of unskilled African labour to fulfil the company's short-term need for labour to undertake shaft sinking, ore digging and various auxiliary jobs (such as woodcutting, clearing vegetation, building bridges, camps and tracks and anti-malarial drainage projects).[77]

It has been believed that when 'the world's mining frontier' passed to the country beyond the Zambesi River, and mines came to be established in increasingly distant areas from markets, it resulted in 'high costs of labour, power, and materials'.[78] This perceived problem of high labour costs did not seem, however, to be a matter of concern for Tanks. Quite the contrary: the low cost of labour was a major asset in mining in Northern Rhodesia and Katanga, as Farrell noted: 'I know of no place where the same amount of mining work could be accomplished for as low a local expense.'[79]

It was recruiting an adequate labour force and the consequent need for a steady food supply that caused the most significant problems for early mining development. From the very outset of the development phase, it became apparent that it would be impossible to purchase a steady supply of food locally, at either Kansanshi or Kambove mines, to sustain all but a small number of local workers. As a result, they adopted the *posho* system (which prevailed in North-Eastern Rhodesia) of supplying local workers with a weekly allowance of calico, with which they could buy their own food.[80] In July 1902 Robert Wright, who was trading on the Luapula River in 1900–4, delivered 'all the calico we had bought', 5,900 yards, to Kansanshi.[81] Later, in 1905, Tanks ordered white and blue calico through Findlay Durham & Brodie, Merchant Bankers, procuring British manufactured goods and finance for their customers. Grey personally instructed to have grey, white and blue calico 'Delver Finished' and 28" wide.[82] According to Robert Rich Sharp (1881–1960), a Tanks prospector noted for discovering in 1911 the Shinkolobwe radium–uranium ore bodies,[83] in 1906 the ordinary monthly wage at the Kambove mine was six to eight yards of 28" wide calico, which represented about three to four shillings in cash. At one time, workers at Kambove were given two yards of calico on a Saturday afternoon and left to try to buy their own rations for the following week.[84] Figure 4.12 depicts paying in calico Africans employed at Kansanshi. Standing is William Whitton, the company accountant, whose responsibilities included payments in calico; sitting next to him is Eriksson. This photograph was later reproduced in a magazine article about the early 'pioneers' in the Copperbelt, but the photographer is not credited.[85]

The *posho* system did not work, however, for those employees whose villages were too far away for food to be regularly brought to them by their own people. As the first mining season (1901–2) advanced, they found it increasingly difficult to buy sufficient food to meet their needs. There were no labour regulations in place until 1904, when the principle of raising revenue from the indigenous population through a hut tax was gradually extended to the concession.[86] For practical as well as ideological reasons the wage labour system was preferred over compulsion for most mining and construction work. The wish to take part in the money economy in order to buy calico, iron cooking utensils or weapons may have been inducements for those who volunteered.[87]

Figure 4.12 Paying in calico, Kansanshi, 1901–2
Source: FHA, PC, VKK871:208.

Nevertheless, in the absence of any other options, the 'pioneers' believed that compulsion to work could be used during preliminary exploration and development work, before a sufficient 'voluntary labour force' could be secured.[88] Ultimately the only real alternative was to coerce unwilling Africans to take up mining work,[89] but the labour recruiting methods employed depended upon individual labour recruiters. Boijer's labour recruiting methods seem to have been notorious. Middleton described how,

> A day or two ago a Native came in who reported that at a kraal about 100 miles to the south-east there was a little-man with two police who was very masterful and used his *sjambok* freely. I expect this is Boyer [*sic*].[90]

Prospectors were often quick to express harsh criticism or mistreat African workers, whose language and beliefs they did not understand and whose perceived incompetence and laziness irritated them. There are clear indications that Tanks employees forced the local population into the workforce as porters or regular workers at mines.[91] The dominant contention is that in the Congo mineworkers very rarely took up waged employment entirely freely until the mid-1920s.[92]

Besides obvious ethical concerns, labour management also involved economic considerations.[93] Sound business depended on precise economic planning, reliable calculations and predictable production estimates, all of which remained elusive without direct supervision of the production process and strict control over the workforce. In Katanga, the early mining industry was concentrated within a region in which villages were widely scattered and rarely had more than 50 inhabitants. The recruitment of workers from farther afield raised a new set of issues: not only the problems of how to secure legal authorisation to recruit and maintain a sustainable level of arrivals (in light of existing local food resources), but also the need to pay greater attention to their workers. Such measures ranged from assessments of physical aptitude and future recruitment needs (in the form of duration of employment contracts) through some codification of working conditions to the very practical issues of nourishment, clothing, accommodation and health care.[94] concerns came to the fore of Tanks' labour management policy after 1906: rules governing labour recruitment were redefined as the industry entered into the era of production on a commercial scale.[95]

Experimental mining and smelting at Kolwezi and Busanga

African copper mining and smelting were thought to have discontinued by the dawn of the twentieth century when colonial prospectors surveyed and staked the seemingly vacant copper workings. This view was obscured by theories of race, class and gender, however. In the wake of colonialism, African metallurgical knowledge in its 'original stage' was thought to have vanished and estimations of African metallurgical achievements were often prejudiced. In 1901–2 the local mining and smelting practices were for the first time systematically documented with maps, photographs and drawings by Tanks' prospectors, mineralogists, geologists and engineers. At Kolwezi, a working of 480 yards by 150 yards at its widest part, situated on the main road to Bihé in Angola, the principal feature was a series of pits in line of three crosscuts up to some 60 feet in length. Shallow pits were circular in shape and timbered in places. Ten men and women, 'Wa-Alunda from Kamimbe's village', were working in the central trench when a party of Tanks prospectors arrived at Kolwezi in early November 1901. The methods of African miners were reported by the party leader, Michael J. Holland, as follows. The mining was done with iron picks and by collecting any loose pieces of malachite that the miners could find. The soil and the ore were pulled to the surface on bark ropes made from local fibres in cylindrical buckets also made of bark, with hard bottoms and softened sides. Ladders were also used, and the rungs were fastened to the uprights with bark rope. On these men and women stood alternately, passing the buckets up and down, or hauling up rocks and blocks of malachite with bark ropes. A basket of soil and crumbly material from the pits was carried to the Kolwezi stream nearby. The basket was placed rim-deep in the running water and the contents then sifted, shaken and handpicked. Only the malachite was left in the basket, which was then turned out on the riverbank and returned to the mine for more soil. The prospectors purchased one basket with its contents immediately after the washing, which was later assayed in order to give some idea of the value of the Kolwezi mine.[96]

Smelting, if not the mining of the ore, was confined to certain guilds or families. Only pure green malachite was used for smelting, for the presence of other chemical elements in copper ores causes differences in colour and affects physical properties such as the melting temperature. The furnaces were supplied with air from bellows made of two bags of antelope skin and were fired by charcoal from the East African Afrormosia (*Afrormosia angolensis*), a particularly dense hardwood. The furnaces were quite small, about 28 inches high and 15 inches in diameter, 'flimsily constructed of pieces of ant-hill' and propped up on all sides with forked sticks. These furnaces were then lit and let burn for an hour and a half, after which the blowers were preparing to play their part, working it like a valve with a quick and panting rhythm. Once the malachite had been smelted, the furnace was broken down and the molten copper refined by the master smelters in the casting furnace of similar construction. Moulds, made of anthill or sometimes clay, were shaped to produce ingots, bars or crosses, and from them were made hoes, bullets and copper wire for ornaments. Ceremonies and ritual accompanied each phase, and these were in the local people's eyes the most vital part of smelting and refining copper.[97]

In the copper industry, vertical integration of mining and smelting capacities was strongly promoted by the move towards larger-scale ore deposits, increasingly remote from major markets. The cost of shipping the product to the markets, as well as greater investments in transport infrastructure, encouraged the vertical integration of smelting capacity, since, as Schmitz (1986) has put it, 'this effectively reduced the cost of shipping each unit of metal.'[98] However, the corporate growth theory, that in colonial Africa 'the lack of domestic capital formation and the absence of a skilled labour force led to external financing of mineral developments and the employment of foreign miners and managerial personnel,'[99] does not seem to fit seamlessly with the case of Tanks.

The first European-produced copper at Kolwezi was reported to have been smelted on 7 July 1905,[100] some six years before a smelter capable of producing copper on a commercial scale came into operation at Lubumbashi.[101] On 16 January 1906 two small water-jacket furnaces were transported from Kimberley to the railhead at Kalomo and then to Kolwezi under Eriksson's command, using a great deal of African labour and at the cost of five carriers' lives.[102] The furnaces had been made in Kimberley for the company as small-scale copies of the full-size water-jacket furnaces that were used by the large copper-smelting outfits in America. Being so small, with a capacity of only 900 lbs, the water-jacket furnaces caused such a lot of work and trouble that their use was soon discontinued. Locally constructed furnaces, using large bricks made from powdered ant-heap, proved much more successful.[103] Figure 4.13 depicts Kolwezi mine after Eriksson's return to Kolwezi in 1906. The ore was sorted by hand but crushed now by a stamp driven by waterwheel.

Figure 4.13 Ore crushing, Kolwezi, 1906
Source: FHA, PC, VKK542:36.

Ultimately, local metallurgical knowledge was an important asset that ensured Tanks' early success in experimental smelting. N. Samwell, mining engineer, who inspected the company's tin-bearing properties at Busanga in 1904, paid attention to local specialised metallurgical knowledge of smelting: '[…] the Natives on the spot are to be recommended – and as they have been smelting both Copper and Iron for generations past for their own requirements, there would be no difficulty in making use of their labour for tin smelting operations.'[104]

Eriksson, the 'pioneer smelter man', as he was nostalgically known in Rhodesiana,[105] carried out experimental smelting of tin ore at Busanga mine during the rainy season of 1904–5. It was found to be possible to smelt on the spot both stream tin – or tin oxide – and lode tin, consisting mainly of cassiterite ore. The tin produced was described as of 'the greatest purity without any need for subsequent refining'. The cost of producing a ton was estimated to be in the region of £2 – depending on the price of labour for mining and making charcoal.[106] In January 1905 the first tin bars were reported to the company accountant based at Kambove.[107] Eriksson had carefully studied the metallurgical and charcoal manufacture processes used by local expert families or guilds that specialised in smelting processes and managed to build an experimental production works for tin smelting at Busanga.[108] Possibly on the basis of a proposal put forward by Samwell (who had experience in tin smelting in New South Wales, Heberton, Queensland and the Malay Peninsula), the furnace at Busanga was later modified according to the model used by Chinese tin smelters in the Malay Peninsula. This type of furnace was built on the spot from fire brick, small iron castings and small portable blowers.[109] Figure 4.14 depicts tin smelting works at Busanga in 1904–5.

Winners and losers of the early mining economy

As it transpired, the Katanga copper and tin deposits were not isolated occurrences but part of a vast geological formation, the like of which was not known outside Africa. Nevertheless, in 1906 Tanks' future seemed to be under threat due to a fall in copper prices and the end of its five-year agreement with CSK over concessionary rights in Katanga. The founding period of the company came to an end on 28 October 1906, when *Union Minière du Haut-Katanga* was formed to exploit mineral deposits pegged for Tanks.

The Katanga interests proved to be something of a lottery ticket for Tanks shareholders.[110] Following the early euphoria, which caused £1 shares in Tanks to touch over £20 in January 1903, the shares fell below par on the market.[111] The financiers were not impressed with the progress made. One of the company's principal financers was Christopher John Leyland (*né* Naylor, 1849–1926), a former naval officer and wealthy landowner, who controlled Haggerston Castle and estates in Northumberland. Leyland had personally spent upwards of £155,000 on Tanks and lost heavily when the company's shares fell on the market.[112] The object of Leyland, a director of Tanks, ZE

Figure 4.14 Tin smelting, Busanga, 1904–5
Source: FHA, PC, VKK542:34.

and the Parsons Marine Steam Turbine Company (an engineering company based on the River Tyne at Wallsend, north-east England, famed for the building of engines for the first two turbine-powered destroyers of the Royal Navy), was now to force the abandonment of the Central African projects at all costs.[113] From 1903 Tanks seemed to have enjoyed little support in the London capital market and was forced to keep itself going by a large distribution of debentures to raise capital, so the company did not have large sums available to invest in the development of its properties, even if it would have wished to do so. With a vast concession to be worked, hampered both by a lack of capital and by its obligations to BSAC, Tanks of the early 1900s was a mining company with huge expenses but little turnover.[114]

The shares in Tanks being undervalued was also reflected negatively in the bonuses of the early white employees of the company, who it was originally agreed would receive £20 per month and, on top of that, under the various agreements with Tanks, secured 4% of the net profits arising from the sale or disposition of the discoveries made. A further 1% was set aside for division among the employees at the manager's discretion.[115] Later arrivals were not always so lucky. Rumours of mineral discoveries attracted so many 'stiffs' (*e.g.* white men inadequately equipped and dependent on donations of foodstuffs, who nevertheless took to wandering across the area in search of work)[116] that Grey felt compelled to issue a warning in *The Livingstone Mail* that there was no chance of securing mining employment with Tanks.[117]

On 27 August 1903, a discovery of a gold deposit in rocks situated 11 miles north-west of the village of Kazembe and bearing the name of Ruwe Hill was reported by the directors of Tanks. The average yield was 4,495 grammes of gold, 3,565 of silver and 3,151 of platinum per ton (sometimes much more).[118] The opening of the Ruwe Hill gold mine in late 1903 and further prospects of locating payable gold-bearing deposits at Kambove were discussed enthusiastically at the company's annual general meeting.[119] The speculation that surrounded the possibility of a payable gold-bearing reef was at least as important to the company's economic viability as the very rich copper deposits. Figure 4.15 depicts alluvial gold from Kambove where gold was found in flat, angular pieces, sometimes with irregularly shaped nuggets weighing from two up to nine ounces. Figure 4.16 depicts gold sluicing at the Ruwe Hill gold mine where the gold was recovered by washing the dirt in riffled sluice boxes.

In 1901–6 most of the company's assets were diverted into the construction of the requisite infrastructure, whilst the mines themselves were starved of working capital. The company was relatively slow to implement mechanisation, and development was heavily dependent on African mining and metallurgy knowledge. By 1906, to mark the end of what had gone before and to commemorate the beginning of a new era in the Central African mining industry, the approximate area of the ancient African mining had been charted, depicted, mapped and renamed with colonial names of mines, mining centres, mineralised zones, concessionary companies and projected railway lines. The prospector brought with him new mining technologies, and he had a better access to capital and a more nuanced understanding of markets. But the mines, metals and even the basic metallurgical principles remained the same for a good many years after the arrival of the colonial prospector. The change from 'blanket' prospecting to a system of scientific prospecting was

Figure 4.15 Alluvial gold, Kambove, 1902–6
Source: FHA, PC, VKK871:75.

Figure 4.16 Gold sluicing, Ruwe, 1903–6
Source: FHA, PC, VKK542:31.

devised after the discovery of the first evidence of the rich ore reserves at depth in the early 1920s.[120] Previously unexploited mineral resources were now exposed, novel metallurgical practices were introduced and new chemical elements in the ore (*e.g.* cobalt, radium and uranium) were brought to the metal markets. Even so, copper continued to define and dominate the mining industry in Central Africa, thus justifying the term 'Copperbelt'.

Concluding discussion

This chapter has discussed the operation of the colonising processes of the London-based mining and mine exploration company Tanganyika Concessions. It has sought to analyse how Tanks' colonising processes took place, why they were considered desirable by various interest groups, and the impact that these processes had on physical and human environments in parts of North-Western Rhodesia and Katanga. In more general terms, the chapter has sought to make a case for analysing the impact of City financing upon empire-building in colonial Southern Africa. Of the numerous registered companies involved in mining and mine exploration in colonial-era South-Central Africa, Tanks was one of the very few successes. It initiated the far-reaching effort to set up a European mining industry in the mineral-rich region that later became popularly and loosely known as the Copperbelt. There is another aspect which makes Tanks a relevant case study: the wide range of available materials – a prospectus, company records as well as personal material (diaries, travelogues and photographs) of the company's many workers in the field – offer a fuller picture of the inception of European mining and mine exploration in Northern Rhodesia and Katanga than is available elsewhere. Mining has been analysed by both economic historians and researchers of colonialism, but the extent to which British capital ultimately revolutionised economies and societies in colonial Southern Africa continues to be a keenly debated subject. Despite extensive existing historiography, very little is known of individual mining companies' operations on the ground.

Previous studies of Tanks' mining and mine exploration operations have focused on powerful capitalists and financiers (Robert Williams, Cecil Rhodes and others). A very much more complex story emerges, however, when written and visual materials produced by the company's employees on the ground are analysed. Descriptions related to the discovery of the Katanga copper deposits, the inception of the wage labour system and the operations related to experimental smelting can differ significantly depending on whether one consults the prospectus, company records, diaries or visual material. The heterogeneous sources can also complement each other, allowing a fuller story to be told and a sounder case to be made. Entries from Middleton's and Eriksson's diaries provide different impressions of the discoveries than the reports submitted by Grey and Farrell. Depictions of Kansanshi Camp during the first mining season (including mining and employed Africans being paid in calico) help us to appreciate how Tanks' colonising processes slowly but irreversibly started to mould physical and human environments for the purposes of colonial economy. Such visual representations show us scenes, processes and people otherwise known to us, if at all, only through the written word. Prior to 1906, before the construction of roads, railways and telegraph lines, Tanks' mining and mine exploring operations were run by local management with the help of engineering firms, suppliers and service sector agencies. With technical and production matters left in the hands of local management, the company's directors sought to attract the attention of investors by circulating favourable reports on discoveries. Share speculation and company promotion was considered an important aspect of the mining business; before 1906 most of the company's assets were diverted into the construction of the requisite infrastructure; at the same time the mines themselves were starved of working capital. The exploitation of mineral wealth was heavily dependent on a cheap supply of African labour. Tanks' early mining industry was concentrated in an area with a relatively small African population: this meant that while there was little pressure upon land, conversely there was only a relatively small pool of labour from which to recruit. White management employees worked in relative solitude, in remote lands, amidst alien peoples, languages and habits; they had very little contact with company-level management and often had to rely on their own initiative. This situation, coupled with the absence of labour regulations and conventional bourgeois taboos of race, gender and class, left the local population vulnerable to abuse at a time when colonial rule was still in its infancy.

When production became a more pressing concern than company promotion, efforts to verify the economic viability of ore lodes intensified. Instead of just being a brass nameplate company in the City, Tanks became increasingly grounded in specific localities and began to transform existing physical and human environments. It set up mining camps, recruited workers (and sometimes apparently used forced labour), created a system of paid jobs, sank shafts, carried out experimental smelting work, cleared vegetation and built roads and railways. In other words the company did everything that was considered requisite for setting up a mining business. Changes caused to the social structure brought new challenges alongside prosperity, especially for the company management, who were also major shareholders. The operation of the early mining economy led directly to large-scale migration of African labourers and the creation of mining communities. Mining development also had a political dimension: most notably the almost invariable restriction of Africans to the lower ranks, thus reinforcing the authority of white workers over African employees. That race, ethnicity, profession and class operated as lines of demarcation and division is evident from relations between various interest groups in the service of the company. The pervasiveness of these hierarchies (both at the time and beyond) can perhaps most obviously be seen in the overemphasis placed on the role of powerful capitalists making their own history at the expense of workers.

In the process of the international development of mining, the role of human capital was just as important as the development of financial institutions. The 'pioneers' – the men on the spot, prospectors, settlers, consulting engineers, traders and labour recruiters – together with the financiers, bankers, stockjobbers, metal merchants, directors and chairmen of the companies were all actively promoting mining in South-Central Africa. The interests of various groups were often intertwined; the exploitation of the area's rich mineral deposits was championed from top to bottom, from company management to petty prospectors in the field. From the reports of the mining engineers, the prospectuses of the mining companies and the statements of their chairmen the impression was created of a centralised, highly efficient and organised industry, in complete charge of itself. This was useful for convincing investors to put their money into mining, yet it often bore little relation to the actual state of affairs at mine level, where there was a desperate shortage of managerial personnel skilled in mining techniques and labour management.

Notes

1 Lonn 1966, 9.
2 Green 1982, 2; Lonn 1966, 5.
3 For further information, see Gann and Duignan 1962.
4 See, for instance, various plaques commemorating pioneers in the Mining District Walk in Johannesburg.

5 On these many roles of colonial photography see Vansina 1992, 193–205; Ranger 2001, 203–215.
6 For further information, see Särkkä 2018.
7 Hutchinson and Martelli 1971, 72.
8 MU, TANKS, ZE/4, Williams' Consolidated Buildings, Limited, Bulawayo, 7 May 1898; *Horizon* July 1962, 2; Pease 1914, 5.
9 Gelfand 1961, 1, 167.
10 MU, TANKS, ZE/4, George Grey to Robert Williams & Co., 29 October 1898.
11 Grey 1901, 62, 76; *The African Review of Mining, Finance and Commerce* 20 May 1899, 326.
12 MU, TANKS, ZE/3, George Grey to Robert Williams, 2 February 1900.
13 MU, TANKS, ZE/3, Robert Williams to ZE, 13 February 1901. Crewe was killed in the fighting at Mafeking (Mahikeng). Farquhar 1914, 21.
14 Gelfand 1961, 121–122.
15 Farquhar 1914, 21–24; Justice 1902, 99–104; Brooks 1944, 81.
16 Grey 1901, 63.
17 Supplement to *The African Review of Mining, Finance and Commerce* 25 November 1899, 31.
18 For further information, see Gann 1964.
19 LMA, SE, CLC, B/004/F/01/MS18000/89B/258, Memorandum of Agreement, 14 June 1901; *Mining World and Engineering Record* 21 December 1901.
20 Justice 1902, 102.
21 DU, BRL, GRE, X/V142, TANKS, 7.
22 Thornhill 1915, 129.
23 *Bulawayo Chronicle* 1901a.
24 Middleton 1963, 8. See also Eriksson 1932, 74.
25 Hutchinson and Martelli 1971, 120.
26 Studt 1909, 159–167; Studt 1913, 44–102.
27 For further information, see Reeks 1920.
28 'Imperial College' 1975, 233–247.
29 Harvey and Press 2000, 101; Harvey and Press 1990, 98–119.
30 Gelfand 1963, 6; Gelfand 1961, 180–182.
31 MU, TANKS, ZE/4, Wm. Whitton, Secretary, Williams' Consolidated Buildings, Limited, Bulawayo, 7 May 1898.
32 Särkkä 2015, 81–91.
33 Särkkä 2021, 303–329.
34 For further information, see Kennedy and Holdridge 2021, 277–301.
35 Thornhill 1915, 154, 170.
36 Middleton 1963, 12, diary entry 3 May 1901.
37 Särkkä 2015, 91–94.
38 MU, TANKS, ZE/4, Williams to ZE, 10 February 1899.
39 DU, BRL, GRE, X/V142, TANKS, 26.
40 MU, TANKS, ZE/3, Williams to ZE, 20 February 1901, copies of Farrell's testimonials.
41 Phimister and Mouat 2003, 22.
42 Eriksson 1932, 172–173.
43 For further information, see Särkkä 2018, 153–154.
44 Eriksson 1932, 70, 72.
45 For further information, see Daly and Hogan 2005, 63–64; Ryan 1997.
46 Eriksson 1932, frontispiece.
47 See, for instance, Clark 1936, 158.
48 For further information, see Särkkä 2018, 141–160.
49 Eriksson 1932, 91, 98, 100.
50 DU, BRL, GRE, X/V142, TANKS, 8–9.

51 Prain 1975, 187.
52 See also Coleman 1971, 172–173.
53 Middleton 1963, 55, diary entry, 9 February 1902.
54 Middleton 1963, 55, diary entry, 8 February 1902.
55 Middleton 1963, 56, diary entry 22 February 1902.
56 See, for instance, an incident reported by Middleton that apparently led to the death of a mining worker (Middleton 1963, 61, diary entry 25 April 1902).
57 Scannell 1961, 12.
58 See Middleton 1963, 52, diary entry 22 December 1901. See also Särkkä 2015, 82.
59 Gann 1964, 106–107.
60 MU, TANKS, TC/12, Robert Laws to Robert Williams, 28 April 1925.
61 Thornhill 1915, 124; Eriksson 1932, 116.
62 TNA, FO 369/3/55, 32269, Application of John Bensley Thornhill of Tanganyika Concessions Limited to be Vice Consul in Katanga District of Congo Free State, 1906.
63 Thornhill 1915, 165.
64 Gale 1969, 41.
65 Roan Consolidated Mines Public Relations Department 1978, 16.
66 Thornhill 1915, 165; Eriksson 1932, 142.
67 Eriksson 1932, 146.
68 DU, BRL, GRE, X/V142, TANKS, Photographs.
69 DU, BRL, GRE, X/V142, TANKS, 92.
70 Middleton 1963, Appendix C, 'Dr. Middleton by William Robert White'.
71 Middleton 1963, 63, diary entry 9 May 1902.
72 Middleton 1963, 63, diary entry 18 June 1902.
73 DU, BRL, GRE, X/V142, TANKS, 129.
74 Harvey and Press 1989, 75.
75 Phimister and Mouat 2003, 22–26. See also van Helten 1990, 176–177; Harvey and Press 1989, 69.
76 Mollan 2009, 230–231, 243.
77 Vellut 1983, 136, 138.
78 Schmitz 1986, 403.
79 DU, BRL, GRE/X/V142, TANKS, 98.
80 DU, BRL, GRE, X/V142, TANKS, 18.
81 Wright 1962, 132–133.
82 MU, TANKS, TC/29, Findlay Durham & Brodie to the Tanks, 8 September 1905.
83 Hogarth 2014, 30–41.
84 Sharp 1956, 27.
85 Scannell 1961, 10–14, 12.
86 Report of the Commission 1938, 29, 111.
87 Jaeger 1981, 76–78.
88 *Bulawayo Chronicle* 1901b, 3–7. See also Katzenellenbogen 1978, 271.
89 Gann 1964, 102–103.
90 Middleton 1963, 52, diary entry 22 December 1901.
91 See, for instance, Eriksson 1932, 164.
92 Lilaka 2009; Roes 2010, 634–670.
93 For further information, see Gardner 2012.
94 Coosemans 1997, 781–784.
95 Dr Pearson and Dr Mouchet were the first medical officers in the Copperbelt to contemplate these concerns systematically (Pearson and Mouchet 1923).
96 DU, BRL, GRE, X/V142, TANKS, 67.
97 Bradley 1952, 34–38.
98 Schmitz 1986, 403.
99 van Helten 1990, 160.
100 *Horizon* November 1959, 26.

101 The first copper in Katanga was brought to the stage of commercial production at Lubumbashi Smelting Works on 16 September 1911 (*The Times* 16 November 1911, 19).
102 Eriksson 1932, 242–252.
103 Thornhill 1915, 86–87.
104 MU, TANKS, TC/29, N. Samwell to Robert Williams, 1 July 1904.
105 *Horizon* November 1959, 24–26.
106 MU, TANKS, TC/29, N. Samwell to Robert Williams, 1 July 1904.
107 MU, TANKS, TC/146, Kambove Accountant, Busanga Tin Smelting Accounts, January to March 1905.
108 Eriksson 1932, 206–210; Sharp 1956, 9.
109 MU, TANKS, TC/29, N. Samwell to Robert Williams, 1 July 1904.
110 The African Review of Mining, Finance and Commerce 21 December 1901, 459.
111 *The Quarterly Review* January 1903, 88–114; MU, TANKS, TC/25, C.J. Leyland to Robert Williams, 23 June 1903.
112 MU, TANKS, TC/25, Tanks to the Shareholders, 4 August 1903.
113 MU, TANKS, TC/25, C.J. Leyland to Robert Williams, 27 May 1903; 14 June 1903. See also Katzenellenbogen 1973, 38–43.
114 LMA, SE, CLC, B/004/F/01/MS18000/129B/277, Balance Sheet, 30 June 1901.
115 MU, TANKS, TC/29, Scotland, the Secretary of the Tanks, 22 June 1907. Later this agreement was the subject of some dispute between the company management and Eriksson, who resigned from his position with Tanks on 31 May 1906 (MU, TANKS, TC/146, Kambove Accountant, Eric Douglas, Kambove, 31 July 1906).
116 Thornhill 1915, 235.
117 Grey 1906.
118 MU, TANKS, TC/29, Report on the Ruwe Bed, Kambove, H. Buttenbach, 26 October 1903.
119 *The African Review of Mining, Finance and Commerce* 16 January 1904, 149.
120 Brooks 1944, 80, 83–84.

References

The African Review of Mining, Finance and Commerce (16 January 1904) 'Big Proposition', XXXVIII:582, 149; (21 December 1901) 'The Tanganyika Concessions, Limited, in the Congo', XXIX:474, 459; (20 May 1899) 'The Tanganyika Concessions', IX:339, 326.

Bradley, K. (1952) *Copper Venture: The Discovery and Development of Roan Antelope and Mufulira*, Mufulira Copper Mines Limited, Roan Antelope Copper Mines Limited, London.

Brooks, R. (May1944) 'How the Rhodesian Coppers Were Found', *Engineering and Mining Journal*, 145:V, 80–84.

Bulawayo Chronicle (March1901a) 'Mr. George Grey's Expedition to North-Western Rhodesia'.

Bulawayo Chronicle (1901b) Christmas number of 1901, 'Progress of Rhodesia', 3–7.

Clark, P.M. (1936) *Autobiography of an Old Drifter*, George Harrap, London, Bombay and Sydney.

Coleman, F.L. (1971) *The Northern Rhodesia Copperbelt, 1899–1962: Technological Development Up to the End of the Central African Federation*, Manchester University Press, Manchester.

Coosemans, R. (1997) 'Occupational Health' in P.G. Janssens, M. Kivits and L. Vuylsteke eds. *Health in Central Africa since 1885: Past, Present and Future*, King Baudouin Foundation, Brussels, 781–798.

Daly, M.W. and Hogan, J.R. (2005) *Images of Empire: Photographic Sources for the British in Sudan*, Brill, Leiden.

Durham University (DU), The Barker Research Library (BRL), Grey Estate Records (GRE), Reports on the Discoveries Made by Mr. George Grey's Expedition in Northern Rhodesia and Congo Free State, and Reports by J.R. Farrell, Mining Engineer, 5 January1903 (X/V142), Tanganyika Concessions Ltd. (TANKS).

Eriksson, C.T. (1932) *Seikkailujeni Afrikka*, K. J. Gummerus, Jyväskylä and Helsinki.

Farquhar, M. (1914) 'The Expedition in 1899' in *Some Account of George Grey and His Work in Africa by Men Who Knew Him There*, Chiswick Press, London, 21–24.

Finnish Heritage Agency (FHA), Helsinki, Picture Collections (PC).

Gale, W.D. (1969) 'The Diaries of Harold Cookson. Part II', *Rhodesiana*, 20, 33–43.

Gann, L.H. (1964) *A History of Northern Rhodesia: Early Days to 1953*, Chatto & Windus, London.

Gann, L.H. and Duignan, P. (1962) *White Settlers in Tropical Africa*, Penguin Books, Harmondsworth.

Gardner, L.A. (2012) *Taxing Colonial Africa: Political Economy of British Imperialism*, Oxford University Press, Oxford.

Gelfand, M. (1961) *Northern Rhodesia in the Days of Charter: A Medical and Social Study 1878–1924*, Basil Blackwell, Oxford.

Gelfand, M. (1963) 'Preface' in M. Gelfand ed. 'Diary of Dr. Richard Watson Middleton, 12th April, 1901, to 18th July, 1902', *The Central African Journal of Medicine*, Supplement to 9:5, 1–6.

Green, T. (1982) *The New World of Gold: The Inside Story of the Mines, the Markets, the Politics, the Investors*, Weidenfeld & Nicolson, London.

Grey, G. (July1901) 'The Kafue River and Its Headwaters', *The Geographical Journal*, 18:1, 62–77.

Grey, G. (18 August1906) 'Notice', *The Livingstone Mail*, I:21.

Harvey, C. and Press, J. (1989) 'Overseas Investment and the Professional Advance of British Metal Mining Engineers, 1851–1914', *The Economic History Review*, New Series, 42:1, 64–86.

Harvey, C. and Press, J. (1990) 'The City and International Mining, 1870–1914', *Business History*, 32:3, 98–119.

Harvey, C. and Press, J. (2000) 'The City of London and International Trade, 1850–1914' in R.C. Michie ed. *The Development of London as a Financial Centre*, Vol. 2: *1850–1914*, IB Tauris, London, 87–105.

Hogarth, D.D. (2014) 'Robert Rich Sharp (1881–1960), Discoverer of the Shinkolobwe Radium–Uranium Orebodies', *Terrae Incognitae*, 46:1, 30–41.

Horizon: The Magazine of the Rhodesian Selection of Trust Group of Companies (November 1959) 'Charles Eriksson – Pioneer Smelter Man', I:11, 24–26; (July 1962) 'George Grey – the Man Who Found Chambishi', IV:7, 2.

Hutchinson, R. and Martelli, G. (1971) *Robert's People: The Life of Sir Robert Williams Bart. 1860–1938*, Chatto & Windus, London.

'Imperial College' (1975) in F.H.W. Sheppard ed. *Survey of London*: Vol. 38: *South Kensington Museums Area*, London County Council, London, 233–247. Retrieved 2 January 2024 from https://www.british-history.ac.uk/survey-london/vol38/v-vi.

Jaeger, D. (1981) *Settlement patterns and rural development: a human geographical study of the Kaonde, Kasempa District, Zambia*, PhD thesis, University of Amsterdam.

Justice, J.N. (July1902) 'Prospecting in Northern Rhodesia', *Travel*, 7:75, 99–104.

Katzenellenbogen, S.E. (1973) *Railways and the Copper Mines of Katanga*, Clarendon Press, Oxford.

Katzenellenbogen, S.E. (1978) 'Labour Recruitment in Central Africa: The Case of Katanga' in C. Dewey and A.G. Hopkins eds. *The Imperial Impact: Studies in the Economic History of Africa and India*, Institute of Commonwealth Studies, University of London, London, 270–279.

Kennedy, W.M. and Holdridge, C. (2021) '"Did You Really Have a Place in the Boer War?": Colonial Conflict and the Contested Production of "Finnish" Nationality, 1899–1908' in R. Merivirta, L. Koivunen and T. Särkkä eds. *Finnish Colonial Encounters: From Anti-Imperialism to Cultural Colonialism and Complicity*, Palgrave Macmillan, Cham, Switzerland, 277–301.

Lilaka, O. (2009) *Naming Colonialism: History and the Collective Memory in the Congo, 1870–1960*, The University of Michigan Press, Madison.

London Metropolitan Archives (LMA), Records of the Stock Exchange (SE), Applications for authority to deal and applications for listing (CLC).

Lonn, G. (1966) *The Mine Finders*, Pitt Publishing Company, Toronto.

Middleton, R.W. (1963) 'Diary of Dr. Richard Watson Middleton, 12th April, 1901, to 18th July, 1902' in M. Gelfand ed. *The Central African Journal of Medicine*, Supplement to 9:5, 1–68.

Mining World and Engineering Record (21 December1901).

Mollan, S.M. (2009) 'Business Failure, Capital Investment and Information: Mining Companies in Anglo-Egyptian Sudan, 1900–13', *The Journal of Imperial and Commonwealth History*, 37:2, 229–248.

The National Archives of UK (TNA), Foreign Office (FO).

Pearson, A. and Mouchet, R. (1923) *The Practical Hygiene of Native Compounds in Tropical Africa: Being Notes from the Experience of the First Eighteen Years of European Work in the Katanga*, Ballière, Tindall and Co., London.

Pease, SirA. (1914) 'Foreword' in *Some Account of George Grey and His Work in Africa by Men Who Knew Him There*, Chiswick Press, London, 1–12.

Phimister, I. and Mouat, J. (2003) 'Mining, Engineers and Risk Management: British Overseas Investment, 1894–1914', *South African Historical Journal*, 49:1, 1–26.

Prain, Sir R. (1975) *Copper: The Anatomy of an Industry*, Mining Journal Books, London.

The Quarterly Review (January1903) 'The Game of Speculation', 197, 88–114.

Ranger, T. (2001) 'Colonialism, Consciousness and the Camera', *Past and Present*, 171:1, 203–215.

Reeks, M. (1920) *Register of the Associates and Old Students of the Royal School of Mines: And History of the Royal School of Mines*, Vols. 1–2, Royal School of Mines (Old Students) Association, London.

Report of the Commission Appointed to Enquire into the Financial and Economic Position of Northern Rhodesia (Report of the Commission) (1938), 145, His Majesty's Stationery Office, London.

Roan Consolidated Mines Public Relations Department (1978) *Zambia's Mining Industry: The First 50 Years*, Roan Consolidated Mines Limited, Ndola.

Roes, A. (2010) 'Towards History of a Mass Violence in the État Indepéndant du Congo 1885–1908', *South African Historical Journal*, 62:4, 634–670.

Ryan, J.R. (1997) *Picturing Empire: Photography and the Visualization of the British Empire*, Reaktion Books, London.

Scannell, T. (March1961) 'Pioneer of 1901 Comes Back to the Copperbelt', *Horizon: The Magazine of the Rhodesian Selection of Trust Group of Companies*, III:3, 10–14.

Schmitz, C. (1986) 'The Rise of Big Business in the World Copper Industry 1870–1930', *The Economic History Review*, New Series, 39:3, 392–410.

Sharp, R.R. (1956) *Early Days in Katanga*, Rhodesian Printers, Bulawayo.

Studt, F.E. (1909) 'Some Notes on the Geology of the Katanga Country and Copper Belt (Read 18th October, 1909)', *Transactions of the Geological Society of South Africa*, XII, 159–167.

Studt, F.E. (1913) 'The Geology of Katanga and Northern Rhodesia: An Outline of the Geology of South Central Africa (Read 30th June, 1913)', *Transactions of the Geological Society of South Africa*, XVI, 44–102.

Supplement to *The African Review of Mining, Finance and Commerce* (25 November 1899), XXI, 31.

Särkkä, T. (2015) 'Imperialists without an Empire? Finnish Settlers in Late Nineteenth- and Early Twentieth-Century Rhodesia', *Journal of Migration History*, 1:1, 75–99.

Särkkä, T. (2018) 'Picturing Colonialism in Rhodesia: C. T. Eriksson's Pictorial Rhetoric and Colonial Reality, 1901–1906' in O. Kleemola and S. Pitkänen eds. *Photographs and History: Interpreting Past and Present through Photographs*, Cultural History 15, University of Turku, Turku, 141–160.

Särkkä, T. (2021) 'The "Pioneer Men": Making of Finnish Settler Identity in Southern Africa Pre-1914' in R. Merivirta, L. Koivunen and T. Särkkä eds. *Finnish Colonial Encounters: From Anti-Imperialism to Cultural Colonialism and Complicity*, Palgrave Macmillan, Cham, Switzerland, 303–329.

Thornhill, J.B. (1915) *Adventures in Africa under the British, Belgian and Portuguese Flags*, John Murray, London.

The Times (16 November1911) 'A Tour to the Great Copper Belt of Katanga, the Mines, Railways, and Work of the Tanganyika Concessions, Ltd. VI. The Smelting Works at Lubumbashi', 39744, 19.

The University of Manchester (MU), Tanks Group Archive (TANKS), Tanganyika Concession (TC), Zambesia Exploring Company (ZE).

van Helten, J.-J. (1990) 'Mining, Share Manias and Speculation: British Investment in Overseas Mining' in J.-J. van Helten and Y. Cassis eds. *Capitalism in a Mature Economy: Financial Institutions, Capital Exports and British Industry, 1870–1939*, Edward Elgar, London, 159–185.

Vansina, J. (1992) 'Photographs of the Sankura and Kasai River Basin Expedition Undertaken by Emil Torday (1876–1931) and M. W. Hilton Simpson (1881–1936)' in E. Edwards ed. *Anthropology and Photography 1860–1920*, Yale University Press, New Haven, CT and London, 193–205.

Vellut, J.-L. (1983) 'Mining in the Belgian Congo' in D. Birmingham and P.M. Martin eds. *History of Central Africa*, Vol. 2, Longman, London and New York, 126–162.

Wright, R. (1962) 'Trading on the Luapula 1900–1904. Part II', *The Northern Rhodesia Journal*, V:II, 123–134.

5 The world of copper mines, railways and labour

This chapter charts the links between the Katangese and Rhodesian mining regimes from the point of view of communications, financial institutions and labour migration networks. It analyses the evolution of the Central African mining industry, from its simple and crude pick-and-shovel beginnings with tent and shack dwellings to the era of commercial-scale mining, smelting and refining. For those with interests in its mineral resources Katanga could be perceived either as a barrier or as a bridge between the southern and central parts of the continent. A barrier for its challenging communications, sparse population and, in addition, for forming the frontier between the neighbouring colonies in the west, south and east. A bridge for its ethnic, cultural, political and economic links with the south, which since the early twentieth century were forged through an integrated rail network system, labour migration networks and the interconnectedness of financial regimes. The chapter concludes that the development of mining in Central Africa required a unique set of financial, technical and management capabilities. Success required the ability to raise the necessary funding, but it also demanded the skill to develop the necessary transport and communications, site installations, infrastructure and auxiliary services, and the management of the very large workforce.

Mapping the bonanza

Early-twentieth-century Katanga held unique characteristics for which it stood out from the rest of the Congo. Not only did it host some of the richest deposits of copper in the world, but, situated where it was, Katanga could not be classed as a purely southern or central African region. In terms of geography, Katanga was an area of extreme contrast between the barren north and the mineral-rich south situated on a high plateau and broken by rounded hills and deep valleys. After the takeover of the colonial government by the Belgian State on 20 August 1908, the Congo became a colony divided into provinces and districts overseen by the Governor General. The administration of Katanga was entrusted to a Vice-governor, however. Stationed in the administrative capital of Katanga, Élisabethville, so named in honour of

DOI: 10.4324/9781003247371-5

Queen Élisabeth of the Belgians, the Vice-governor held similar administrative powers over Katanga to those of the Governor General over the whole of the Congo. The colonial administration of the Congo was decentralised on account of the lack of communication between Élisabethville (Lubumbashi) and Léopoldville (Kinshasa) – the capital from 1923 and 1,000 miles away as the crow flies – and because the entire financial power of Katanga, the hinge of the Congo's economy, was in the hands of the directors of the mining and railway companies, with significant British holdings.[1]

But Katanga was not only geographically and administratively diverse – it was also one of the most ethnically complex areas of the whole of the Congo. The people categorised as 'Baluba' inhabited most of north Katanga and they comprised several distinct subgroupings. In the eighteenth century they had formed a powerful copper empire based on trade with the Portuguese on the Atlantic Coast. The mineral-rich south-east area, adjoining neighbouring Northern Rhodesia, was on the other hand dominated by the 'Balunda', with close links to the south.[2] The Province of Katanga was about the same size as France or Spain, but its population was scarce and widely scattered within the region. The mining industry was concentrated within the south-eastern region in Katanga in which villages rarely had more than 50 inhabitants.[3] This meant that in order to develop the copper mines of Katanga into payable mining properties, and to operate them on a large enough scale for global trade, labour had to be attracted to work on the mines and the railways from regions more densely populated, either from the other provinces of the Congo, from neighbouring colonies or, in the case of white management and mining experts, even from more distant sources of labour such as North America.[4] Ultimately, local, regional and global labour migration networks all had to be used to satisfy the very large demands for labour. The biggest supplier of African labour was Northern Rhodesia, and the most common languages spoken in the mines of Katanga were consequently Lunda and Bemba (which the Kazembe-Lunda had adopted from their neighbours).[5] In terms of settler colonialism, British South Africa Company (BSAC)-administered territories had an initial advantage. During the pre-1920 era a full one-third of the white settlers in Katanga had moved up from the south, and English was as commonly spoken in Katanga as French or Flemish.[6] At the same time, up to half of the African migrant labour force was recruited from the BSAC-administered territories.[7] The heterogeneous provenance of both white management and low-wage African labour contributed to the considerable ethnical diversity of the mining settlements in Katanga.

The interconnectedness of Rhodesian and Katangese mining regimes was another feature which set Katanga apart from the rest of the Congo. In principle the Congo formed a single economic unit. There were no trade, customs or fiscal barriers between the provinces, and the economy of the Belgian Congo was run with a budget based on her own currency, the Congolese franc, introduced in 1887, denominated in centimes and francs, and fixed at parity with the Belgian franc.[8] Yet on account of several contributory factors there was not a complete financial separation between Katanga and the neighbouring Northern Rhodesia. Historically the frontier had made Katanga open to infiltration and influence from the south. Katanga's natural resources were developed by giving exclusive concessions to private mining and railway corporations, with significant British holdings. They exploited their experience in the South African and Rhodesian mining industries that geographically were relatively close to Katanga, and made use of their extensive mining finance networks in the City of London, Johannesburg and Bulawayo, to expand their operations in the Copperbelt.

Another feature that strengthened the interconnectedness of Rhodesian and Katangese mining regimes was that the two major railway systems which would ultimately connect the Central African Copperbelt to the world's markets – the Benguela Railway and the Rhodesia Railway – were mostly British financed. The miners' most immediate need was to secure a railway connection to the mine, for without one no copper mine could operate on any large scale. By the late nineteenth century, the mining companies had become dependent on the railway for operational capability, cost management and the long-distance haulage of mineral wealth. Before the Bas-Congo to Katanga line was completed in 1928 linking the navigable stretches of the Congo River by rail to Port Francqui (Ilebo) on the mouth of the Kasai River, so that in principle exports from distant Katanga could reach Europe via the port of Matadi, more than 80 miles up the Congo River estuary, communications between Élisabethville and Léopoldville were infrequent and slow.[9] The distances from Élisabethville to the nearest ports in Mozambique (Beira) and Tanzania (Dar es Salaam) on the east coast, and Angola (Benguela) on the west, were calculated as 1,750, 1,619 and 1,120 miles respectively, showing a 500-mile saving by the latter route in addition to some 2,700 miles' saving in ocean transport to the principal shipping ports in the UK. It is not therefore entirely surprising that the colonial miner of the early days faced the west, in the direction of Benguela, with the nearest natural deep-water harbour in Lobito Bay on the Atlantic Coast (Figure 5.1).

Communications and mineral wealth

The greatest obstacle for the development of the Central African copper mines into payable mining properties was the lack of adequate means of steam transport and telegraph communications. As the mine and mineral seeking expeditions of the 1890s and early 1900s had demonstrated, transport costs by means of the porterage system were exorbitant. Each porter could transport a load between 40–55 lb. at one time but had to carry his own provisions in addition to the commercial load. From the miner's perspective carriers were liable to desert or to fall ill and had proven difficult to manage. Then again, transport by ox-wagons or by pack animals was impeded by the prevalence of tsetse fly and a variety of biting midges that could transmit diseases such as horse sickness.[10]

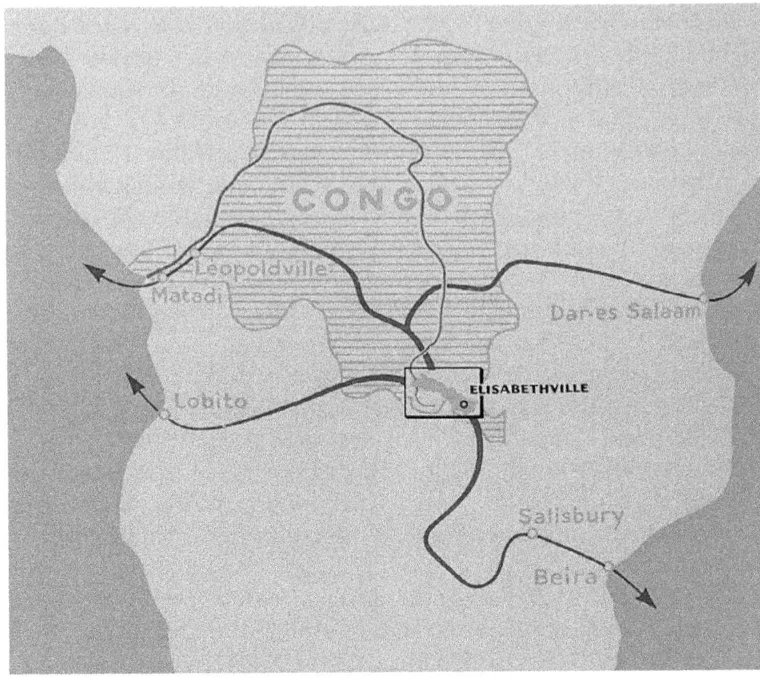

Figure 5.1 The four major railway systems of Central Africa
Source: Modified after *Union Minière du Haut-Katanga Rapport Annuel* 1965.

In 1903 Tanganyika Concessions (Tanks), a landlocked operator whose economies were to a large extent dependent on an efficient railway, approached railway contractors Messrs. George Pauling & Co. with a proposal to construct a railway from Benguela to the mining district of Katanga.[11] In his address 'The Milestones of African Civilization' the Managing Director Robert Williams highlighted the importance of the Benguela Railway not only from the commercial point of view but also from the perspective of settler colonialism.

> Because it [the Benguela Railway] will bring thousands of tons of ore hundreds of miles nearer Europe; it will bring the High Plateau of the great Zambesi-Congo divide, with its vast possibilities of cattle ranching, stock raising, and cereal cultivation, into close touch with the meat needs of Europe; and it will take the settler from the sea to the Bihé highlands, and far beyond them to Katanga.[12]

Besides having purely commercial objectives, the Benguela Railway project was also implicitly imperial by nature. It involved the surveying of seemingly empty lands for the railway and mining and for the promotion of a colonial settlement scheme and, in general, was inspired by Williams' conviction in

British technical superiority, the Victorian belief in progress and in the notion that Britain was the leader of humanity in Africa. Besides deeming the influence of the railway itself to be civilising, Williams believed that the Benguela Railway would give to Tanks a degree of strategic independence from Belgian mining interests which supported the idea of the 'all Belgian route' of rail and river (*i.e. Voie Nationale* or transCongo) via the port of Matadi and which saw the expansion of the Rhodesian railway system from the south as a way to further British railway imperialism.[13]

On 6 May 1903, the Benguela Railway Company (BRC), registered as *La Companhia do Caminho de Ferro de Benguela* in Lisbon, was incorporated, with the principal aim to raise capital to finance a railway from Benguela on the Angola–Congo border. The majority of the directors were Portuguese, and General Joachim Machado, the former Governor of Mozambique, whom Williams had met in Beira in 1891, was appointed as the Managing Director. The company's issued capital was the substantial sum of £3 million, of which Tanks registered 2,700,000 fully paid shares of £1 each (*i.e.* 90% equity), with the remaining shares taken up by the Portuguese Government.[14] The capitalisation of Tanks' shareholding was arranged so that a group of financiers headed by Frank Hilder and Athol Thorne raised £2 million of debenture stock. Among the other gentleman capitalists was Lord Howard de Walden (Thomas Evelyn Scott-Ellis, 1880–1946) – dubbed at the time 'Britain's wealthiest bachelor' for his estates in the West End of London, including the aristocratic mansion Seaford House in Belgrave Square – who participated in the venture with £500,000 cash in shares.[15]

After only about six months of construction work the Benguela Railway project halted because of the massive technical challenges caused by the steep 3,000-foot escarpment from the Atlantic Coast. Messrs. George Pauling & Co. found it impossible to continue the project, and a contract was now signed with Messrs. Griffiths & Co. Nicknamed 'Empire Jack', the swashbuckling John (Sir John in 1922) Norton-Griffiths (1871–1930) has been described as being every inch a *Boys' Own* hero for his pluck and determination. Norton-Griffiths had emigrated to the Witwatersrand goldfields at the age of 17, took part in the Raid on the Transvaal in December 1895 and served in the Second Matabele War and the South African War. With the financial backing of another veteran of the South Africa War, Lord de Walden, he founded Messrs. Griffiths & Co., a firm of railway contractors.[16]

Besides being technically a very challenging project, the main problem was the dearth of labour. In the aftermath of the South African War the Witwatersrand gold mining industry developed exceptionally rapidly, and the prevailing regional economic system was dominated by the powerful Rand mines and their need for low-wage labourers. With a longer working life for their mines, larger profits and greater capital resources, South African mining companies could afford to make sizeable investments, which meant a higher salary and better wage structure than the other, more marginal, regional mining and related infrastructure projects could afford to pay. Their success forced the Benguela Railway project to compete for its labour supply in ways that were difficult to sustain. To minimise costs and secure low-wage labourers, Norton-Griffiths resolved to use the well-tried method of many other large-scale railway projects in the British Empire and beyond – the importation of low-wage Asian labourers. In early 1903 an agreement was reached between Messrs. Griffiths & Co. and the Government of Natal for the shipment of 1,500 'Indian Coolies' from Natal to Angola. Besides the grave shortage of labour, fresh water and food, almost every conceivable tropical illness was encountered, delaying the project even further. Despite these massive challenges, by May 1905 a hundred miles of railway had been built, connecting Lobito and Benguela to the inland as far as the Catumbela River, which was bridged over in the same year. Messrs. Griffiths & Co. continued the work until 1908 when the recession in the world copper market (and the subsequent drop in share prices) halted the project,[17] and the outbreak of the First World War brought it to a complete standstill as it was impossible to purchase and import construction material. By this time 325 miles of rail had been laid from Lobito Bay but more than 500 miles was still required before the Congo border was reached.[18]

The discovery of payable coal deposits in Wankie (Hwange), Southern Rhodesia in 1894 was an event of fundamental importance in the laying of the foundations for the integrated Rhodesian railway system. Getting access to the vast reserves of Wankie coal to power furnaces and the locomotives themselves was just as important to developing this system as were its objectives of importing supplies of necessary materials and the export of mineral resources to the metal markets. The line from Bulawayo in a north-western direction towards the Victoria Falls reached the Wankie Colliery in September 1903, boosting the development of the mine so that output rose to 50,000 tons of coal in 1903.[19] The Bulawayo–Victoria Falls line was completed in April 1904, and 14 months later the Zambezi Bridge to span the vast gorge below the Victoria Falls was inaugurated for traffic. After this the contractors, Messrs. George Pauling & Co., extended the line through the Tonga Plateau to Kalomo, the first administrative capital of North-Western Rhodesia, where Tanks and The Standard Bank of South Africa had their first modest offices in North-Western Rhodesia.[20] After spanning the Kafue River, the line was directed through the area where Lusaka now stands, reaching in January 1906 the Broken Hill (Kabwe) lead and zinc mine, 250 miles from Katanga's southern border. The mine had commenced its operations in 1904 under the Rhodesian Broken Hill Development Company, controlled by Edmund Davis (Sir Edmund in 1927) (1861–1939), an Australian-born financier who provided major investment for exploration and mining in Northern Rhodesia and who was a director on the boards of BSAC and the Wankie Colliery Company, among numerous others.[21] The significance of the railway for the development of Northern Rhodesia was immediate and enormous. In its first financial year since the arrival of the railway, 1906, Broken Hill exported 8,965 tons of calcinated zinc ore, valued on the rails at the mine at £10 per ton, dwarfing the value of the other export items such as hides, skins, ivory, 'native curios' and rubber (worth a measly £1,625 in total). In the same year, the value of the chief imports, railway materials and manufactured iron goods, was already £68,000, signalling a strong upward curve in investments.[22]

The same trend can be detected from the returns of the Wankie Colliery Company. Seven years after the arrival of the railway to Wankie, in 1910, the company's output was already 180,000 tons of coal and the company's issued capital had gone up to £202,000. By 1919, the output had risen tenfold compared to 1903 (510,000 tons) and the issued capital to £567,000.[23] Despite their relative success, the Wankie Colliery and the Broken Hill mine struggled to return regular profits and dividends. Setting up site infrastructure and auxiliary services, and the management of the very large workforce, involved considerable outlays which did not return a profit for a long time after the initial expenditure. A complex system of cross-subsidisation, in which each of the many companies involved in or affiliated to the Rhodesian mining industry had capital invested in some of the others, was key to persuading investors to risk their money in a potentially profitable but also risky business.[24]

Although no large-scale mine could operate profitably without a railway, the rail alone did not guarantee a successful mining operation, as was illustrated by the case of the Bwana Mkubwa copper mine, one of the 'ancients' situated close to the Congo border, on the huge bend (or the 'Hook') of the Kafue River. This mine was staked for Davis's Bechuanaland Exploration Company and thence transferred to the Rhodesia Copper Company, one of the offshoots of Davis's mining finance group, which was incorporated on 31 January 1902 and subsequently renamed in 1911 as the Rhodesia Copper and General Exploration and Finance Company.[25] From its humble beginnings the production of the mine, an outcrop of oxide and carbonate ore somewhat similar to the occurrences in Katanga, was boosted by the arrival of the railway in 1909, followed by the flotation of The Bwana M'Kubwa Copper Mining Company in the next year. In 1912 a small concentrator was erected at Bwana Mkubwa, but the work was hampered by numerous technical challenges in treating the ores. The plant could treat about 75 tons of ore per day, but recovery was only about 40% of the total copper content.[26] The plant continued to operate for two years in a desultory way until it was closed down, but operations were resumed in 1916 on account of the high wartime demand for copper. After the First World War the work was resumed on a development programme which aimed to put production on a profitable, permanent footing by utilising the so-called Perkins process invented by an American consulting metallurgist, W.G. Perkins, for treating oxidised ores. In 1922 the enterprise was reorganised with a substantial £1.5 million in capital, and the company erected a pilot plant with a capacity of 100 tons in preparation for a reduction plant of 1,000 tons daily, which was achieved with the reduction and ammonia leaching process. The copper produced in the pilot plant ran as 'Superior Best Selected' at the London Metal Exchange (LME), but despite being prominently situated by the Rhodesia Railway, Bwana Mkubwa constituted only a minor event from the perspective of the rise of the Northern Rhodesian copper industry.[27]

While its many mines in Katanga had already proved their worth for further development, in Northern Rhodesia Tanks controlled only one mining property which was at the time considered worth developing further, namely the Kansanshi copper mine, pegged off by Grey's first expedition in 1899. The Kansanshi ore assayed a few pennyweights of gold per ton but far less than would have been sufficient to defray the cost of transport to the railhead at Broken Hill, some 300 miles away. On 25 January 1909 Tanks registered the Rhodesia-Katanga Junction Railway and Mineral Company (RHOKAT), with the significant sum of £1.6 million capital. The company took over the development of the Kansanshi mine and the Northern Rhodesian prospecting rights, and, under an agreement in Brussels on 11 July 1908, it undertook the project to construct the last stretch of the line to connect the Rhodesian railway system with that in Katanga. The major signatories were Tanks and BSAC which received 50,000 fully paid shares in return for an interest in the Kansanshi mine. £750,000 was issued in 5.5% debentures at par, charged over all its assets and repayable in 50 years.[28]

The Rhodesia-Katanga Junction Railway reached the border, near Sakania, at the end of 1909 and the ceremonial opening took place on 31 December 1909.[29] The railway reached The Star of the Congo on 27 September 1910 and the Kambove mine three years later, before arriving in May 1918 at the port of Bukama on the mouth of the Lualaba River. Once completed, the railway system of Katanga, stretching from Bukama on the Congo River to Sakania on the Rhodesian frontier (457 miles), rendered an integrated rail transport system possible: trains could haul copper from Katanga to the Port of Beira in Mozambique and return with coal and coke from the Wankie Colliery in Southern Rhodesia.[30]

Being denied a railway connection, the Kansanshi mine was unable to realise its full potential during the colonial era. The early assays showed that Kansanshi was blessed with a seemingly unlimited supply of high-grade oxidised ore, averaging between 3% and 5% of the red metal, and the initial processing cost estimates were remarkably low, but the development was hampered by the lack of the railway, which bypassed the mine to build a direct line from Bwana Mkubwa to the Congo border. It was deemed by the miner that The Star's ore could be mined and treated relatively cheaply because it was more highly concentrated than ore found at Kansanshi, and because most of it was found close enough to the surface to be worked by open-cast methods.[31]

An initial attempt to transport Kansanshi ores over a wagon road by means of traction machinery supplied by John Fowler & Co. of Leeds, initiated in 1910 from Kansanshi to the railhead, then at Baya Station in Katanga (a distance of about 80 miles), proved a failure.[32] The first shipment of Kansanshi copper sold in London in 1911 realised £56.12.6 per ton. Copper was produced at a cost of £15 per ton.[33] In 1913 the Kansanshi mine yielded 2,400 tons of copper, all of which was obtained by smelting with charcoal and wood.[34] Besides unwieldy communications and heavy transport costs (the railage from the Congo border to the port of Beira was £3.1.0 per ton in

1912),[35] a great many other deductions and expenses were incurred by the miner at Kansanshi, including freight, dock charges, and expenses attending the shipping of copper from Beira to London. From the perspective of smelting technologies, operations at Kansanshi were inefficient and depleted with many technical problems. At LME, Kansanshi copper ingots were sold under the heading of 'Rough Copper' (between 94% and 95% Cu), which incurred an automatic deduction of £1.10.0 per ton. This was due to the Standard Copper Contract, which dictated the standard grade of refined to be between 99% and 99.3% Cu, and instituted premiums for electro and discounts for rough copper down to 94%. By way of comparison, the copper content of Chili bars, delivered to London under the Standard Copper Contract, was often below the agreed standard (down to 97% Cu), but these bars also contained an appreciable quantity of gold and silver, which made them much more sought after by the refiners than Kansanshi ingots.[36]

In 1912 Mr Gibb, who had designed the Kansanshi Plant, noted that there was only a limited supply of direct smelting ore remaining at the mine, and by the outbreak of the First World War practically all the remaining reserves of this high-grade oxidised ore had been cleaned up and smelted, so that no large ore reserves could be counted on in any future work. As it turned out, at Kansanshi the paying ores were found at much greater depth, requiring expensive shaft sinking. In 1913–14, Mr C. Grey, with Mr Magee acting as a drillman and assisted by Mr Kerr, exposed a sulphide zone at deeper parts of the mine which was assayed at 3.2% Cu (mixed ore reserves averaged 4.5% Cu).[37] It was concluded by the miner, however, that neither Kansanshi nor any other large mine could be developed further without a railway, so the future of the mine was put on hold. Little was done to develop this property until 1928 when the arrival of the Benguela Railway on the Angola–Belgian Congo border rekindled speculation over the future of Kansanshi.

The emergence of financial feudalism in Katanga

British mining and railway interests in Northern Rhodesia were served by free trade and foreign direct investments, with something akin to financial feudalism coming into existence in the Katangese mining industry with its complex business structure that was like no other. The birth of the European mining industry in Katanga was a classic case of monopoly capitalism evolving from a crude state of free competition over large concessions and new markets. In the centre of it all was the *Comité Spécial du Katanga* (CSK), which was formed by Royal Decree in Brussels on 19 June 1900. The formation of CSK was aimed at bringing a solution to a problem which had arisen from the delimitation of the lands of King Léopold II in the name of the Congo Free State (CFS) in the Upper Congo Basin and those lands (one-third of the whole) ceded in 1891 with full ownership rights to the *Compagnie du Katanga* (CK) on its creation. As a joint organisation CSK facilitated the development of the said lands and functioned as a holding company for the interests of both parties. When the administration of CFS was taken over by the Belgian State, a two-thirds interest in CSK was transferred to the state while CK continued to control one-third. Though not approaching the scale of BSAC in Rhodesia, CSK possessed attributes that amounted to a quasi-sovereign power in some respects, so that its actual and potential influence on the economic development of its territory and on such matters as settler colonialism was very significant. To attain the avowed aims of its charter, CSK maintained a variety of essential services for the miner. The most important was the mining service, concerned with such issues as prospecting, concessions and licences, and the enforcement of the colonial Mining Law. Besides the mining service, the other respective services provided by CSK included the geographical and geological service (*i.e.* the study and evaluation of surface soil and subsoil as well as the classification of geological samples and maintaining the geological map of its territory); the topographical and hydrographical services; the forestry and agricultural service; the engineering service; and the colonisation service (*i.e.* providing advice and help for the settler, including loans and subsidies, and supervising enterprises set up through its offices).[38]

CSK was managed by a committee which comprised six members, four including the president appointed by the state (initially CFS but later the Belgian State) and two by CK. The committee assumed the rights of CK, including for ownership of the land and a 99-year concession for the exploitation of the substrata of the said lands. It also held an administrative role in the territory under its domain. Its charter stated that it had the widest powers of administration management and legal conveyance of property to others, without any exception and reserve. The revenue, profits and other benefits accruing, and costs and charges incurred by the committee, were divided in the ratio of two parts to the state and one to CK. CSK did not itself exploit the land directly. The land under its domain was worked by concessionaires who had obtained their grants from CSK, which obtained its revenue from dividends of its investments, rent from its mines, proceeds of sales and leases of its land and sales of its timber. The conditions of concessions were determined, as far as mining was concerned, by the Mining Law, but the committee evolved its own regulations for surface concessions and mortgages, subject to the restraint and control of the colonial legislation. The fact that two-thirds of its lands were state property, and that the Treasury had a two-thirds interest in the results of its activities, gave CSK the nature of a parastatal organisation responsible to the public. As a matter of fact CSK was an administrative body acting under a charter – it was not a colonial *holding d'État* in the true meaning of the term. CSK merely managed the joint interests of the state and CK, and, in general, epitomised a close bond with the state and its main financier in Katanga, the *Société Générale de Belgique* (SGB), Belgium's biggest investment and holding company.[39]

The direct financial interest of CSK in many businesses operating in Katanga led it to ensure that leased and sold land or subsidised concerns were soundly developed and efficiently run, at least from the financial point of view.

Of its many businesses in Katanga the most important was the *Union Minière du Haut-Katanga* (UMHK), incorporated on 28 October 1906 by Royal Decree in Brussels to exploit all the mines already discovered or to be discovered in Katanga under Congolese law. The authorised capital of the company was a modest 100,000 capital shares of 100 francs each (equivalent to some £4 per share). SGB and Tanks subscribed 50,000 shares each, with the object of developing the mineral wealth in Katanga that had already been discovered, including copper, tin and gold ores, with coal and the necessary fluxes for smelting, and any new discoveries. UMHK constituted the biggest and most valuable affiliate of SGB and their respective boards of management were as a consequence closely intertwined. The concessionary's ownership was to reflect the voting rights: the first administrative council of UMHK was composed of five directors nominated by Tanks and five by CSK. Baron Ferdinand Baeyens (1837–1914), the governor of SGB, became the President (*i.e.* the Chairman) of UMHK, with Robert Williams as the Vice-President.

The concessionary company (*i.e.* UMHK) had the right also to free use of land as necessary for the support of white settlers employed in the mines for a period of 15 years, on condition that the colonists employed in the cultivation of these lands were brought into the country at the cost of the company. The concession was initially granted for a period of 30 years (until 1936), with the possibility of an extension up to 1990.[40] In return for the concession, CSK and Tanks held 100,000 Preference stock units of nominal value in UMHK, allotted in the proportion of 60% to CSK and 40% to Tanks, which increased in equal proportion (*i.e.* 60%–40%) with the increase of Ordinary stock units, thus ensuring that the ratio of voting power in UMHK held by CSK and Tanks remained the same (as far as the preferred shares were concerned).[41] Special rights vested in Tanks and CSK substantially reduced the normal prerogatives of the other shareholders. They included, for example, the right to oppose capital expansion, the issue of new shares, bonds or loans and the right to nominate the chairman and representatives on the board of UMHK.[42] As a result of these vested interests, the whole formed a parastatal hybrid, engaged in private, purely for-profit interests, whilst being endowed with quasi-governmental powers and functions.

The Star is born

It was due to those 'ancient workings' pegged off by the Tanks prospectors in 1901–2 that the important copper mines in Katanga were first mapped. The Copperbelt was spread over an area of some 14,000 square miles, roughly forming a rectangle of 280 miles in length, with a width of 35–60 miles, lying from the north-west to the south-east, and concentrating in and around Kolwezi in the west, Kambove, which may be regarded as the centre, and The Star which was located south-east about nine miles from Élisabethville. The first property to be exploited systematically in Katanga was The Star – for its luxuriance of mineral resources and its proximity to the railway. The assays revealed that the early finds at The Star were of oxidised ore, much of it malachite, an easily converted, high-grade copper carbonate ore, averaged at 10%–20% Cu, with some samples even as high as 30% Cu. In 1909, Tanks and UMHK commenced construction of the first of three 30-ton blast furnaces, supplied by Allis-Chalmers Co. of Milwaukee, on the Lubumbashi River to treat the oxidised ore from The Star and the nearby Luushia (Luiswichi) mine.[43] Overseeing the erection work was entrusted to an American mining engineer, P.K. Horner.[44]

Commercial smelting of copper began on 30 June 1911, when the Lubumbashi Smelter was run off for the first time. The first copper in Katanga was brought to the stage of commercial production on 16 September 1911.[45] From the outset of the smelting operations the labour shortage was the greatest worry and hampered work in every direction.[46] Ore arriving on trains from the mines had to be unloaded by African labour by hand in the yard and then loaded to charging trucks to get ready for the furnace. During the rainy season the ores were exposed to rains and were often muddy masses, and naturally such a state of the charge meant increased fuel consumption, not only on account of the extra water to be driven off but also on account of the packed nature of the charge resulting from this muddiness. As there was no coal washery in the Wankie Colliery at the time, the coal had to be washed at the smelter. This work was also done in the open yard, greatly interfering with the free use of the yard for the large amount of riveting work done at the smelter and the bricklaying at the coke oven plant which had been begun at the same time.[47] Coke could not be obtained from the Wankie Colliery at less than £5 per ton,[48] so the company was desirous to coke its own fuel. All these simultaneous processes taken in conjunction – the dearth of labour, faulty methods in ore handling and coal washing, the rainy season, poor-quality fuel, and ongoing construction works – led to high fuel consumption per ton of metal produced. In 1913 the smelter was using some 3.8–3.9 tons of Wankie coal per ton of fine Cu produced. The cost of production was relatively high, at £26.10.0 per ton,[49] and the cost of marketing and refining brought the total cost at the smelter to £38.10.0 per ton.[50] The average LME market price for London Standard Cash in the same year was over £72 per ton, however.[51] Therefore, UMHK was already realising very healthy profits, despite the high production costs and freight charges.

There was a system of dual control in the management in place in Katanga until it was abandoned in 1913 as it resulted in confusion, laxity and inordinate management expenses. In 1914 a system of a technical committee and a general manager was implemented. The technical committee had full control of all operations in Katanga, and it consisted of Jean Jadot (1862–1932), the appointed Governor of SGB in 1913, Robert Williams and Franz Studt representing interests of Tanks, one other Belgian member and two secretaries. In 1914 the committee nominated Archer E. Wheeler, an American mining engineer connected with the Great Falls and Anaconda copper companies, as the General Manager in Katanga.[52] Following Wheeler's appointment, construction of a new plant, consisting of a leaching plant, four new blast and reverberatory furnaces (on top of the three furnaces already in place) and a concentrating plant capable of treating 3,000–4,000 tons of ore per day, commenced in Lubumbashi in mid-1914. As a consequence of the simultaneous development work on many fronts, the smelter doubled its production from 1914 to 1916. At the same time the average LME price had almost doubled to £136 per ton owing to the high demand for small arms and artillery ammunition (*i.e.* self-contained metallic cartridges made from copper, zinc, lead and nickel) during the height of trench warfare.[53]

Copper production went on virtually without interruption during the war, but owing to the shortage of labour, only The Star, Luushia and Kambove were mined on any commercial scale – the company had to sacrifice development work of the other mines to keep the smelter supplied with ores and fluxes. UMHK's operations at the rich Kambove mine, with ores assaying on average 10% Cu, were inaugurated in December 1907 but industrial-scale mining commenced only in mid-1913, when the railway reached the mine, whilst the deposits at Kamatanda along with other neighbouring deposits at Kambove West (Kambove No. 2), Likasi (Likasye) and Shituru (about five miles distant) were left undeveloped until thc labour situation improved.[54] Later development work in the Kambove West and Likasi mines would indicate that these were among the richest mining properties of the company.[55] The general development work of the mines did not keep pace with production, however, creating serious technical problems which could not be solved until hostilities ceased. Production in 1918 (20,238 tons) represented roughly 1.4% of total world production in the same year (1.43 million tons).[56]

The production figures at Lubumbashi from the start of the smelting operations until the end of the war are shown in Table 5.1.

Table 5.1 The Lubumbashi Smelter copper output, 1911–18 (tons and %)

	Tons	*% Share*
1911	997	0.9
1912	2,492	2.4
1913	7,407	7.0
1914	10,722	10.2
1915	14,054	13.3
1916	22,149	21.0
1917	27,463	26.0
1918	20,238	19.2
Total 1911–18	105,522	100.0

Sources: MU, TANKS, TC/180, Mr Studt's Reports, Élisabethville, January 1913 to September 1915; 'Tanganyika Concessions, Ltd' 1919.

Wastage of labour

The Province of Katanga being very thinly populated relative to its size meant that labour had to be attracted to the mines from the other provinces of the Congo, from neighbouring colonies or from countries more densely populated. Like in the Benguela Railway project, importing low-wage Asian labour was initially considered as a viable means to boost development work. Nevertheless, in view of the rapid development of the Rand mines going on at the same time there was little hope of getting migrant labour from South Africa. Similarly, attempts to obtain 'Chinese coolies' directly from the Straits Settlements floundered early, as the colony did not allow the export of labour for mining.[57] Building on earlier recruitment patterns established by African miners, the vast majority of early workers in the Katanga mining industry continued to be of Rhodesian origin. Lamba people from North-Western Rhodesia had worked as tribute labourers in Katanga's copper mines prior to the Yeke dominance of the region.[58] The first labour recruitment had its origins in the porterage system, which sought to provide men to carry goods along transport routes. Recruitment of the Bemba from North-Eastern Rhodesia followed from their earlier engagement as porters along Katanga's eastern supply route.[59] In 1901 Tanks transport routes were organised to convey goods and food to the Luapula River and thence to Kambove (from Karonga on Lake Nyasa and later from Blantyre) and to Kansanshi (from Bulawayo and later from the railhead at Kalomo).

Recruitment of labour intensified after 1906 when Messrs. Robert Williams & Co. of Bulawayo took over labour recruitment on behalf of the newly constituted UMHK. At the turn of 1905 and 1906, Paul MacDonald, the former member of Grey's first expedition, established a recruiting centre called 'Madona' to the south of Johnston Falls.[60] In May 1906 Madona was already described as a rising township in need of a missionary, on account of the population and the great traffic passing to and from the Katanga mines. In the course of the first four months of 1907, MacDonald recruited as many as 1,138 miners and 2,437 carriers from the Mweru and Luapula Districts of North-Eastern Rhodesia for loads destined for the Kambove mine. A similarly large number of Luapulans were engaged to work on the completion of the Rhodesia Railway to the Congo border.[61]

At the time when the transformation of North-Eastern Rhodesia into a reservoir of both labour and food for the mines of UMHK was well under way, the presence of the tsetse fly of the *Glossina palpalis* species that transmits sleeping sickness became apparent along the Luapula River and the eastern shore of Lake Mweru, a factor which brought further labour recruitment from those districts to a standstill. In late 1906 Dr Sheffield Airey Neave (1879–1961), a director in the boards of ZE, Tanks and UMHK whose varied career spanned medicine, sport and agriculture as well as mining finance, was sent to Katanga to undertake medical research on the prevalence of sleeping sickness among the mining workers. Neave's work as a Katanga Medical

Commission entomologist from 1906 to 1908 could be interpreted as the 'academicisation' of colonial medicine,[62] but equally it could be seen as a means for the promotion of railway, mining and colonial settlement schemes. From a strictly financial point of view, every sick worker was an added expense, and every death among the labourers represented a financial loss for the company.

By 1911 the sleeping sickness epidemic had subsided, and recruitment operations and development work got under way again. In the same year Mr G. Adams, then the mine manager at The Star, reported that 'we have now some 700 boys here, of which over 200 are time expired this month. News is that MacDonald should be back in Ft. Rosebery [Mansa] with labour in the beginning of June.'[63] Initially the only approach to labour management was strict discipline. In the words of a missionary, commenting on the Rhodesia Railway construction work on the Broken Hill–Sakania line, workers were treated 'as so many dogs'.[64] From these early experiences, Williams drew attention to the importance of diet as a means to 'stabilise' labour in and around the mines. It is known that MacDonald purchased sizeable quantities of locally produced foodstuffs, mostly dried fish and cassava, as a means of inducing men to work at the mines and railways.[65]

The urge to earn persuaded and the hut tax coerced African men to leave their families in rural homes to work in the mines and railways in Katanga, but in order to make the system work, the workers had to be paid in British coin. Currency was not only very hard to get on account of the drastic scarcity of cash money, but its use for salary payments was against the prevailing colonial legislation, which required the use of Congolese francs. The stipulation was winked at however by the government officials, who in practice had little choice but to go along with the prevailing unsatisfactory situation.[66] Small patches of so-called voluntary labour arrived at the mines irregularly, but generally Katangese were very slow in reaching the mines. The influx of Europeans and their needs for low-wage labour – over 1,200 settled at Élisabethville alone in 1911 – was the main obstacle for the dearth of local labour at the mines. In the same year John H. Hayes lamented that about 500 loads of the company's provisions were lying at Élisabethville for 'these new people are paying most exorbitant rates for whatever natives they get, and the natives are quite out of hand, and have too much money for having any need to work.'[67]

The dearth of labour led in 1910 to the formation of the parastatal *Bourse du Travail du Katanga* (BTK), which took over UMHK recruiting operations within the Congo,[68] especially in the more populous Kasai Province and the Lomami District in Katanga. BTK's labour recruiting methods were rapidly generating a bad reputation in their own right as illustrated in a complaint by Dr Walter Fisher, a British surgeon and missionary then stationed at Kalene Mission Hospital, North-Western Rhodesia, regarding the treatment of certain migrant labourers in 1911. The report details the story of a group of 23 Angolese who had been arrested by labour recruiters because they were not wearing their hut tax medal and had no pass to prove that they were in fact

'Portuguese subjects' (*i.e.* the Pass Law restricted mobility and was designed to cope with the problem of desertion and to direct labour to regions that were suffering most from labour shortages). The men were sent to the Kambove mine to work out their tax, and while doing their forced labour they were so brutally treated that one of them, a mining worker called Kasonda, died as a result. The rest of the group managed to escape from their compound by digging a hole under the wall of their hut. The men wandered off without food or provisions in the Lualaba District where they encountered a headman, who gave them food and salt and persuaded the 'deserters' to return to Kambove. But though already malnourished and very weak by this stage, the ill-fated group were given neither work nor food at Kambove. Instead, these Angolese men – who had at this stage become a bit of a nuisance to the mine manager – were sent on their way towards Broken Hill to see if they had better luck finding food and work there.[69] As earlier in South Africa and the Rhodesias, racial segregation encouraged the indiscriminate and wasteful use of African workers in mining. This 'wastage of labour' (*i.e.* repatriates, deserters and deaths) can be detected from BTK's labour returns. Table 5.2 exemplifies the situation of BTK's recruits at the Lubumbashi Compound, from 1 October 1912 to 30 September 1913.

The mine manager may have been a king – or a tyrant – within the confines of his own mine, but nothing humbled him faster than a summons to report

Table 5.2 Labour returns, *Bourse du Travail du Katanga*, Lubumbashi Compound, 1 October 1912 to 30 September 1913 (persons)

1912	*Work-force, first of month*	*Engaged*	*Dis-charged or trans-ferred*	*Deser-ted*	*Died*	*Work-force, last of month*	*Dif-fer-ence*
October	0	134	0	0	0	134	0
November	134	273	0	32	0	375	241
December	375	104	92	91	10	286	−89
1913							
January	286	133	15	117	38	249	−37
February	249	59	1	78	9	220	−29
March	220	61	40	7	5	229	9
April	229	115	7	0	3	334	105
May	334	158	45	0	2	445	111
June	445	64	5	0	0	504	59
July	504	5	204	2	0	303	−201
August	303	0	149	0	2	152	−151
September	152	46	153	2	0	43	−109

Source: MU, TANKS, TC/180, *Bourse du Travail du Katanga*, Lubumbashi Compound, Sept. 1912 to Sept. 1913.

to the company Head Office. The constant effort by the local management to keep the mines operating and their production quotas fulfilled put extra strain on the labour. Roughly 20% of the operational costs were due to the recruitment of thousands of African workers, often at very significant distances from the mines themselves. Feeding, clothing, housing and providing them with at least some rudimentary sanitary and health services, so that the often unacclimatised workers would survive the very hard manual labour in three shifts, was the greatest worry in terms of labour costs. On paper the cost (recruiting expenses, salary, food, camp maintenance, general expenses) was 55 Frs. per worker per month in June 1913. This sum had to be corrected, however, for incidental costs such as morbidity, mortality and desertions, which brought the total cost to about 75 Frs., respectively. On 30 June 1913, the total African labour force at The Star and the Lubumbashi Smelter was 1,422 workers, whilst the 'wastage' of that month (repatriates, deserters, deaths) represented 19 workers (1.3% of the total).[70] On account of the large number of physically weak or under-aged workers, no more than 50% of African workers were classified as 'effectives' (*effectifs*) who could be put to regular shifts on mining work, which meant that the equivalent cost of the labour rose to roughly 150 Frs. per worker per month in June 1913.[71]

Besides the dearth of labour, another problem was its temporary nature. In Katanga a 12-month engagement period was the standard, but workers recruited from Rhodesian territories were usually engaged to work out six tax tickets of 30 shifts each on the UMHK payroll. A 'ticket' (*i.e.* a booklet containing 30 slips of paper, each representing a shift) was the method by which the length of service by African labourers was measured. The accountant marked the completion of each day's work on a ticket, and salaries were paid after 30 shifts were fulfilled. Workers were induced to prolong their contracts for another six tickets, but many of them did not.[72] The shorter contract was a way to lure Rhodesian labour to the Katangese mines but ran contrary to the needs of UMHK. In order to develop sound mining business, precise economic planning was needed, which entailed reliable production cost estimates and predictable employment of a definite amount of labour for night and day shifts. All of these remained elusive without strict control over the workforce in such matters as the terms of the contract, accommodation, nutrition and health. These concerns came to the fore of UMHK's labour management policy after the First World War. The rules governing labour recruitment were redefined as the industry entered into the era of production on a commercial scale.

Finance capitalism pure and simple

Despite the many challenges UMHK faced during its first operating years, the development of payable mining properties was so satisfactory that the company directors estimated that the profits for 1913–14 justified the declaration of a substantial dividend in 1915. Following the German occupation of Belgium in 1914 the Head Office was evacuated to London, saving the company from further vexations, but the impossibility of holding shareholder meetings in Brussels prevented the company from making board decisions. After Belgium had been liberated, UMHK was discounting its first dividend in 1919. A major part of the profits (*c*. 80%) was taken over by the Treasury levying an exceptional tax on all Belgian companies, which between 1 July 1914 and 31 December 1918 had realised higher profits than in 1912, 1913 and the first six months of 1914.[73]

In this unique situation the majority of the early profits resulting from the development of the Katangese mines were divided between SGB, CK, CSK and Tanks. The Zambesia Exploring Company, the parent company of the Tanks Group, controlled a majority stake in Tanks, influenced its direction and helped to raise capital for its needs through its many Rhodesia-based businesses, whilst BTK and Messrs. Robert Williams & Co. brought further managerial resources in terms of labour recruiting. In terms of cash flow, the financial situation of Tanks remained poor, and the company struggled to fulfil its many obligations. Since its creation in 1899, all balance sheets of Tanks had shown a deficit, and the company was able to continue business only thanks to numerous increases of debenture capital. The first debenture was secured by the trust deeds of 13 June 1905 and the second for £120,000 was issued to Christopher John Leyland on 22 November 1906. On 13 June 1907, the Board of Directors was forced yet again to exercise its powers contained in its Memorandum and Articles of Association and created a series of 250,000 First Mortgage Debentures of £8 each, bearing 5% interest per annum. This time capitalisation was secured in an indenture made between the company on the one hand and Sir Howard Melliss (b. 1847), the Inspector-General of Imperial Service Troops of India under the direction of the Foreign Department,[74] and the Right Honourable Arthur Stanley (1869–1947), the Conservative MP for Ormskirk, the Trustees, on the other.[75] At the same time, Tanks' indebtedness to ZE increased to over £200,000 in 1910. ZE accepted an allocation of Tanks shares credited as fully paid at £5 per share in satisfaction of the debt, so that the fortunes of the companies were practically bound together.[76]

Tanks' balance sheet showed a positive credit balance for the first-time in 1917, thanks to advances which UMHK had been able to grant.[77] Subsequently the company was able to pay off two of the coupons in arrears on its debentures. The principal assets in the company's portfolio may be summarised as follows: 2,700,000 shares of £1 each and £38,000 debenture capital in BRC (a 90% interest), 100,000 fully paid cash shares of 100 Frs. each and 60,000 bearer shares in UMHK (a 39.2% interest), and 495,814 shares of £1 each in RHOKAT (a 70% interest).[78] Furthermore, in 1908 Tanks had acquired holdings from the Wankie Colliery Company to secure its future needs for coal and coke.[79]

In 1919, issued capital of Tanks had risen to nearly £2 million, whilst debentures were slightly more at £2.2 million.[80] By 1919, most of Tanks' mining properties acquired during the prospecting era 1899–1906 had been floated off, and were exploited by its two subsidiaries, namely UMHK, formed to develop the copper deposits of Katanga, and RHOKAT, formed to develop the Kansanshi mine and prospect the concession in Northern Rhodesia. Among the other major interests in Katanga the Kundelungu-Lualaba Exploitation Committee was important. It had been formed in 1910 by Tanks and CSK to exploit diamond pipes which had been found in the Kundelungu Plateau and also various copper and tin deposits which had been discovered by Tanks' prospectors subsequent to the formation of UMHK. The initial capitalisation was 2.5 million francs of which CSK and Tanks subscribed half each. The results of this enterprise were disappointing, however, and in 1924 Hubertus (Hubert) Droogmans (1858–1938), the President of CSK, was forced to announce that there 'is not much possibility of finding payable ground in them'.[81]

Despite the many changes in the Tanks business structure in the first 20 years of the company's existence, management at Head Office was kept firmly in the grip of Robert Williams, the Managing Director, and Tyndale White, the Chairman who had run the company since its inception. More significant changes in the London management took place after the First World War. In 1925 General Sir Francis Reginald Wingate (1861–1953), the former Governor-General of the Sudan (1899–1916) and High Commissioner in Egypt (1917–1919), replaced White as Chairman. Sir Cecil Budd (1865–1945), the Chairman of LME and Managing Director of the British Metal Corporation, joined Tanks' board as a director in 1922. The other prominent directors included Major Charles Robert Grey, 5th Earl Grey (1879–1963) of Howick, Northumberland, whose family interests had been represented in ZE since the pioneering years of Rhodesian gold prospecting; Lord Arthur Butler (James Arthur Wellington Foley Butler, Marquess of Ormonde, 1849–1943); Mr Godfrey Cresswell Hutchinson, Barrister at Law and husband of Ann Williams, elder daughter of Robert Williams; Captain Sheffield Neave, the medical doctor for Katanga Medical Commission from 1906 to 1908; and a Mr Thomas Honey and a Mr Charles Frederick Roswell, both gentleman capitalists. The vested interests in the Katangese mines and railways were reflected in the management of Tanks by Théodore P.J.A. Heyvaert representing CSK's interests in its board.[82]

The domicile of Tanks was initially at 30 and 31 Clements Lane, off Lombard Street but after being damaged in a Zeppelin raid the registered office was transferred to Frias House, New Broad Street, City of London. Built in 1907–8, it was the sort of speculative, multiple-occupancy building that made up a considerable portion of the City from the late Victorian era onward. In Northern Rhodesia the office buildings in Kambove were given up, and new offices were set up at Tanganyika House, *Avenue de l'Étoile du Congo*, Élisabethville. Franz Studt, who had arrived in Katanga as the geologist of George Grey's second expedition in 1901, oversaw Tanks' Katangese interests. Captain A.A. Thomson, the Manager of the Kansanshi mine and the nephew of Robert Williams, and J.G. Watson, the Manager of the Kambove mine, were the company's head engineers in 1919. The company's bankers continued to be the London City and Midland Bank and The Standard Bank of South Africa which in 1920 merged with the African Banking Corporation. The Élisabethville branch of the *Banque du Congo Belge* was handling the company's assets in Katanga.[83]

Concluding discussion

Evidently then, the exploitation of Central African mineral resources was a complex and extensive process, requiring much wider managerial skills in the operational companies than just simply managing the extraction of metalliferous ores. The major problem that needed to be solved first was the lack of communications. The Central African Copperbelt is situated in a landlocked country, with significant distances from the nearest navigable waterways and suitable ports for ocean-going vessels. To become viably connected with the world's metal markets meant that an entire integrated railway communication network had to be built from scratch. Once completed, it opened up access to the Central African mineral resources and facilitated the transport of supplies of necessary materials, including machinery and fuel.

As in many other parts of the world, remote from the established economic heartlands, mining companies themselves had to raise capital for very large infrastructure projects and acquire the required expertise before full-scale commercial mining could start. It was one thing to organise mine-seeking expeditions with a limited financial risk and hope the prospectors would hit a goldmine. But it was quite another to induce investors to take on the very high risks involved in the requisite infrastructure projects which preceded the commercial-scale copper mining operations. Even if enough capital were forthcoming, technical obstacles that had to be overcome were substantial, sometimes requiring the old mining methods and metallurgical processes to cope with the local conditions, or in some cases even the development of entirely new methods and processes to exploit the mineral deposits in a viable way. Even then success was by no means guaranteed. In order to operate on a large enough scale, and to offset the extra costs generated by the sheer tyranny of distance from metal markets, companies were operating under a number of disadvantages on the Central African Copperbelt. They included higher salaries, and benefits and bonus costs for the white management, which arose from the need to be able to lure skilled labour to Katanga, which was quite justifiably known as a dangerous place to work and live. The risk of sickness or death by diseases such as malaria, or the collapse of physical or mental health from the strain including the sheer sense of solitude were never far away. Suicides among white workers were not uncommon. The case of Mr M. Mangan who committed suicide by shooting himself on 23 September 1913 was typical. Mangan had lost his left arm as a result of a mining accident at The Star and the continual brooding over the loss of his arm resulted in 'slight mental derangement', as Studt explained the course of the incident in his report to Williams.[84]

The management costs were also high, and arose from the very complex, multilayered business structure which the mining companies employed. In the case of Tanks, the Head Office was located in the City of London, and the operational African management had their offices in Bulawayo, Kansanshi and Kalomo, and later in Élisabethville and Kambove. The Bulawayo office of Messrs. Robert Williams & Co. handled labour recruiting operations on the ground, while the directors in London concentrated on steering Tanks' business relations at the top level with the directors of BRC, UMHK, CSK, BSAC, the Wankie Colliery Company and many others. Such a multilayered business structure required extensive telegraph and mail communication, record-keeping and travel, all of which again increased costs.

The Central African Copperbelt was located at significant distances from the nearest navigable waterways and ports, with the tyranny of distance making the transport problems immediate and immense. Until the outbreak of the First World War, the most feasible means to travel from Katanga to Europe was either via German East Africa, embarking at Dar es Salaam, or by rail as far south as possible and thence by Cape mail steamer to Southampton. Commercial operations were resumed in 1919, but communications improved painstakingly slowly. Evidence suggests that the high management, operational, transport or labour costs, unwieldy communications, lack of capital or even its uneven distribution were not the main problems for Central African development, but the unprofitable nature of many of the early investments. The balance sheets of Tanks showed a deficit for the first 17 years of the company's existence. The Benguela Railway tied up most of Tanks' working capital, and the company struggled to return regular profits and dividends until the early 1920s.

Notes

1 *Bulletin de la Société Belge d'Études Coloniales* Juin 1910, 423–424, 452; Lemarchand 1964, 55–60.
2 Hoskyns 1965, 6–7; Ranger 1980, 363–364.
3 Coosemans 1997, 784.
4 See, for instance, Fetter 1976, 34.
5 White 2000, 269–271.
6 TNA, CO 795/123/8, British Consulate General, Léopoldville, 10 September 1943.
7 Henderson 1972, 47.
8 Hoskyns 1965, 1–5.
9 Katzenellenbogen 1974, 65.
10 Bancroft 1961, 45–53; Gann 1958, 120, 127.
11 MU, TANKS, TC/29, the Tanks to Messrs. Emile Erlanger & Co., 6 October 1903. On the financial alliance between BSAC, the railway contractors George Pauling & Co. and the merchant bankers the House of d'Erlanger see Andersen 2011, 76.
12 Williams 1925, 4. *Cf.* Stratham 1922, 116, 119.
13 TNA, FO 367/4, Sir A. Harding to Sir Edward Grey, 30 April 1906. See also *Boston News Bureau* 26 March 1925.
14 LMA, SE, CLC, B/004/F/01/MS18000/129B/277; Prospectus, no date.

15 Hutchinson and Martelli 1971, 152–153; Davies 2001.
16 Hobson 1969, 26; Tabor 2003, 214. See also Varian 1953.
17 MU, TANKS, TC/31, Construction account, 4 April 1907; Benguela Railway Contract, 4, 8 and 9 April 1907; 11 August 1908.
18 Hobson 1969, 26. See also Varian 1953; Hutchinson and Martelli 1971, 161, 183–190.
19 MU, TANKS, TC, 179, Mr Studt's reports, April 1926.
20 Hunt 1959, 9–13.
21 Bancroft 1961, 37–38, 57, 60, 68, 71, 116; Gann 1955, 2, 4; Gann 1964, 117–119, 122–126; Wills 1965, 195; Phimister 1994, 16.
22 *The Livingstone Mail* December 1906, II; Bancroft 1961, 115.
23 MU, TANKS, TC, 179, Mr Studt's reports, April 1926.
24 Phimister 1994, 1, 16.
25 Brooks 1944a, 80–81.
26 MU, TANKS, TC/180, Mr Studt's reports, January to June 1913.
27 Rickard 1926; Brooks 1944a, 81.
28 TNA, BT 31/32010/101258, Rhodesia-Katanga Junction Railway and Mineral Company, Memorandum and the Articles of Association, n.d.; Prospectus, n.d.; MU, TANKS, TC/29, A.T. Millar, the Assistant Secretary of BSAC, to Robert Williams, 8 September 1908; Hutchinson and Martelli 1971, 171–172.
29 The Katanga Railway was laid through the mineralised zone by the *Compagnie de Chemin de fer du Katanga* – a 40% Tanks- and 60% CSK-controlled railway company formed on 11 March 1902 to construct a railway through the mining district to Ruwe – and the *Compagnie de Chemin de fer du Bas-Congo au Katanga*, formed in 1906 with the object of constructing the Sakania–Bukama line (BCK 1956).
30 TNA, T 1/12009, Budget des Recettes et des Dépenses pour ordre du Congo Belge 1916; Katzenellenbogen 1974, 65; Hutchinson and Martelli 1971, 174, 208.
31 Copeman 1954, 23; Katzenellenbogen 1974, 65.
32 MU, TANKS, TC/30, John Fowler & Co. to Tanks, 29 November 1911.
33 LMA, SE, CLC, B/004/F/01/MS18000/159B/986, The stage reached of copper production, 2 June 1911; *Mining World and Engineering Record* 19 December 1908; 25 February 1911.
34 *The Engineering and Mining Journal* 28 June 1913, 1302.
35 MU, TANKS, TC/30, Mashonaland Railway Company to Tanganyika Concessions, 17 August 1912.
36 MU, TANKS, TC/30, Messrs. Vivian Younger & Bond to Tanganyika Concessions, 9 and 10 August 1911. See also Gibson-Jarvie 1976, 37–38.
37 MU, TANKS, TC/179, Kansanshi Mine ore reserves, Mr. Studt's reports, April 1926 and 12 May 1926; TC/180, F.E. Studt to Robert Williams, 5 March 1913.
38 *Bulletin de la Société Belge d'Études Coloniales* Avril 1910, 323–329; Juin 1910, 423–452. See also CSK 1950; Radmann 1978, 26–27.
39 TNA, CO 795/123/8, British Consulate General, Léopoldville, 10 September 1943. See also CSK 1950; Radmann 1978, 26–27.
40 TNA, FO 367/1, Société Union Minière du Haut-Katanga, 1906. See also UMHK 1956.
41 MU, TANKS, TC/29, L. Scotland, the Secretary of Tanks, 22 June 1907.
42 TNA, FO 371/176725, Lord Clitheroe and Captain Waterhouse, 27 February 1964.
43 MU, TANKS, TC 29, Allis-Chalmers Co. to Tanganyika Concessions, 1 and 29 August 1907; 9 September 1907; 18 March 1908; 17 April 1908.
44 MU, TANKS, TC/180, Mr Studt's reports, Élisabethville, 20 September 1913.
45 *The Times* 16 November 1911.
46 See also Higginson 1989, 21–22.
47 MU, TANKS, TC/180, Mr Studt's reports, Élisabethville, 5 March 1913.

48 *The Engineering and Mining Journal* 28 June 1913, 1302.
49 MU, TANKS, TC/180, Mr Studt's reports, Élisabethville, 5 February 1913; 3 October 1913.
50 *The Engineering and Mining Journal* 22 August 1914, 337.
51 Schmitz 1979, 271.
52 *The Engineering and Mining Journal* 22 August 1914, 337; Hutchinson and Martelli 1971, 165–166, 198–199.
53 Schmitz 1979, 271; Ball 2004, 452; Hutchinson and Martelli 1971, 199, 204.
54 MU, TANKS, TC/180, Mr Studt's reports, Élisabethville, 5 February 1913; 6 May 1913.
55 *Bulletin of the American Geographical Society* 1910, 667–670.
56 *The Belgian Congo* 1944, 401–404.
57 MU, TANKS, TC/180, Mr Studt's reports, Élisabethville, 18 June 1913.
58 Siegel 1988, 61–84.
59 Musambachime 1974, 39–65.
60 Davison 1952, 41–42.
61 Macola 2000, 191–192.
62 Baker and Bayliss 2009, 21–28; Coosemans 1997, 785; MacKenzie 1990, 208. See also Neave 1908.
63 MU, TANKS, TC/180, Mr Studt's reports, Élisabethville, 11 June 1913.
64 Quoted in Macola 2000, 191–192.
65 Macola 2000, 192.
66 MU, TANKS, TC/30, Eric Douglas to Rev. James Anton, Kapiri, 2 November 1911. See also Perrings 1977, 237–259; Higginson 1989, 26–29.
67 MU, TANKS, TC/30, John H. Hayes to F. Schindler, Kapiri, 3 July 1911.
68 *Bulletin de la Société Belge d'Études Coloniales* Novembre 1910, 725–727; Higginson 1989, 26.
69 MU, TANKS, TC/30, Dr W. Fisher to F. Schindler, Kanele Hill, 5 December 1911.
70 MU, TANKS, TC/180, Summary of company's boys, Lubumbashi section, 7 June 1913.
71 MU, TANKS, TC/180, Mr Studt's Reports, Élisabethville, 13 August 1913.
72 Brooks 1944b, 96–97; Juif and Frankema 2018, 321–322; White 2000, 269–306.
73 *Agence Économique et Financière* 22 January 1919.
74 Buckland 1906, 285.
75 TNA, J 13/7437, File of proceedings in the matter of Tanganyika Concessions Ltd., 27 April 1915.
76 MU, TANKS, TC/30, Zambesia Exploring Company to Tanganyika Concessions, 14 June 1910.
77 *Agence Économique et Financière* 22 January 1919.
78 TNA, J 13/7437, The High Court of Justice in the matter of Tanganyika Concessions Ltd., 8 March 1915; TNA, FCO 45/609, Interest of Tanganyika Concessions, Limited in railways and mineral areas, 1916.
79 LMA, SE, CLC, B/004/F/01/MS18000/129B/277, Mr Tom Bayne's report on coal, Bulawayo, 30 October 1908; A. Pingstone, The Bulawayo Assay Office and Public Laboratory, Report No. 3368, Bulawayo, 31 October 1908.
80 *South African Who's Who* 1920.
81 MU, TANKS, TC/12, Notes on Kundelungu-Lualaba Exploitation Committee, F. E. Studt, 10 December 1923; H. Droogmans, 13 March 1924.
82 MU, TANKS, TC/31, List of directors, 10 May 1922.
83 *South African Who's Who* 1920.
84 MU, TANKS, TC/180, Mr Studt's reports, 26 September 1913.

References

Agence Économique et Financière (22 January1919).

Andersen, C. (2011) *British Engineers and Africa, 1875–1914*, Pickering & Chatto, London.

Baker, R.A. and Bayliss, R.A. (2009) 'Two Naturalists in Africa: Sheffield Airey Neave (1879–1961) and James Jenkins Simpson (1881–1937) with Particular Reference to Their Work on Insects and Ticks from 1910 to 1915', *The Linnean*, 25:1, 20–28.

Ball, J.S. (2004) 'The German Octopus: The British Metal Corporation and the Next War, 1914–1939', *Enterprise & Society*, 5:3, 451–489.

Bancroft, J.A. (1961) *Mining in Northern Rhodesia: A Chronicle of Mineral Exploration and Mining Development*, British South Africa Company.

The Belgian Congo (1944) Great Britain Naval Intelligence Division, Geographical Handbook Series, London.

Boston News Bureau (26 March 1925) 'Who Developed Katanga Copper?'

Brooks, R. (May1944a) 'How the Rhodesian Coppers Were Found', *Engineering and Mining Journal*, 145:V, 80–84.

Brooks, R. (July1944b) 'Other Factors in Success in Rhodesian Exploration', *Engineering and Mining Journal*, 145:VII, 94–97.

Buckland, C.E. (1906) *Dictionary of Indian Biography*, S. Sonnenschein, London.

Bulletin de la Société Belge d'Études Coloniales (Avril 1910) 'Le Katanga', 4, 323–338; (Juin 1910) 'Le Katanga', 6, 423–452; (Novembre 1910) 'Bourse Du Travail Du Katanga', 11, 725–727.

Bulletin of the American Geographical Society (1910) 'Katanga's Communications and Mineral Wealth', 42:9, 667–670.

Comité spécial du Katanga 1900–1950 (CSK) (1950) L. Cuypers, Bruxelles.

Compagnie de Chemin de fer du Bas-Congo au Katanga (BCK) (1956) L. Cuypers, Bruxelles.

Coosemans, R. (1997) 'Occupational Health' in P.G. Janssens, M. Kivits and L. Vuylsteke eds. *Health in Central Africa since 1885: Past, Present and Future*, King Baudouin Foundation, Brussels, 781–798.

Copeman, E.A. (1954) 'George Grey', *The Northern Rhodesia Journal*, II:3, 23–25.

Davies, W.L. (2001) 'SCOTT-ELLIS, THOMAS EVELYN (1880–1946), 8th BARON HOWARD DE WALDEN and 4th BARON SEAFORD, Landowner and Sportsman, Writer, and Patron of the Arts' in *Dictionary of Welsh Biography.* Retrieved 12 January 2024 from https://biography.wales/article/s2-SCOT-EVE-1880.

Davison, A.I. (June1952) 'Subscriber Number One', *The Northern Rhodesia Journal*, I:5, 41–42.

The Engineering and Mining Journal (28 June 1913) 'The Copper Mines of Katanga', 95:26, 1302; (22 August 1914) 'Union Miniere du Katanga', 98:8, 337.

Fetter, B. (1976) *The Creation of Elisabethville, 1910–1940*, Hoover Institution Press, Stanford University, Stanford, CA.

Gann, L.H. (1955) 'The Northern Rhodesia Copper Industry and the World of Copper, 1923–1952', *Rhodes-Livingstone Journal*, 18, 1–18.

Gann, L.H. (1958) *The Birth of the Plural Society: The Development of Northern Rhodesia under the British South Africa Company, 1894–1914*, Manchester University Press, Manchester.

Gann, L.H. (1964) *A History of Northern Rhodesia: Early Days to 1953*, Chatto & Windus, London.

Gibson-Jarvie, R. (1976) *The London Metal Exchange: A Commodity Market*, Woodhead-Faulkner and Metallgesellschaft AG, Cambridge.

Henderson, I. (1972) *Labour and politics in Northern Rhodesia, 1900–1953: a study in the limits of colonial power*, PhD thesis, University of Edinburgh.

Higginson, J. (1989) *A Working Class in the Making: Belgian Colonial Labour Policy, Private Enterprise, and the African Mineworker, 1907–1951*, The Wisconsin University Press, Madison.

Hobson, D. (1969) 'John Norton-Griffiths: A Rhodesian Pioneer', *Rhodesiana*, 20, 23–32.

Hoskyns, C. (1965) *The Congo since the Independence: January 1960–December 1961*, Oxford University Press, London, Toronto and New York.

Hunt, B.L. (1959) 'Kalomo–Livingstone in 1907', *The Northern Rhodesia Journal*, IV:1, 9–17.

Hutchinson, R. and Martelli, G. (1971) *Robert's People: The Life of Sir Robert Williams Bart. 1860–1938*, Chatto & Windus, London.

Juif, D. and Frankema, E. (2018) 'From Coercion to Compensation: Institutional Responses to Labour Scarcity in the Central African Copperbelt', *Journal of Institutional Economics*, 14:2, 313–343.

Katzenellenbogen, S. (1974) 'Zambia and Rhodesia: Prisoners of the Past: A Note on the History of Railway Politics in Central Africa', *African Affairs*, 73:290, 63–66.

Lemarchand, R. (1964) *Political Awakening in the Congo: The Politics of Fragmentation*, University of California Press, Berkeley and Los Angeles.

The Livingstone Mail (December1906) 'Livingstone 1906. A Retrospect', II.

London Metropolitan Archives (LMA), the Records of the Stock Exchange (SE), Applications for authority to deal and applications for listing (CLC).

MacKenzie, J.M. (1990) 'Experts and Amateurs: Tsetse, Nagana and Sleeping Sickness in East and Central Africa' in J.M. MacKenzie ed. *Imperialism and the Natural World*, Manchester University Press, Manchester and New York, 187–212.

Macola, G. (2000) *A political history of the Kingdom of Kazembe (Zambia)*, PhD thesis, School of Oriental and African Studies, University of London.

Mining World and Engineering Record (19 December 1908); (25 February 1911).

Musambachime, M.C. (1974) 'Labour Migration from Mweru-Luapula 1900–24' in R. H. Palmer ed. *Zambian Land and Labour Studies*, II, National Archives of Zambia, Lusaka, 39–65.

The National Archives of the UK (TNA), Kew, Board of Trade (BT); Colonial Office (CO); Foreign Office (FO); Royal Courts of Justice, Chancery Division (J); Treasury (T).

Neave, S. (1908) *Portions of Report on Work of Katanga Medical Commission, 1906, 1907, 1908, with Map*, Whitehead, Morris, London.

Perrings, C. (1977) '"Good Lawyers but Poor Workers": Recruited Angolan Labour in the Copper Mines of Katanga, 1917–1921', *The Journal of African History*, 18:2, 237–259.

Phimister, I. (1994) *Wangi Kolia: Coal, Capital and Labour in Colonial Zimbabwe 1894–1954*, Witwatersrand University Press, Johannesburg.

Radmann, W. (1978) 'The Nationalization of Zaire's Copper: From Union Minière to Gecamines', *Africa Today*, 25:4, 25–47.

Ranger, T. (1980) 'Making Northern Rhodesia Imperial: Variations on a Royal Theme, 1924–1938', *African Affairs*, 79:316, 349–373.

Rickard, T.A. (2 January1926) 'A Journey to South Africa – VI', *Engineering and Mining Journal*, 121:1, 13–21.

Schmitz, C.J. (1979) *World non-Ferrous Metal Production and Prices, 1700–1976*, Frank Cass, London.

Siegel, B. (1988) 'Bomas, Missions, and Mines: The Making of Centres on the Zambian Copperbelt', *African Studies Review*, 31:3, 61–84.

South African Who's Who (1920) *Social, Business, and Farming 1919 - 1920*, K. Donaldson ed. John Wright & Sons, Cape Town, 'Tanganyika Concessions, Ltd.'.

Stratham, J.C.B. (1922) *Through Angola, a Coming Colony*, William Blackwood & Sons, Edinburgh and London.

Tabor, G. (2003) *The Cape to Cairo Railway & River Routes and the Principal Hotels en Route through Africa*, Genta Publications, London and Cape Town.

The Times (16 November1911) 'A Tour to the Great Copper Belt of Katanga, the Mines, Railways, and Work of the Tanganyika Concessions, Ltd. VI. The Smelting Works at Lubumbashi', 39744, 19.

Union Minière du Haut-Katanga 1906–1956 (UMHK) (1956) L. Cuypers, Bruxelles.

Union Minière du Haut-Katanga Rapport Annuel (1965) UMHK, Bruxelles.

The University of Manchester (MU), Archives of the Tanks Group of Companies (TANKS), Tanganyika Concessions (TC).

Varian, H.F. (1953) *Some African Milestones*, George Ronald, Wheatley, Oxford.

White, L. (2000) *Speaking with Vampires: Rumor and History in Colonial Africa*, University of California Press, Berkeley.

Williams, R. (1925) 'The Milestones of African Civilization', *The African World*, London.

Wills, A.J. (1965) *An Introduction to the History of Central Africa*, Oxford University Press, London.

6 The growth of the Central African Copperbelt

This chapter considers the growth of the operations of the *Union Minière du Haut-Katanga* (UMHK) up to the end of the colonial era. After 1920 the operations of UMHK were spread around three large mining centres, namely Élisabethville, Jadotville (Likasi) and Kolwezi, which were several dozen miles apart from each other and in an isolated area of about 14,000 square miles, forming a rough rectangle 280 miles long and 35–60 miles wide. The smelting and concentrating plants, dams and hydroelectric plants, various workshops, offices, and towns with their housing complexes, hospitals and schools were all built within this area. The communication between the various operational sites was improved by the laying of some 300 miles of railway line, over 600 miles of roads and a network of over 1,000 miles of high-tension cables. This immense geographically dispersed network of communications formed an industrial metabolism which was complicated by the importance of the timely exchange of materials between the mining centres. The chapter maintains that mining provided the spur for the economy and society of Katanga: Progressively after 1920 UMHK emerged as a significant provider of employment, accommodation, training, and medical and social services. But at the same time the single-company mining economy put the vulnerable Katangese at the mercy of the world metal markets.

Copper and cartels

In the interwar-era copper industry, the vertical integration of mining, smelting and refining capacities was strongly promoted by the move towards larger-scale and lower-grade ore deposits, increasingly remote from major markets. At the backdrop of this development was a considerable improvement in copper metallurgy which resulted in lower production costs and an economically viable grade of copper. The development was particularly notable in the North American West. In 1924 the Utah Copper Co., for instance, treated over 12.1 million tons of 1.07% Cu-grade sulphide ores and produced 107,300 tons of copper, which represented a recovery rate of 82.6% Cu of the original ore. In 1925 Nevada Consolidated extracted 91% Cu from copper sulphide ores of 1.1% Cu grade.[1] Improved metallurgical practices were reflected in the world's metal

DOI: 10.4324/9781003247371-6

production in the immediate post-war years when production rates were surpassed year after year. In 1924, the world average of mining, treating and industrial consumption of raw metals (aluminium, copper, zinc, lead, tin, nickel, mercury and silver) reached nearly four million tons (3.99 million) compared to the 3.67 million of 1923. These were higher figures than the mean of the wartime years, from 1914 to 1918 (3.58 million tons p.a.) or of the four years preceding the war, from 1909 to 1913 (3.18 million tons p.a.). In 1924, the turnover of aluminium, zinc, lead and tin increased all round compared with the mean for the years 1909–1913 – aluminium rose 27.6%, zinc by 11% and lead and tin each by 13% – but the sharpest increase was in the world's copper production which improved 43% over the same period.[2] In 1925, the world's copper output amounted to about 1,588,000 tons of which American producers achieved 60%. Together with the Chilean and Peruvian outputs, largely controlled by the American copper corporations, the United States produced nearly three-fourths of the world's output (74.6%). The world's refinery shipments of copper in 1925 amounted to 1,416,000 tons of which American refiners supplied 58.7% (831,192 tons). This was nearly 96,000 tons more than a year earlier.[3]

While the world's copper production increased in the immediate post-war years, the price for London Standard Cash copper collapsed to the pre-war level. Variations in prices for London Standard Cash from 1920 to 1925 are shown in Table 6.1.

In 1925 the price of copper was below its proper value based on supply and demand, especially in comparison with other metals in the same class of base metals which were traded at considerably higher prices than in 1913. Undoubtedly a big factor in bringing down the price of copper was the UK stock in 1925, which increased from 41,500 tons in January to over 56,000 tons at the end of the year.[4] Despite having a relatively small stock, it was generally recognised that LME determined the world's copper prices – in spite of the fact that American producers controlled about three-quarters of the world's output. The stagnated price of copper, coupled with increased rough and refined copper production, led to a considerable effort at price-fixing and market-sharing arrangements during the interwar era.

Table 6.1 Variations in the LME prices for Standard Cash copper, 1920–5 (£ per ton)

	Highest	*Lowest*
1920	122.5.0	70.0.0
1921	75.5.0	65.5.0
1922	66.2.6	57.0.0
1923	76.12.6	59.2.6
1924	68.15.0	60.7.6
1925	67.18.9	59.1.3

Source: MU, TANKS, TC/179, Mr Studt's reports, Variations in the LME prices for Standard Cash copper, 9 March 1926.

UMHK of the interwar era entered a very competitive copper market, with rapidly increasing global production and declining prices. In 1919, as the first step of its vertical expansion strategy, UMHK acquired its own refinery, a former *Metallgesellschaft* refinery located at the Scheldt River, in Hoboken, south of Antwerp, Belgium. The refinery was reconstructed under the *Société Générale Métallurgique de Hoboken* (SGMH) and its sales were conducted through the *Société Générale des Minerais* (SGM). The acquisition of the Hoboken Refinery was followed in 1925–7 by the erection of a 32,000-ton electrolytic refinery at Olen, in the province of Antwerp.[5] The location of Olen was ideal from the point of view of refining rough copper produced in North America that was aimed at European markets. As part of a strategic alliance against Northern Rhodesian producers whose sulphides started to emerge on the London markets in the mid-1920s, in 1925 UMHK entered negotiations with the American copper producers to form a joint sales organisation. As a result of these negotiations, UMHK and the majority of the North American producers agreed to form the Copper Exporters Inc., an association for the joint sale of copper in Europe.[6] UMHK retained full liberty in respect of its production, which it sought to increase through market-sharing agreements and by avoiding free competition with the American copper giants over market share.[7]

By setting up the Copper Exporters Inc., UMHK and American producers endeavoured to change the very free-market principle on which LME was founded. By taking the sale of the great majority of the world's copper out of the hands of the London metal brokers and selling their production directly to their consumers, the members of the new cartel sought to eliminate the speculation and hedging of copper stocks on the London market. The parties hoped to achieve greater stability in the price of the copper and to bring the price in line with the other base metals. The American producers were also trying to achieve the same by buying standard copper warrants for copper lying in LME warehouses. It was estimated at the time that shipping only 15,000–25,000 tons of copper from the LME warehouses to the American refiners would have created abnormally short copper stocks in Britain, and as a consequence the price of copper would have likely shown a rapid rise.[8] It is notable that in 1925 the world consumption of copper was larger than in any previous year, and was considerably greater than the actual output, so it was unlikely that the price of copper would have fallen materially, even if there had been an increase in output. So from the point of view of the American producers the problem did not lie in the increased production of copper but in the free-market principles of the London metal market.

In the period from 1926 until the outbreak of the Second World War, UMHK's Katanga production was sold at fixed prices to its customers. UMHK guaranteed to deliver a minimum of 40,000 tons to the Nichols Copper Company of New York in 1926 and Nichols for its part undertook to take up to a maximum of 60,000 tons if required. Most of its concentrate was exported to UMHK's refiners at Hoboken and Olen, or Lauren Hill, New

York, which was controlled by the Nichols Copper Company. The agreement affected the market logic of copper but it did not materially change the price of copper – the prices set by the cartel roughly followed the course of the average LME quotation of London Standard Cash for the month.[9] UMHK's copper sale contracts for 1926 are listed in Table 6.2.

The role of tin, radium, uranium and cobalt in the interwar business strategy

While it was copper that laid the foundation for the interwar-era mining in Katanga, tin, radium and cobalt mining and smelting campaigns were also expanding and put on a commercial footing in the 1920s. The early tin smelting operations at Busanga, inaugurated by Tanks' prospectors in 1904 and conducted until 1909,[10] had been important in the sense that these operations generated revenue at the time when the copper mining was still in its infancy and balance sheets showed a deficit. The Busanga tin smelting campaigns continued after the First World War due to the peaking prices, realising well over £300 per ton at LME in 1920.[11] There was no doubt as to the value of the ground at Busanga, but the problem lay in poor communications. The nearest railhead was some 40 miles to the east of Busanga as the crow flies, and this mileage was across some very difficult mountainous country which was some of the worst in Katanga. It would have been a questionable policy to try to bring the traction road across this country, and to transport tin bars from Busanga and food and supplies from the railway to the mine by means of traction engines.[12] In the 1920s development of the Busanga tin mine was overshadowed by the rapid development of the copper mines, and UMHK left finding economies of scale in the tin industry to the *Société Belge Industrielle et Minière du Katanga* (SIMKAT) and the *Compagnie Géologique et Minière des Ingénieurs et Industriels Belges* (Géomines), both already formed in 1910 but rising to significance in the 1920s. In 1926 only 37.5% of the cassiterite smelted was any longer mined by UMHK, the rest being mined by Géomines and SIMKAT.[13]

Table 6.2 UMHK copper sale contracts for 1926 (tons)

Nichols Copper Co., New York	40,000
American Smelting and Refining Co., Baltimore	15,000
United Metal Selling Co., New York	500
British Metal Corporation, Liverpool and Swansea	14,400
Compagnie française des métaux, Givet	2,400
Metallgeselschaft, Frankfurt	6,375
Lissaner, Cologne & A. Hirsch & Son, Halberstadt	750
Total	79,425

Source: MU, TANKS, TC/179, UMHK Technical Committee minutes, No. 508, 19 January 1926.

In 1911 uraninite ore was found at Shinkolobwe, and in 1913 further discoveries were made at Luushia,[14] but processing of the ore began only after the First World War. Market-sharing agreements helped to transform the new deposits into marketable products by removing fear of excessive competition in the markets, which at the time were expanding but still very limited. Initially the most important chemical element in uraninite ore proved to be radium, the known deposits of which UMHK held a virtual monopoly over at that time. The first consignment of the ore was sent to Belgium in 1921, and the manufacture of radium started in the next year.[15] In September 1922, UMHK made a contract with the Standard Chemical Company to facilitate sales in North America and to compete against its principal competitor, the United States Radium Corporation. The agreement between UMHK and the Standard Chemical Company fixed the price at $70 per milligram and guaranteed a minimum sale of 9 grammes per year.[16] The sales were conducted through *Radium Belge*, a commercial department of UMHK. In 1925, besides its usual consignment to the Standard Chemical Company, *Radium Belge* delivered radium to various clients in 15 different European countries and in Japan. Of the major importing countries, France took 3.15 grammes, England 2.44, Germany 1.81, Italy 1.68 and Spain 1.02. These deliveries represented practically the entire virgin radium production in the world in 1925. The sales of uranium salts were through Messrs. Maurice & Co. and were sporadic in nature. For instance, in November 1925 they totalled 3,176 tons.[17] When compared to the scale and scope of the copper trade, it will be realised that radium and uranium salts constituted only a minor fragment of UMHK's business in the interwar era.

In 1926, the staff of the radium works was transferred to the Olen cobalt plant and the various sections or radium works were progressively closed. After September 1926, the manufacture of radium continued irregularly because of its dependence on the availability of ore and on the level of demand.[18] In November 1925 exceptionally rich cobaltiferous zones (over 6% Co) were reported by the Mines Department from the Ruashi and Luushia mines, and secondary-nature cobalt deposits were also found at The Star, Kambowe West, Kalabi and Shinkolobwe mines and in certain northern deposits.[19] Initially the production of cobalt concerned largely the question of refining costs: Whether it would be best to refine its ore in Katanga or Europe was examined from the point of view of the role of cobalt in UMHK's future business strategy.[20] Ultimately there was no doubt about the preference for cheaper European refining. The Olen Plant enabled the manufacture of cobalt metal and black cobalt oxide, with regular production commencing on 1 July 1926.[21] The production decision was preceded by a market-sharing agreement with the Deloro Smelting and Refining Company of Ottawa, which controlled the bulk of the world's cobalt market at the time. This agreement led to the formation of a clearing house in New York where both companies had authorised representatives. The clearing house carried out the division of sales and received copies of all contracts, invoices and records so that all deliveries by the parties could be properly adjusted. UMHK considered that this contract secured, on good terms, the sale of a substantial part of the annual output of cobalt and had the further advantage of leaving the two companies free to develop their markets unafraid of damaging competition.[22]

The birth of industrial metabolism

As it transpired, it was copper that laid the foundation for mining in inter-war-era Katanga. The arrival of the railway at Kambove hurled the building of a gravity-fed smelter, a large concentrator and a leaching-electrolytic plant to Panda near to the Likasi mine and some 18 miles from the Kambove mine. The Panda Plant comprised seven blast furnaces together with one reverberatory furnace which started operations in June 1924. The running of this operation was entrusted to an experienced engineer, T.S. Carnahan, formerly with the Utah Copper Co., Bingham.[23] The copper output expansion programme at Panda was embodied in the launching of the first of four new reverberatory furnaces, each of 400 tons' daily capacity, in July 1927. A steam-powered 30,000-ton leaching plant commenced its operations in October 1927, while the first unit of the hydroelectric leaching plant went into operation in July 1929 and the second in July 1930.[24]

UMHK's growing need for electric power led to the establishment of a vast complex of hydroelectric installations. When completed its four power stations had a combined generating capacity of 2.5 billion kilowatt hours per year. After the damming in 1925 of the Cornet Falls on the Lufira River at Mwadingusha, some 40 miles from Jadotville, in 1930 electric power for the smelting operations started to be delivered from the Émile Francqui hydroelectric power station on the Lufira River.[25] The Francqui Power Station – belonging to the 1925-established *Société Générale des Forces Hydro-Electriques du Katanga* – required the construction of a dam 500 metres long, forming a reservoir lake of 1,250 million cubic metres. The energy production was further boosted in early 1950 by the commencing the operation of the Bia Power Station, located some four miles downstream from the Francqui Station. On the Lualaba River a dam 72.5 metres high and 162 metres long created an artificial lake of 1,800 million cubic metres. The waters of this lake fed the Delcommune Power Station as well as the most powerful of the four, Le Marinel Power Station, 20 miles downstream.[26]

From 1919 to 1930 UMHK's copper output increased from roughly 23,000 tons to roughly 139,000, concomitant with the development of the railway and the establishment of new hydroelectricity power plants, concentrators, leaching plants, furnaces as well as labour-saving mining equipment such as steam or electric shovels and transportable ore-loading devices. For a few years in the 1920s, UMHK produced more copper than any other single company in the world. In 1923, the Congo (virtually UMHK alone) ranked third in world copper production, producing 3.6% or 57,886 tons of the total 1,588,000 tons. It held this rank, following the United States and Chile, until

1930. After this, because of the Great Depression, it agreed, largely due to US wishes, to curtail its production.[27] UMHK copper output from 1911 to 1960 is shown in Figure 6.1.

The interwar-era copper output was primarily divided between the Kambove, Ruashi and Luushia mines. Kambove supplied 36% of the total smelting ore shipped from the mines in 1926, while Ruashi yielded 34% and Luushia 9%. The rest of the production was divided between seven other mines which were being exploited at the time.[28] Of the new mines brought to the operational stage the most important was Kipushi, which lay a few hundred yards from the Northern Rhodesia border and about 17 miles south-west from Élisabethville, the administrative capital. The initial ore deposits at Kipushi had been oxidised, but drilling work which commenced in December 1922 exposed rich copper sulphide ores at depth. The sulphides and mixed reserves assayed at about 12% Cu, containing sufficiently oxidised ores to justify blast furnace smelting at the Lubumbashi Smelter. The railway connecting the mine to the main line at Munama was completed in April 1926 and a loading platform was finished at roughly the same time.[29] Baptised 'Mine Prince Léopold' at its inauguration, Kipushi greatly added to the company's high-grade ore reserves.[30] The first load of concentrate (104 tons on 6 October 1926) assayed 46.4% of Cu and 2.015 grammes silver per ton (65 ounces per ton).[31] Owing to its high grade of silver, Kipushi copper was more valuable than the ore extracted from The Star, which began to wane in importance as a consequence. The rest of the sulphide and mixed-ore reserves at the same group of deposits at Fungurume and Ruashi mines were of low-grade ores, averaging about 4.2% of Cu. Prospecting at Fungureme was started in 1918 and development work two years later. The work was done by

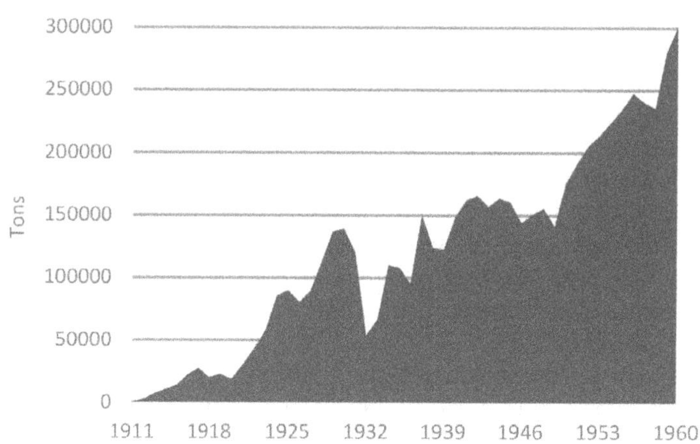

Figure 6.1 UMHK copper output, 1911–60 (tons)
Source: MU, TANKS, TC/179, Tanganyika Concessions and Union Minière du Haut-Katanga annual reports, 1911–60. See also Katzenellenbogen 1975, 377.

drilling and by crosscut tunnels, exposing ore reserves which led an eyewitness in 1926 to remark, 'By gosh, it's a wonderful mountain of ore.'[32] In addition to the aforementioned mines, in the western part of the Copperbelt there was a group of mines in the vicinity of the junction of the Lualaba and the Lufupa rivers, the most important of which was Ruwe, yielding copper, gold, silver and platinum, as well as Musonoi and Kolwezi where extraction of copper and other metals commenced in the 1940s. Apart from Kipushi, where it was necessary to mine two shafts of a little over 1,000 feet to extract the ore, all the other copper mines were suitable for quarry working.[33] In most of the open pit mines steam or electric shovels were used along with other modern mining equipment, including drilling machinery and transportable loading devices.[34]

Cost of production

Despite the great developments both in mining methods and in copper metallurgy, mining operations in Katanga remained inefficient, especially compared to the exploitation of the low-grade pyrites in the North American West. The damning verdict of T.A. Rickard, a mining engineer active in the United States, Europe and Australia, is illustrative in this respect. Speaking about the two centres Lubumbashi and Panda, Rickard stated that:

> The Lubumbashi Smelter, near Elisabethville, is situated in a depression, this unsuitable site having been chosen by a British metallurgist, with the idea of facilitating a supply of water by gravity. The concentrator at Panda is likewise badly placed; in this case the blame rests with an American metallurgist.[35]

Whereas UMHK was at the time discarding ore of 4%–5% Cu grade, the Utah Copper Co. was making money on ore of only 1% Cu. Such a drastic difference in the underlying ores and production methods reveals how the economic viability of the ore at any given time depended on local conditions, particularly the cost of labour and transport, as well as artificial factors such as tariffs.

The original export duty paid by UMHK was a sort of mining royalty and came within Article 3 of the royal decree of 1906 which approved the constitution of the company. A new customs tariff was imposed on 1 January 1924 which increased the export duties of copper, cobalt–copper alloy and cassiterite ingots significantly. The export duties levied by the Ministry of Colonies are listed in Table 6.3.

The new tariff regime included three additional effects. First, assistance for UMHK by a reduction in duty for their largest imports (machinery, coke and coal); second, an increase in the cost of living in Katanga as a result of the general increase in duty; and third, an attack on the southern transport route in favour of 'the Belgian National Route' of rail and river (*i.e. Voie Nationale* or transCongo) via the port of Matadi.

Table 6.3 Export duties levied in Katanga before and after 31 December 1923 (Frs. per ton)

	Before 31 December 1923	*After 1 January 1924*	*% Increase*
Copper	90	147	38.8
Co–Cu alloy	45	78	42.3
Cassiterite	390	635	38.6
Uranium ore	360	360	–

Source: MU, TANKS, TC/31, New tariffs, E.R. Heath, n.d.

Besides tariffs, transport and labour costs, the cost of smelting in Katanga depended on the cost of fuel, limestone and ore delivered to the furnaces. The difficulty of estimating the value of the cobalt in the crude copper brought further challenges to the production cost estimates as the market for cobalt was still a restricted one during the interwar era.[36] Reverberatory smelting was considered to be the cheapest method of smelting Katanga ores. Although various improvements for the blast furnace smelting economy had been instituted, the real cost difference between blast and reverberatory smelting proved significant. In July 1926 the cost of copper from the Panda blast furnaces was estimated at £30.0.4 per ton on rail at the smelter, whilst the cost of copper from the reverberatory furnace was estimated at £22.5.5 per ton.[37] Being a selective mining practice, the leaching method resulted in lower transport, concentrator, smelting, coal handling and tailings treatment costs. In addition, the leaching method was less labour intensive than other methods, which effectively reduced labour costs.[38]

The widening use of electric smelting had a double effect on the cost of production. UMHK's own coal reserves were limited to the Luena coal mine, operated by the *Charbonnages de la Luena* some 420 miles north of Élisabethville, but these deposits were not fully exploited partly because of the decision to use electric smelting and partly because of the ready availability of Wankie coal.[39] Incidentally, there was no need to be apprehensive about dependence on the Wankie Colliery because they were as anxious to sell fuel as UMHK was keen to buy it,[40] as revealed by the returns of the Wankie Colliery Company. In 1925 the actual coal mined at Wankie totalled 723,000 tons of which 56% was sold directly, 29% was coked, 2% was used at the Colliery and 13% discarded. In the same year company profit was a substantial £164,250, justifying the declaration of a 20% dividend. The authorised capital of the company was £900,000 in 10/- shares, of which £881,000 had already been issued.[41]

The same tendency applied to the dependence of the Rhodesia Railway on the Katanga transit traffic, as is evident from the following figures. Until October 1930, the railage for coal by the Rhodesian Railway from Wankie to Sakania was 28/- per ton for 583 miles (0.398 penny per ton kilometre). In October 1931 a completely new agreement was reached which reduced the cost of railage on coal to 24/- per ton when quantities between 60,000 and 100,000 tons of fuel were carried annually, and down to 22/- per ton when the annual quantity exceeded 100,000 tons (equivalent to 0.341 and 0.313 pence per ton kilometre, respectively). The cost at the Wankie Colliery remained the same as previously, namely 10/6 per ton. For coke, the cost at the Colliery was 24/- per short ton and the railage from Wankie to Sakania for fuel quantities under 60,000 tons per annum was 34/- per ton; for quantities between 60,000 to 100,000 tons it was 32/- per ton; and for quantities over 100,000 tons per annum it was 30/- per ton.[42] The Rhodesia Railway's dependency on Katanga transit traffic thus progressively lowered the cost of coal and coke as well as the cost of railage.

The rise of the Northern Rhodesian copper empire

The Benguela Railway, completed by means of a guarantee given by the British Government, arrived at Luao, on the Angola–Belgian Congo border, on 28 July 1928, and joined up with the Rhodesia–Katanga line at Tenke junction, near Tshilongo, on 10 March 1931.[43] Its inaugural ceremony was held nearly 30 years after the initial construction work had started.[44] The Benguela Railway was specifically designed to supply the Copperbelt and to extract its ores by linking it up with the Katanga Railway and the Rhodesia Railway. As a result, a 90% Tanks-owned access to the Congo border, with its much-sought strategic freedom, had been created. Quantities of ores and minerals could now flow from Katanga to the metal markets via Benguela, whilst supplies, machinery and fuel could be transported as return cargo to the mines.[45]

The launching of the Benguela Railway changed the logic of the Katanga copper trade. Until then the Rhodesia Railway had been the only reliable route to the Katangese mining district, and the imports and exports of that territory provided a very substantial portion of its total traffic and revenue. In fact, this valuable transit traffic to and from Katanga was for many years a more important factor for the development of BSAC territories than the progress of the Northern Rhodesian and Southern Rhodesian mining industries combined. After completion of the Benguela Railway, the future of the Rhodesia Railway increasingly depended on the potential expansion of the copper mining industry in Northern Rhodesia. It was very important for the parties with interests in the Northern and Southern Rhodesian mining and railways that the whole of the traffic to and from Katanga should continue to pass over the Rhodesia Railway, to and from the port of Beira and the Union of South Africa ports of Port Elizabeth (Gqeberha) and Cape Town.[46]

The future of the Kansanshi copper mine had an important bearing here. After the completion of the Benguela Railway, Tanks proposed to the Northern Rhodesia Government that a siding should be constructed from the Kansanshi to the Musonoi mine in Katanga. In considering the prospects of this siding, the most important factor was the cost of freight, including the

Crown Agent's expenses, freight, port charges and railage, which usually absorbed about 70% of the total transport costs. The distance by rail from Kansanshi (via Musonoi) to Lobito Bay was calculated at 839 miles and to Wankie 867 miles, and it was possible that if the proposed railway was ever constructed, the mine could land good-quality coal from Britain via the Benguela Railway at lower rates than from the Wankie Colliery. The proposed railway would have therefore linked not only Kansanshi but the emerging Ndola group of copper mines in Northern Rhodesia to Lobito Bay.[47]

The important emerging sulphide copper mines in the Ndola group included the Roan Antelope and Mufulira Copper Mines of the Rhodesian Selection Trust of Companies, incorporated in 1928 and controlled by an American-born mining engineer Alfred Chester Beatty (1875–1968).[48] The other important mines of the group were N'Kana, controlled by Rhodesian Anglo American, a subsidiary of Anglo American Corporation of South Africa, controlled by Sir Ernest Oppenheimer (1880–1957) and listed on the Johannesburg Stock Exchange, with a secondary listing on the London Stock Exchange on 9 October 1917.[49] The parent organisations – Selection Trust and Anglo American – provided managerial, administrative, financial and technical services to the individual mining companies of the Ndola group which were floated for operating the mines. By the mid-1930s, some of the mines in this group had grown into a considerable and cost-effective copper producer at the LME. In 1935, N'Kana was producing copper at the rate of 60,000 tons per annum. The corresponding figure for Roan Antelope was 40,000 tons, whilst Mulufira was closed owing to the depressed state of the copper market. The cost of N'Kana and Roan copper landed in the LME warehouses in England was in the region of £20 a ton.[50]

In view of these powerful mining interests operating in Northern Rhodesia, the ultimate justification for the rejection of Tanks' proposal to link Kansanshi by rail was as much strategic as commercial – the exploitation of the mineral resources of Northern Rhodesia for the British markets by using the 'all British' financed routes via the ports of Beira, Cape Town and Port Elizabeth. The question which received special consideration – if Lobito Bay was to become the port of entry and exit for the Northern Rhodesia mining industry – was port charges at Lobito Bay. There appeared to be a big disparity between the charges levied in respect of British and Portuguese ships, with especially low rates quoted for the latter.[51] Another factor was the limited availability of low-wage labour. The northern portions of the Mwinilunga and Solwezi districts in Northern Rhodesia were sparsely populated, a factor which was another hindrance for the development of the railway according to Tanks' proposal. These districts had possibilities as pasture, and a forestry officer believed a portion of the Mwinilunga District was eminently suited for softwood plantations,[52] which were in high demand for pit props, sawn and hewn wood, as well as pulpwood at the time. However, the political economy dictated that forestry and agricultural development, independent of mining activity, did not as a rule alone justify the construction of a railway in colonial-era South-Central

Africa.[53] The colonial-era railway projects were primarily linked to mining, and its demand for high transport capacity of ore, fuel and supplies of manufactured goods and machinery.

The most important underlying reason for the denial of Tanks' proposal was financial, however. The boards of the Rhodesia and Mashonaland railways had vested interests in the Rhodesian mining industry and if a considerable portion of traffic were directed away from the Rhodesia Railway system to the Benguela Railway, the only result would have been a worsening of the financial situation of the Rhodesian mining and railway companies. It was therefore in the interests of the other Rhodesian mining companies for the status quo to be maintained and the Kansanshi mine to be left underdeveloped. In 1935, the combined debenture capital of the Rhodesia Railways, the Mashonaland Railway & Co., Beira Railway Co. and the Beira Works was over £24 million, all raised in Britain. Bearing in mind that the average LME price for standard copper had dropped to an average of £30 a ton in 1935 (in 1931 the average had been £39), the Rhodesian railway companies were operating at a loss of about £1.25 million per annum (after the fixed charges), forcing them to enter into moratorium schemes with their debenture holders.[54]

Local resistance to the project was an issue as well.[55] The interested parties voted against the construction of the proposed Kansanshi–Musonoi line, in accordance with the Agreement of 29 September 1923, which dictated that:

> no new railway or railways shall be constructed in Northern Rhodesia except under the authority of the special legislation in each case and that such legislation shall not be enacted unless His Majesty's Government after full consideration are satisfied that the new railway or railways to be constructed will not have an unduly adverse effect on the railway Companies operating in Northern and Southern Rhodesia.[56]

For a third of a century (1890–1923), BSAC was the sole administrative body in Northern Rhodesia that had powers to determine which financiers and companies were awarded grants and concessions over the land. BSAC had the full backing of the British Government, which was relieved from the expensive necessity of maintaining very extensive police supervision and from the direct collection of the fees, rates and taxes for mining, and other local payments by outsourcing supervisory tasks to the chartered company. The government therefore approved the concessions and over a long period of years recognised that in practice the chartered company effectively owned the mineral rights throughout Northern Rhodesia – a recognition which was further strengthened by a statement to this effect in the Mining Proclamation of 1912 which was confirmed by the government. The Agreement of 29 September 1923 brought to an end BSAC's administration of Northern Rhodesia, but the rights of BSAC were again recognised by the government. Ultimately the greatest beneficiary of the imperial-era business system in Northern Rhodesia was BSAC, which after 1924 continued to receive its income (in either cash or shares) in respect of concessionary rights granted to mining and railway companies.[57] Local opposition to the ownership rights of BSAC started to grow over the interwar years as a result of increased copper production, and especially after the Second World War, when the opposition intensified further as a result of the high price of copper. In 1947–8 BSAC receipts from the royalties on minerals produced in Northern Rhodesia had risen to over £2 million and they continued to rise towards the end of the colonial era.[58]

Labour management from a financial point of view

> All the efforts of the Medical and the Native Labour Affairs Departments will be in vain as long as the European staff, from the Brussels and African managements down to the lowest supervisor of works, does not appreciate that the native is not a machine into which it is sufficient to put some food and combustible to obtain a given result, but that he is a human complex who has a thinking individuality which one must know how to manage. He is a child whom one cannot induce to work by simply offering good food and lodging with cold discipline. We must know how to talk to him, understand him and listen to his complaints, encourage him as a teacher does his pupil, but maintaining a paternal authority. This is the transformation which has to be induced into the UMHK staff which has – from the lowest to the highest – been hypnotized by a single word – production.[59]

For 60 years (1906–66) the Katangese copper mining was carried out by UMHK, which was a private concern and was run strictly on business lines. During this time the company carefully kept vital statistics of their labour force, and since 1924 statistical information has also been available on women and since 1926 on children living in the mining camps. In analysing UMHK's vital statistics it is important to note at the outset that the directors of the company, the managers of its mines and the officers of the Medical and Native Labour Affairs departments of the mines were primarily concerned in producing copper economically and were interested in the welfare of the population living in the mining camps only insofar as it affected the production of copper or the cost of production. Considering that UMHK was a private concern and not a government institution or a philanthropic one it is interesting to note that the directors nevertheless authorised the spending of large sums of money on improving living quarters, providing better nutrition, the prevention of diseases, general sanitation, the education and welfare of children, the care of women and the treatment of the sick – being fully convinced that such expenditure would improve the productivity of the labour force and ultimately lead to cheaper production costs. These new principles governing labour management came to the fore during the first 12 years of UMHK's post-First World War existence (1919–31). Throughout this period the officers of the Medical Department (*Hygiene Industrielle*) lamented that managers frequently gave preference to questions relating to production as against those relating to labour health and that the medical personnel were powerless to improve local conditions unless aided by the general management. The situation improved progressively, and in 1932 the Principal Medical Officer of the Medical Department, Dr L. Mottoulle, was finally able to state that 'the financial point of view and the humanitarian point of view have met in a common role'.[60]

For the first 20 years of UMHK's mining operations (1906–26) up to half of the workforce was recruited annually by Messrs. Robert Williams & Co. and classified as being 'Balunda' from the Lualaba and Lozi districts, and to a lesser extent 'Nyassa, Balovale and Barotse' peoples who formed on average 6% of the total recruited workforce.[61] On 1 January 1927 UMHK took over recruiting operations in Rhodesia from Messrs. Robert Williams & Co. and passed them to Mr Yule, who was authorised by UMHK to recruit labour in Northern Rhodesia formally in his own name but in practice on the company's account.[62] This development was due to restrictions placed by the Government of Northern Rhodesia on the export of labour to Katanga, which forced UMHK to look for new sources of low-wage labour. This meant a new intense recruitment drive in Katanga, where the returns shown by the *Bourse du Travail du Katanga* (BTK), the office charged with recruiting operations in the Congo, remained poor. The general management's discontent with BTK became evident on 24 September 1926 when the office *Central du Travail* took over recruiting operations in the Congo.[63] BTK thus disappeared from the business scene after a chequered career of 16 years.

Once communications between Katanga and the rest of the Congo improved, towards the end of the 1920s, Bantu speakers from the populous Lomani District (a part of the Katanga vice-government formed in 1913) and the Ruanda-Urundi District (a former colonial territory of German East Africa which was administered by Belgium under military occupation from 1916 to 1922 and held thence under the Mandate of the League of Nations) became prominent new sources for labour. In Ruanda-Urundi, the success of recruitment work was largely credited to Mr Freygang, the *Chef de Mission de Recrutement*, but precious little is known about recruiting methods in Ruanda-Urundi. Force or trickery in recruiting labour was forbidden by the colonial legislation but it is difficult to estimate just how much this edict was heeded. The medical reports say that 'the Ruanda cluster of ethnicities belonging to the Bantu were of a docile and sensitive character' who rapidly accustomed themselves to the camp life and work.[64] Assimilation into the camp life here meant docile black bodies as a labour force for mining. Those that found it difficult to assimilate posed a potential threat to the company and colonial society as a whole.

The very competitive copper market of the 1920s, with rapidly increasing global production and declining prices, induced the management to introduce labour-saving technologies and to minimise labour costs. Some of the technological advances such as the improvement of concentration due to adding flotation treatment of tailings were made from the point of view of economy of labour. Despite technological transformation in mining and smelting methods, the work at the mines remained very labour-intensive. From 1919 to 1930 the total number of UMHK's African labour force increased year by year along with the increased copper production. By 1929 UMHK's African mining population had risen to over 20,000 (Table 6.4). In the same year, it was calculated that every new worker brought to work on the mines cost the company £16 before even a day's work had been carried out.[65] Once the management had established that every sick worker was an added expense and that every death amongst labour represented a total loss of this sum, it is no wonder that the directors started to slowly but unavoidably appreciate that it was a matter of economics to keep their labour force fit and well. This the company tried to achieve, first by preventing sickness (*e.g.* by providing better living quarters, food and clothing, distributing inoculations and training women and children); second by the provision of hospitals and medical facilities for the care of the sick, ensuring that no labourer remained ill longer than was necessary; and finally by creating mining centres suitable for a stable workforce of employed volunteers (as opposed to labour drafted for half of a year or a year at a time so that the personnel of the labour force completely changed every 12 months).

When the first mining camps were established in the early 1900s UMHK was averse to granting permission to women and children to accompany men to the camps. The presence of women and children in the camps was not officially recognised, and no specific compound accommodation, food, medical or welfare services were provided for them. As a consequence the infant mortality was extremely high. According to UMHK's vital statistics, as many as 509 of the children died in the mining camps in the first years of the European mining economy. The camps' reputation for immorality was regarded as justified by officials and missionaries, who principally assigned responsibility for the high infant mortality to the ignorance of the expectant women and their 'congenital debility'. Women were blamed for being ignorant of the most elementary rules of hygiene and transmitting venereal diseases such as syphilis.[66]

Table 6.4 UMHK mining population, 1924–30 (persons)

	Men	*Women*	*Children*	*Total*
1924	10,318	1,793	n.a.	12,111
1925	11,343	2,506	n.a.	13,849
1926	10,335	2,940	940	14,215
1927	11,815	3,662	1,423	16,900
1928	10,643	4,702	2,105	17,450
1929	11,440	5,817	3,149	20,406
1930	9,667	6,673	4,457	20,797

Source: TNA, CO 795/49/12, Report on the condition of mining camps of the UMHK, Dr H. de Boer, Deputy Director of Sanitary Services, 5 January 1932.

The system by which men were separated from their families and rural homes for half of a year or a year at a time proved to be very destructive for the social welfare of the labour. A complete turnaround was made in 1926 when the officers of the Medical and Native Labour Affairs departments managed to convince the directors of the need for a new policy which would 'stabilise' the African population in and around the mines.[67] From then on the Medical and Native Labour Affairs departments of the mines endeavoured to recruit only men accompanied by women and even went so far as to assist recruits to obtain women for the mining camps. Some were employed for camp maintenance and women could even be made of use of in the work of ore picking on the sorting belts, though this stabilisation policy had not been with a view to actually employing women (apart from performing jobs such as housekeeping, sewing and cooking).[68] Instead, the scheme intended the various ethnicities to eventually blend, so that over time the mining population of UMHK would form a common identity.[69]

The stabilisation policy stemmed from findings from UMHK vital statistics. First, recruited labour (as opposed to employed volunteers) suffered the worst morbidity and mortality rates; second, most cases of sickness or death occurred during the first few months in the mining camps (*i.e.* the morbidity and mortality rates dropped the longer the period of time spent in the camps); and finally, family men were relatively fitter than bachelors. Therefore, from a financial point of view, it was extremely advantageous to the company to encourage the stability of their workforce. Not only did it help to keep their labour fit, but it also effectively diminished recruiting expenditure. The backdrop of this development was 'wastage' of labour in the early years of the European mining economy in the Central African Copperbelt. Especially severe was the Spanish flu pandemic in 1918 when as many as 12.7% of all African miners crowded in the compounds died.[70] After this the situation improved gradually but remained severe. For instance, 51 deaths from sickness were registered in July 1925. Among the fatalities 26 were due to pulmonary complaints classified as 'pneumonia', the most destructive of all diseases amongst the UMHK workers, and 14 to cerebro spinal meningitis, which also resulted in a high mortality rate.[71] Recruits were brought from far and near to the camps where very little had been done in preparation of their reception, resulting in overcrowding – one of the chief causes of the high death rate as shown by the vital statistics. The recruits were straightaway expected to start work and keep on for 12 or even 15 hours per day, seven days a week.[72]

As a first step in the stabilisation scheme, UMHK started to invest in the construction of sizeable, square, wooden and sheet iron roofed compounds – the buildings that were to constitute the core of African housing in the mining centres for years to come. Previously the bulk of compound accommodation was based on huts constructed in provisional grass camps by the workers themselves using local building materials. This system had been popular with the mine managers because the use of their own workforce and local materials constituted an enormous saving of the very expensive and scarce building materials and rendered employment of skilled builders unnecessary. As a result, accommodation was always inadequate – periodically in quantity and almost always in quality. Then temporary sheet iron huts were introduced. They remained unpopular among the labour, and many preferred rough camping because of the iron sheets which all too easily transmitted seasonal fluctuations in temperature.[73]

From the beginning of 1927 the Native Labour Affairs Department took up the building of all houses for African labour. This was due to the labour stabilisation scheme which encouraged women and children to settle in compounds, causing a large increase in demand for accommodation.[74] The first permanent housing was large single-sex dormitories built on the Rand model which housed up to 60 men, were poorly lit and had earthen floors and iron sheet roofs. Men were crowded together in large rooms, each room taking three rows of bunks. The total absence of privacy was often accompanied by various social problems as a consequence of workers from different cultural backgrounds being shuffled together. Then single rooms each holding a family were provided. These were still poorly lit and concreted flooring impervious to damp was not yet provided. Then the floors were concreted, roofs thatched and soon after windows fitted and small kitchens built adjoining the rooms. Lighting and ventilation were also given some consideration. Finally, single cottage construction for family men was adopted.[75]

In these ways the bleak and barracks-like appearance of the mining camps was done away with by providing the most elementary facilities and improving comfort and hygiene. Some camps were even serviced with a piped water supply and bathing accommodation which were provided in fairly close proximity to most buildings. Smoke pit latrines (*i.e.* fires producing smoke that were kept going continuously during the daytime) were the means of preventing flies that could transmit contagious diseases such as bacillary dysentery. The planting of trees and gardens of flowers and ornamental shrubs was the other means to improve the quality of life in the camps.[76]

Another continuing problem was feeding the ever-growing labour force in Katanga. Instead of buying large quantities of foodstuffs produced in the British-administered territories, harvesting of crops by the company was introduced. It was not possible to increase the output of local agriculture very rapidly, however, because of the heavy vegetation in parts of the mining district. The land had to be cleared before it could be cultivated and this itself involved the use of further large quantities of labour. Nutrition improved progressively, however, and by 1931 problem solving had been placed on a scientific footing, involving the distribution of designated rations to the workforce. A ration, except meat, was issued weekly for each labourer, excluding those who were employed underground or on arduous surface work who were provided with hot drinks and food whilst at work. The designated weekly ration included the following: Mealie meal (2.5 kg); manioc (2.5 kg); meat (1.4 kg); palm oil (0.5 kg); sweet potatoes (8 kg); fruit and vegetables (0.76 kg); salt (0.1 kg). The ration was later supplemented by a kilogram of ground nuts weekly per worker.[77] The ordinary ration for females and children was half that of an adult male worker. Expectant women and nursing mothers were issued with a full male worker ration, which was intended as an inducement to attend instruction and medical checks at the Child Welfare Centre.[78]

Work clothing was another concern that was given attention. Usually recruits arrived from their villages with very little clothing and without money to buy clothes to protect themselves against cold and damp. Volunteers on the other hand generally arrived with much more clothing.[79] To combat the effects of cold and damp and to reduce the risk of pneumonia and other chest complaints the Medical Department drew up a plan to supply workers with clothing, especially for night work and for sleeping.[80] In addition, free clothing was issued to those mothers and children whose spouses earned less than five francs a day.[81]

Another delicate and difficult task – in view of the fact that UMHK was trying to make their labourers work as efficiently as possible – was discussion on the abandonment of night and Sunday work. The Meeting of Departmental Managers on 29 September 1926 decided that, as far as possible, the night shift in the mines from 11 p.m. to 7 a.m. would be closed down, and that, in cases where it had to be retained (*e.g.* for work at the smelter, for the concentrator, and for the shipment of ores, which necessitated continuous reliable labour shifts), the only labour used for night work should be employed volunteers. The new recommendation was eight-hour shifts followed by a rest period of an hour and a hot midday meal. In most mining centres Sunday rest had not been observed previously but its indispensability was now recognised too.[82] Furthermore, from October 1925 a penalty of 1,000 Frs. was imposed on any mining centre for each labourer who died while employed. This penalty fee was intended to encourage the mine managers to pay more attention to matters of health in order to cut down on their operating cost.[83]

The stabilisation scheme reduced the continual coming and going of new workers but did not do away with it altogether. Regarding the question of the re-engagement of time-expired workers, UMHK introduced premiums payable to those workers who were willing to extend their terms of engagement. They received a premium of 50 Frs. if they engaged for an additional year, 125 Frs. for two years and 200 Frs. for three years. These premiums were also given to those volunteers who at the end of their term went on leave and returned with more of their tribesmen for work (proportioned to the number of volunteers brought back).[84]

Improved facilities and medical practices were reflected positively in the mortality figures. In just five years the overall death rate declined from 45.9 per 1,000 persons in 1925 to 16.28 in 1930.[85] Of the various diseases transmitted in the mining camps pneumonia was by far the deadliest. It accounted on average for 65% of the deaths occurring each year but the gravity of the health situation greatly varied each year and with each epidemic.[86] At times pneumonia existed amongst the newly arrived African workers to such an extent that it does not seem an exaggeration to say that an attack of pneumonia formed a part of the acclimatisation to camp life. Overcrowded dormitories were among the main contributors to the severity of the epidemic. The general fatigue and cold of the labourers were gradually also acknowledged to have a major impact on the prevalence of disease. Distribution of blankets, clothing and waterproofs were means to fight the disease as were hot food and drinks which were provided in the yards according to the season. Pneumococcal vaccination was first tried in 1919, but in 1924 it was decided to limit the distribution of preventive inoculations to recruits from Northern Rhodesia. The decision was rationalised by the system of short contracts which were usually limited to six months or one year (and which effectively ran against the stabilisation policy). The distribution of preventive inoculations to African labour was abolished altogether in 1930.[87] By then the number of short-term recruits from Northern Rhodesia had dropped, and employed volunteers from the Congo formed a major part of the stable workforce.

Some other diseases of a severe nature such as sleeping sickness and cerebrospinal meningitis were also endemic in Katanga but declared themselves more sporadically than pneumonia. Smallpox, tuberculosis, typhoid fever, bacillary dysentery, measles and tick fever were some of the other diseases which regularly caused death. They were fought back with the gradual improvement of compound accommodation (*e.g.* by replacing the earth floors of huts by concrete floors), with hygiene measures (*e.g.* disinfection of the huts) and with preventive inoculations (in the cases of smallpox, typhoid fever and meningitis). Significant progress was made in the reduction of the death rate from pneumonia after the introduction of the stabilisation policy, which gradually put an end to the continual coming and going of most of the labour force. In 1930 there were 987 cases of pneumonia which caused 173 deaths amongst the 16,340 men and women living in the UMHK camps. This represented a death rate of 10.59 per 1,000 men and women from pneumonia, but the statistics further reveal that it was considerably lower among employed volunteers (6.6 per 1,000) than with recruits (14 per 1,000).[88] The careful selection of recruits before their introduction into the camps, and the exclusion of certain ethnicities which had proven difficult to acclimatise to the camp life, were the other means to prevent sickness and premature deaths. This policy mainly concerned people from the Lulua territory, whose mortality in respect of the Ruashi and The Star mines alone was 18.3 per 1,000 workers in the first part of 1926.[89] The improvement of working conditions and the introduction of machinery that rendered work less hard, in certain mines, and the development of the living quarters and hygienic measures throughout the camps had an impact on the mortality rate from sickness as well.

While UMHK endeavoured to combat scientifically many of the diseases occurring in their mining concession, very little attention was given to mosquito control by netting, draining pools of stagnant water and swamps, or bush-clearing. The control of malaria was largely restricted to the use of prophylactic quinine distributed to Europeans, on whose medication against malaria UMHK spent nearly one million francs each year. The perceived relative immunity of the African population against blood parasites did not stop them from contracting malaria and in fact acute cases were very frequent amongst Africans in the camps. As a rule malaria was not specified in the morbidity figures, however, though it was recorded that among survivors sickness from malaria caused an average of four days of sick leave. In 1930, one-third or 5,420 of the 16,340 men and women living in the UMHK camps were treated for malaria.[90]

Hospitals were means to ensure that sick persons were treated as early as possible and to keep the period of absence from work at a minimum. The nursing of the patients was in the hands of the White Sisters of the Roman Catholic Sisterhood (*Sœurs missionnaires de Notre-Dame d'Afrique*, The Missionary Sisters of Our Lady of Africa), who were assisted by male African orderlies. The value of the hospitals is well shown by the vital statistics. In 1931 the Lubumbashi Hospital catered for about 2,000 men and about 1,500 women and children. The hospital provided 150–200 beds and had a staff of one European doctor, four White Sisters and 35 African orderlies.[91]

Welfare work among women and children was social, medical and moral and aimed to ensure that every child born and raised in the mining camps would eventually be available to the company as a labourer (not training children to work elsewhere than on the mines). Of the various mining centres, preliminary work was conducted in 1925 at the Lubumbashi Compound as well as The Star, Ruashi and Kipushi mines. The welfare work was organised by the Medical Officer and the Superintendent of the camp representing the Medical and the Native Labour Affairs departments. The work comprised the following: first, the creation of the Child Welfare Centres, kinds of maternity wards purported to instruct pregnant women in their duties as mothers and staffed by the White Sisters acting as nurses and midwives; second, the creation of primary schools for children between 5 and 12 years old (up to 15 years old for those who were perceived as talented and were destined to enter a vocational school later); third, the control of the apprenticeship of children between 12 and 15 years old. The welfare work was coupled with moral and religious instruction, organised under the Benedictine Fathers. The Reverend Fathers of the Benedictine Mission were in charge of the schools and of the recruitment of African *instituteurs* to deal with the education and instruction of the children.[92]

While the stabilisation scheme improved labour productivity and the health and welfare of the workers and the women and children at large, it also increased labour costs. The increase in cost was due to:

1 A higher scale of wages and premiums given to retain and stabilise labour
2 Better and more abundant food rations
3 More ample clothing being supplied
4 Extra expenditure on child welfare
5 An increase in the cost of foodstuffs, salaries and hospitals
6 An increase of 20% in stores consumed
7 Allocation from the extraordinary fund to the stabilisation scheme.

Of the aforementioned factors, systematic information is only available on the development of the wages scheme. From 1925 onwards wages were divided into five classes. In the first class (15–20 Frs. per day) belonged those African labourers who were generally considered to have achieved their position by showing 'intelligence and perseverance'. They were performing jobs which earlier were considered work of a poorly paid European (*e.g.* the use of power shovels, jackhammer drills and other labour-saving machines). The second class (12–20 Frs. per day) included unsupervised workers in the quarries and yards. The third class (15 Frs. per day) comprised miners working underground, whilst the fourth class (4–8 Frs. per day) included workshop hands and sanitary workers among many others performing tasks considered secondary by nature. The fifth and lowest-paid class (2.50–5 Frs. per day) included those labourers who worked under supervision in work gangs, and generally those who were categorised as being outside of the 'effective' workforce (*e.g.* the sickly and children). Certain taxes payable by labourers to the government were deducted from their salary. For some workers, like those from the Eastern Province (Province Orientale), one-third of the wages were paid in Katanga and two-thirds on their return after the expiration of their contract. In the case of death of a worker the balance of his salary was to be paid to his heirs – such balance being not less than 150 Frs.[93] These were means to ensure that the recruits worked for UMHK only and were not to be ceded to contractors working for UMHK (which as a rule paid higher salaries). The wages paid by UMHK to its African workers were lower than those paid in Northern Rhodesia too. In some mining centres such as the Kipushi mine, which lay in the vicinity of the border where the Rhodesian Congo Border Concessions were employing workers for the Bwana Mkubwa mine at Ndola, it was necessary to institute a pay rate similar to that of Northern Rhodesia.[94]

The end of the colonial epoch

In the 1920s UMHK experienced an outstanding transfer of technology that brought it to the premier position it was to occupy in the field of non-ferrous metals for decades to come. The company had a major impact on the expansion of industrialism in Katanga and on the lives of the African mining population which it had brought into existence, first with cold discipline and then from the mid-1920s onwards with a labour management programme aiming at stabilising the African population in and around the mines. For 25 years the prosperity of Katanga was bound to the fortunes of UMHK, and all production figures showed a strong upward trend. The Great Depression signified a turn for the worse. Between 1930 and 1932 UMHK's copper output plummeted from 139,000 to 54,000 tons, its staff of European descent dropping from 2,300 to 600 and its African workforce from 14,000 to 5,000.[95]

It does not seem an exaggeration to say that the whole economic and social life of Katanga was at the mercy of UMHK.[96] In 1938 when UMHK had recovered from the Depression and resumed regular dividend-sharing with its shareholders, the company provided employment for some 1,000 workers of European descent and some 14,000 Africans. The company owned a large share in the metallurgical and chemical industries, maize milling, cattle farming, insurance, explosives, cement, real estate, railways and roads, and controlled the entire production of hydroelectric power. In addition, UMHK owned and operated numerous schools, hospitals and other welfare centres for its employees and their families.[97] The value of UMHK's participation in the Katangese economy, judged by the value of its purchases made and contracts placed locally, was 13 million francs in 1933, rising to 51 million in 1938, then to 133 million in 1942.[98] In light of these figures, it was therefore not entirely surprising that the mining moguls of UMHK should have come to believe that what was good for them was good also for the Katangese.

Following the German occupation of Belgium in 1940 UMHK transferred its corporate domicile to the Congo which effectively saved the company from having its assets confiscated. Demand for copper was unprecedentedly brisk but the loss of the refining facilities in Belgium meant that the whole output had to be exported to Britain where it was sold on a cash-and-carry basis at prices fixed by the British Government. In 1941 Britain refined a Congo copper ore equivalent of 126,000 tons of the red metal that was vital for her war effort.[99] Most cobalt was exported to the United States where it was used towards the end of the war in the manufacture of jet engines. UMHK was also the principal supplier of uranium for the US atomic bomb programme (The Manhattan Project) and therefore the company had a strategic importance for the 'Free World' as a whole.[100]

Meanwhile, a cloud of economic and political anxiety joined the cloud of sulphurous fumes hovering over smelters and concentrators. There were still bitter memories of the Great Depression. The whole economy of the Congo was at the mercy of the world metal markets and extremely vulnerable as a consequence. In view of the strategic importance of metals produced in Katanga, the desire to maintain industrial peace understandably grew.[101] Traditionally, white workers had enjoyed a privileged position in the industry. They were engaged for a period of three years after which a holiday, or *congé*, of six months was granted,[102] but following the Depression the white workers saw their wages reduced by 10%, their family allowances docked, the length of the contract extended from three to four years, and the suppression of all kinds of bonuses and allowances, culminating in widespread protest among the labour force during the war.[103]

Another cause of anxiety was that the African worker might one day try to push for greater independence in managing his own affairs. The traditional docile outlook of the African worker was a legacy of the colonial rule when he was transferred to his new rulers in complete and unquestioning submission formerly accorded to tribal chiefs. In a mining centre the African was not recognised as an individual but as an effective unit of the labour force when fit for work or as wastage when sick, a runaway or dead. Labour relations were based on a system of military discipline, and little or no effort was made to understand the difficulties of the African on the job. A completely new look in African labour relations came about with the emergence of the stabilisation policy. Drafted recruits took a medical inspection, received their prophylactic injections and attended training which consisted of instructions in company rules, safety and hygiene and aptitude tests, before being assigned to productive work under the very close supervision of selected Africans and Europeans.[104]

Urbanisation was one of the most striking symptoms of the impact of Western industrialism in Central Africa. Initially the African workforce on UMHK mines and its satellite commercial organisations was migratory labourers who remained in employ for a short period and then returned to their tribal areas. No elaborate system of social relations between African and African and between African and European was necessary where their interaction was transitory. Progressively since the mid-1920s, following the stabilisation of the African population in and around the mines, it was becoming evident that more and more Africans were cutting themselves adrift from their tribal areas and becoming increasingly urban dwellers. By 1965 the average length of an employee contract had risen to nine years.[105] The size of the urban African population was increasing at an unprecedented rate, and the formerly unarticulated and somewhat apathetic masses were beginning to develop a voice.[106] This development was stimulated by contact with European workmen, their standards of living, their outlook and trades unionism and by the sympathetic interest of public opinion abroad. As a result of these influences, the traditional outlook of the African towards European authority changed completely. The African started to look upon himself as an industrial worker and to refer to the employment of the white workers as a yardstick by which to measure their own labour relations.

While mining provided both the spur and the source of finance for the greater part of the economy of the Congo, the same applied also to Central Africa as a whole. The preponderant role played by its parents, Tanks and SGB, with their significant and numerous subsidiary companies, conferred on UMHK the status of a first-class mining company, with combined assets of the order of £300–400 million. At the end of the colonial era UMHK provided employment for some 2,000 workers of European descent and some 20,000 Africans, and indirectly the source of their livelihood for a population of about 100,000. The main statistical elements of the demographic situation of UMHK's personnel from 1940 to 1965 are given in Table 6.5.

By the end of the colonial era, UMHK had built more than 200,000 dwellings for its African personnel, creating at the same time access roads, churches, clubs, mine stores, playing fields and recreational centres. Of the African workforce, 85% lived in the company-owned compounds and the rest in their own homes. The compound had therefore lost some of its former significance as an African housing unit. Another significant population trend concerned the training of African workers. Africanisation of the supervisory staff was still rather modest. The strength of the supervisory staff was 1,708 of which 163 were Africans. Furthermore, 291 Africans held responsible jobs assisting the supervisory staff.

Table 6.5 The population trends of UMHK, 1940, 1945, 1950, 1955, 1960 and 1965 (per 1,000 workers [w.] or inhabitants [i.])

	Women	*Children*	*Birth rate*	*Death rate*	*Death rate*
	per 1,000 w.	*per 1,000 w.*	*per 1,000 i.*	*per 1,000 w.*	*per 1,000 i.*
1940	577	592	37.33	4.60	12.34
1945	697	937	52.90	4.31	10.80
1950	782	1,430	63.62	4.18	9.43
1955	822	1,904	72.85	2.81	7.12
1960	837	2,929	71.10	3.40	5.62
1965	780	3,041	52.53	2.66	6.81

Source: TNA, FO 371/161517, UMHK, Reports of Directors and Auditors Presented on the Annual General Meeting, 24 May 1962; TNA FO 371/187757, The Annual General Meeting of the Union Minière du Haut-Katanga on May 26, 1966, Reports of the Board of Directors regarding 59th financial year 1965.

The company had 70 of its own schools, including 15 kindergartens, 33 primary schools and 22 professional, technical, teacher training schools. The number of children attending the primary schools directly managed by UMHK or financially supported by it was 20,455.[107]

Despite the growing uncertainties in the operating environment, maintaining a high level of investment did not seem a questionable policy to the owners. In its last colonial-era years UMHK invested directly (excluding investments by its subsidiary companies) approximately 15 billion francs in plant equipment and social installations.[108] UMHK's importance to the Congolese economy can scarcely be exaggerated. It was the largest company in the Belgian Congo, earning annually some 60%–70% of its revenue. Thanks to UMHK, the Congo ranked third among world copper producers, accounting for 7%–10% of the world's annual supply of copper. In addition, it provided more than 60% of the world's cobalt,[109] a large part of its germanium and virtually all of its radium.[110]

The mineral exploitation activities of UMHK were spread around three large mining centres: Élisabethville, Jadotville and Kolwezi. The major mines worked by the company were:

a Western Group: Musonoi (copper, cobalt); Ruwe (copper); Kamoto (copper, cobalt); Kolwezi (copper)
b Southern Group: Kipushi – Mine Prince Léopold (copper, zinc, germanium); Ruashi (copper); Karavia (copper)
c Central Group: Kambove (copper, cobalt); Fungurume (copper, cobalt); Kamatanda (copper)[111]

The second stage of the highly automated copper electrolytic plant at Luilu, just north of Kolwezi, started operations in March 1961, and the cobalt plant in June of the same year. This highly automated concentrator was among the most modern plants of its kind in the world. The complicated operations of crushing the ores and processing them by electrolysis into copper and cobalt metal were regulated automatically from a central control room. Work on the West Kambove Concentrator had begun in 1959 and this new facility became operational in mid-April 1961. Work constructing the Kakanda Concentrator began in 1960. Other planned installations included the underground works and concentrator at Kamoto, the company's largest copper mine so far. It was expected that the Kamoto mine would come into full operation only in 1970, and that it would take 15 years to develop before reaching its full production capacity.[112] About two-thirds of UMHK's copper was obtained by electrolytic processes at the plants in Jadotville, and at the new automated Luilu Plant, through hydrometallurgical treatment of oxidised concentrates coming mainly from the Western Group of mines. The refined metal was 99.95% pure. Blister copper (98.5%–99% pure) was obtained from the Lubumbashi Plant by thermal treatment of sulphuretted and oxidised concentrates mainly from the subterranean Mine Prince Léopold at Kipushi and was refined at Olen.[113]

Post-war production increasingly diversified to other metals than copper. About three-quarters of the cobalt mined in Katanga was obtained by a hydrometallurgical process at Jadotville and Luilu and transformed locally into marketable granules. The remainder was in the form of cobalt alloy refined at Olen. The Shinkolobwe mine, which had furnished uranium for the US atomic bomb programme during the war, was closed on 15 April 1961 and its mining equipment dismantled, but the company still produced nearly all of the world's radium, and they were also producing high volumes of zinc, cadmium and germanium concentrates. The latter metal was partially recovered from the furnace dusts of the Lubumbashi Plant. Final processing took place at Olen, where it was refined to extraordinary purity (impurity tolerance of one part per billion). Cadmium was obtained by electrolytic treatment of dusts and cements containing the metal recovered during metallurgical operations on copper and zinc concentrates. After concentration, most of the zinc was treated in roasting furnaces at Jadotville. Some of the concentrate was treated by hydrometallurgical methods in Katanga and some sent untreated to Olen.[114]

Concluding discussion

The development of mining in Central Africa required a unique set of financial, technical and management capabilities. Success meant the ability to raise the necessary funding, but it also meant the development of the requisite transport and communications, infrastructure including site installations and auxiliary services, and the management of the very large workforce. Besides needing to undertake major railway concerns, mining companies also embarked on financing other large-scale infrastructure projects such as hydroelectric power stations and dams and a great variety of ancillary services. Capital was also needed to erect the mills, smelters and plants themselves to process the ores. Vast amounts of coal had to be provided for railways and power plants, creating another large demand for capital. To facilitate and support the settlement of the workforce on a permanent basis, entire mining centres had to be constructed to house thousands of mining workers and their families. Living in large mining communities created new demands for accommodation, nutrition and sanitation as well as for clothing and various services such as health and social services. Mining companies therefore provided an important stimulus to the development of the society of the Central African economy, crossing as it did numerous ethnic and political boundaries across the Southern and Central African regions and triggering far-reaching changes in the social structures of the traditional African societies. Ultimately, capital gave an important stimulus to far-reaching changes in social structures of the mineral-rich countries in Central Africa and beyond. As Duignan and Gann (1975) have made clear, this multiplier-accelerator process pushed mineral-rich countries towards modernity.[115]

Notes

1 MU, TANKS, TC/179, Mr Studt's reports, 9 March 1926.
2 MU, TANKS, TC/179, A summary of statistics published in September 1925 by the *Metallgeselschaft* and the *Metallbank und Metallurgische Gesellschaft* of Frankfurt.
3 MU, TANKS, TC/179, Mr Studt's reports, 9 March 1926.
4 MU, TANKS, TC/179, Mr Studt's reports, 9 March 1926.
5 Heinrich 1958, 289; SGMH 1958; Declercq 2022b, 266–267.
6 MU, TANKS, TC/179, Mr Studt's reports, 9 March 1926. See also Declercq 2020, 207–215; Declercq 2022a, 254–256; Declercq 2019, 215–253.
7 MU, TANKS, TC/179, UMHK Technical Committee minutes, No. 516, 22 February 1926.
8 MU, TANKS, TC/179, Mr Studt's reports, 9 March 1926.
9 MU, TANKS, TC/179, Nichols Copper Contract, 8 December 1925; Nichols Refining Contract, 8 June 1926.
10 'Background to a Punctuated History' 2015, xxiv.
11 Hillman 1997, 153.
12 MU, TANKS, TC/180, F.E. Studt to Messrs. Robert Williams & Co., Élisabethville, 31 October 1913.
13 MU, TANKS, TC/179, Mr Studt's reports, 24 September 1926. See also Hillman 1997, 154–156.
14 MU, TANKS, TC/180, F.E. Studt to Messrs. Robert Williams & Co., Élisabethville, 5 February 1913.
15 Adams 1993, 491–501.
16 MU, TANKS, TC/179, UMHK Technical Committee minutes, No. 505, 4 December 1925.
17 MU, TANKS, TC/179, Mr Studt's reports, 23 February 1926.
18 MU, TANKS, TC/179, UMHK/Hoboken Joint Committee minutes, No. 71, 19 November 1925.
19 MU, TANKS, TC/179, Mr Studt's reports, 8 December 1925.
20 MU, TANKS, TC/180, F.E. Studt to Messrs. Robert Williams & Co., Élisabethville, 13 August 1913.
21 MU, TANKS, TC/179, Mr Studt's reports, 18 August 1926.
22 MU, TANKS, TC/179, Deloro Contract, 21 December 1925.
23 Rickard 1926, 20.

24 MU, TANKS, TC/179, Mr Studt's reports, June 1926.
25 *World Trade Information Service* 1954, 6–7.
26 TNA, FO 371/161517, UMHK, Reports of the Directors and Auditors Presented on the Annual General Meeting, 24 May 1962. See also Hutchinson and Martelli 1971, 227.
27 MU, TANKS, TC/179, Mr Studt's reports, 9 March 1926; *An Economic Survey of the Colonial Empire* 1935, 512–513; Pascual and Nadal 2008, 18–19; Birchard 1940, 430, 434–435.
28 MU, TANKS, TC/179, UMHK mines, work during first half 1926, 16 November 1926.
29 MU, TANKS, TC/179, Mr Studt's reports, 11 October; 2 December 1926.
30 MU, TANKS, TC/179, A.A. Thomson to R. Williams, 14 June 1925.
31 MU, TANKS, TC/179, Mr Studt's reports, 16 November 1926.
32 TANKS, MU, TC/179, Mr Studt's reports, 2 December 1926; quotation from Rickard 1926, 18.
33 *The Belgian Congo* 1944, 401–404.
34 Birchard 1940, 430.
35 Rickard 1926, 16.
36 MU, TANKS, TC/30, Riley & Harbord, metallurgical chemists, Report on the smelting of copper ores at the Girod Works, Ugine, 13 April 1912.
37 MU, TANKS, TC/179, Mr Studt's reports, 24 September 1926.
38 MU, TANKS, TC/179, R. Williams to Smith, 27 September 1924.
39 MU, TANKS, TC/179, R. Williams to A.A. Thomson, 8 January 1925.
40 MU, TANKS, TC/179, Smith to R. Williams, 10 October 1924.
41 MU, TANKS, TC/179, Mr Studt's reports, April 1926.
42 MU, TANKS, TC/179, Comparative cost of British and Wankie fuels, 31 December 1932.
43 MU, TANKS, TC/179, J.G. Watson, Élisabethville, 24 September 1926.
44 Hutchinson and Martelli 1971, 219–220. See also Varian 1953.
45 MU, TANKS, TC/127, F.E. Studt, 29 November 1944.
46 TNA, DO 35/385/5, Kansanshi Railway project, 12 June 1931.
47 TNA, CO 795/63/2, A.E. Owen, Controller of Stores & Transport, to the Chief Secretary, N. R. Government, Livingstone, 24 October 1933.
48 TNA, BT 31/36447/230671, Report of the Directors with Statement of Accounts, 30 September 1939.
49 TNA, BT 31/23845/148637, Memorandum and Articles of Association of the Anglo American Corporation of South Africa, 9 October 1917.
50 TNA, CO 795/63/2, Memorandum 'Railway connection with Kansanshi', n.d.
51 TNA, CO 795/63/2, The relative steamship fares between England and Lobito Bay and Cape Town, 24 October 1933.
52 TNA, CO 795/63/2, The Chief Secretary, Livingstone, 18 October 1933.
53 TNA, CO 795/63/2, Governor's Office, Livingstone, Northern Rhodesia, 27 November 1935. See also Särkkä 2021.
54 TNA, CO 795/63/2, The Rhodesia Railway, 5 May 1933.
55 *Bulawayo Chronicle* 25 February 1933.
56 TNA, CO 795/63/2, Memorandum 'Railway connection with Kansanshi', n.d.
57 TNA, CO 795/105/6, Memorandum 'British South Africa Company', n.d. See also Rönnbäck and Broberg 2022, 777–803.
58 TNA, PREM 8/1066, Northern Rhodesia mineral rights, Secretary of State for Colonies, 3 August 1949.
59 MU, TANKS, TC/179, Dr L. Mottoulle, the Principal Medical Officer of the Medical Department of UMHK, 4 September 1926.
60 MU, TANKS, TC/179, Dr L. Mottoulle, the Principal Medical Officer of the Medical Department of UMHK, 4 September 1926. See also Hanretta 1999, 305–335.

61 Henderson 1972, 47.
62 MU, TANKS, TC/179, Technical Committee minutes, No. 553, 15 October 1926.
63 MU, TANKS, TC/179, Technical Committee minutes, No. 547, 3 September 1926. See also Higginson 1989, 56.
64 MU, TANKS, TC/179, UM Native Labour on 24 October 1926.
65 TNA, CO 795/49/12, Report on the condition of mining camps of the UMHK, Dr H. de Boer, Deputy Director of Sanitary Services, 5 January 1932.
66 TNA, CO 795/49/12, Report on the condition of mining camps of the UMHK, Dr H. de Boer, Deputy Director of Sanitary Services, 5 January 1932.
67 For a literature review, see Parpart 1983; Perrings 1979; Fetter 1976; White 2000; Straube 2021.
68 MU, TANKS, TC/179, Use of native women labourers, January 1926.
69 Fetter 1976, 466; van Onselen 1976, 174–175; Cooper 2017, 148.
70 Coosemans 1997, 785; Higginson 1989, 35–36.
71 MU, TANKS, TC/179, Medical report for July 1925.
72 MU, TANKS, TC/179, UM natives on 12 September 1926.
73 MU, TANKS, TC/179, UM natives on 12 September 1926.
74 MU, TANKS, TC/179, UM native labour at the end of January 1926; UM native labour on 5 May 1926.
75 TNA, CO 795/49/12, Report on the condition of mining camps of the UMHK, Dr H. de Boer, Deputy Director of Sanitary Services, 5 January 1932. See also Higginson 1989, 40; Straube 2021, 27.
76 TNA, CO 795/49/12, Report on the condition of mining camps of the UMHK, Dr H. de Boer, Deputy Director of Sanitary Services, 5 January 1932.
77 MU, TANKS, TC/179, Native Labour on 15 July 1926; TNA, CO 795/49/12, Report on the condition of mining camps of the UMHK, Dr H. de Boer, Deputy Director of Sanitary Services, 5 January 1932.
78 TNA, CO 795/49/12, Report on the condition of mining camps of the UMHK, Dr H. de Boer, Deputy Director of Sanitary Services, 5 January 1932; Medical Department Order No. 54, Élisabethville, 22 December 1930.
79 MU, TANKS, TC/179, UM native labour on 5 June 1926.
80 MU, TANKS, TC/179, UM native labour on 25 October 1925.
81 TNA, CO 795/49/12, Report on the condition of mining camps of the UMHK, Dr H. de Boer, Deputy Director of Sanitary Services, 5 January 1932.
82 MU, TANKS, TC/179, UM natives on 12 September 1926.
83 MU, TANKS, TC/179, Mr Studt's reports, 23 November 1925.
84 MU, TANKS, TC/179, UMHK native labour, 6 December 1925.
85 TNA, CO 795/49/12, Report on the condition of mining camps of the UMHK, Dr H. de Boer, Deputy Director of Sanitary Services, 5 January 1932. *Cf.* Katzenellenbogen 1975, 386.
86 MU, TANKS, TC/179, UM medical reports Oct. 1925 – Dec. 1926.
87 TNA, CO 795/49/12, Report on the condition of mining camps of the UMHK, Dr H. de Boer, Deputy Director of Sanitary Services, 5 January 1932.
88 TNA, CO 795/49/12, Report on the condition of mining camps of the UMHK, Dr H. de Boer, Deputy Director of Sanitary Services, 5 January 1932.
89 MU, TANKS, TC/179, UM natives, 12 September 1926.
90 TNA, CO 795/49/12, Report on the condition of mining camps of the UMHK, Dr H. de Boer, Deputy Director of Sanitary Services, 5 January 1932.
91 TNA, CO 795/49/12, Report on the condition of mining camps of the UMHK, Dr H. de Boer, Deputy Director of Sanitary Services, 5 January 1932.
92 TNA, CO 795/49/12, Report on the condition of mining camps of the UMHK, Dr H. de Boer, Deputy Director of Sanitary Services, 5 January 1932. See also Higginson 1989, 73–74.

93 MU, TANKS, TC/179, UM native labour on 24 October 1926; TNA, CO 795/123/8, British Consulate General, Léopoldville, 10 September 1943.
94 MU, TANKS, TC/179, Technical Committee minutes, No. 550, 24 September 1926.
95 TNA, CO 795/8/154, British Consulate General, Léopoldville, 10 September 1943; Katzenellenbogen 1975, 377.
96 *Cf.* Young and Turner 1985, 289–290.
97 *The Belgian Congo* 1944, 404.
98 TNA, CO 795/123/8, British Consulate General, Léopoldville, 10 September 1943.
99 *The Belgian Congo* 1944, 401–404; Birchard 1940, 434–435; Hutchinson and Martelli 1971, 241–242.
100 TNA, WO 276/203, Memorandum on the International Defence Scheme of the Copper Belt, n.d. See also James 1996, 31.
101 TNA, CO 795/123/7, The Katanga Workers' Union Association, 1942.
102 Rickard 1926, 19. See also Money 2022.
103 Higginson 1988, 199–223.
104 TNA, CO 1015/938, '"New look" in African labour relations', O.O. Bennett, the General Manager of Rhokana Corporation, 15 August 1955.
105 Fabian 1973, 301.
106 Mitchell 1951, 20–27.
107 TNA, FO 371/161517, UMHK, Reports of the Directors and Auditors Presented on the Annual General Meeting, 24 May 1962.
108 TNA, FO 371/161517, Background information concerning UMHK, 9 August 1962.
109 TNA, FO 371161/557, Figures giving the position in regard to cobalt imports from Katanga, I.C.L. Alexander, 29 August 1962.
110 TNA, FO 371/161517, UMHK, Reports of Directors and Auditors Presented on the Annual General Meeting, 24 May 1962.
111 TNA, FO 371/161517, UMHK, Reports of Directors and Auditors Presented on the Annual General Meeting, 24 May 1962.
112 TNA, FO 371/187757, J.R. Cotton, H.M. Ambassador, Léopoldville, 2 May 1966.
113 TNA, FO 371/161517, UMHK, Reports of Directors and Auditors Presented on the Annual General Meeting, 24 May 1962.
114 TNA, FO 371/161517, UMHK, Reports of Directors and Auditors Presented on the Annual General Meeting, 24 May 1962.
115 Duignan and Gann 1975, 17–29.

References

Adams, A. (1993) 'The Origin of the Early Development of the Belgian Radium Industry', *Environment International*, 19:5, 491–501.

'Background to a Punctuated History' (2015) in M.J. de Wit, F. Guillocheau and M.C. J. de Wit eds. *Geology and Resource Potential of the Congo Basin*, Springer, Heidelberg, xi–xxxvii.

The Belgian Congo (1944) Great Britain Naval Intelligence Division, Geographical Handbook Series, London.

Birchard, R.E. (1940) 'Copper in the Katanga Region of the Belgian Congo', *Economic Geography*, 16:4, 429–436.

Bulawayo Chronicle (25 February1933) 'How to Get a Port on the West'.

Cooper, F. (2017) 'From Enslavement to Precarity? The Labor Question in African History' in W. Adebanwi ed. *Beyond the Margins: The Political Economy of Everyday Life in Africa*, James Currey, Martlesham, 135–156.

Coosemans, R. (1997) 'Occupational Health' in P.G. Janssens, M. Kivits and L. Vuylsteke eds. *Health in Central Africa since 1885: Past, Present and Future*, King Baudouin Foundation, Brussels, 781–798.

Declercq, R. (2019) 'Red Fever: Natural Resource Companies and the Global Copper Mining Frontier 1890–1939' in S. Joseph ed. *Commodity Frontiers and Global Capitalist Expansion: Social, Ecological and Political Implications from the Nineteenth Century to the Present Day*, Palgrave Macmillan, Cham, Switzerland, 215–253.

Declercq, R. (2020) 'Forging Cartels: A Transatlantic Perspective on Business Collusion and the Interwar Copper Industry (1918–1940)', *Scandinavian Economic History Review*, 68:3, 204–221.

Declercq, R. (2022a) 'The Congo Cartel: Governing Raw Materials Chains and Socio-Economic Stability 1918–1950' in M. Shanahan and S. Fellman eds. *A History of Business Cartels: International Politics, National Policies and Anti-Competitive Behaviour*, Routledge, New York and London, 249–265.

Declercq, R. (2022b) 'Katanga and the American World of Copper: Mechanization, Vertical Integration, and the Territorialization of Colonial Capitalism, 1900–30' in R. Declercq, D. Money and H.O. Frøland eds. *Born with a Copper Spoon: A Global History of Copper, 1830–1980*, The Chicago University Press, Chicago, IL, 253–273.

Duignan, P. and Gann, L.H. (1975) 'Introduction' in P. Duignan and L.H. Gann eds. *Colonialism in Africa 1870–1960*, Vol. 4: *The Economics of Colonialism*, Cambridge University Press, Cambridge, 1–30.

An Economic Survey of the Colonial Empire (1935) His Majesty's Stationery Office, London.

Fabian, J. (1973) 'Kazi: Conceptualizations of Labor in a Charismatic Movement among Swahili-Speaking Workers', *Cahiers d'Études africaines*, 50, 293–325.

Fetter, B. (1976) *The Creation of Elisabethville, 1910–1940*, Hoover Institution Press, Stanford University, Stanford, CA.

Hanretta, S. (1999) 'Space in the Discourses on the Elisabethville Mining Camps: 1923 to 1938' in F. Bernault ed. *Enfermement, prison et châtiments en Afrique: Du 19e siècle à nos jours*, Karthala, Paris, 305–335.

Heinrich, E.W. (1958) *Mineralogy and Geology of Radioactive Raw Materials*, McGraw-Hill Book Company, New York.

Henderson, I. (1972) *Labour and politics in Northern Rhodesia, 1900–1953: a study in the limits of colonial power*, PhD thesis, University of Edinburgh.

Higginson, J. (1988) 'Bringing the Workers Back in: Worker Protest and Popular Intervention in Katanga, 1931–1941', *Canadian Journal of African Studies / Revue Canadienne Des Études Africaines*, 22:2, 199–223.

Higginson, J. (1989) *A Working Class in the Making: Belgian Colonial Labour Policy, Private Enterprise, and the African Mineworker, 1907–1951*, The Wisconsin University Press, Madison.

Hillman, J. (1997) 'Chartered Companies and the Development of the Tin Industry in Belgian Africa, 1900–1939', *African Economic History*, 25, 149–173.

Hutchinson, R. and Martelli, G. (1971) *Robert's People: The Life of Sir Robert Williams Bart. 1860–1938*, Chatto & Windus, London.

James, A. (1996) *Britain and the Congo Crisis, 1960–63*, Macmillan, Houndmills, Basingstoke and London; St. Martin's Press, New York.

Katzenellenbogen, S. (1975) 'The Miner's Frontier, Transport and General Economic Development' in P. Duignan and L.H. Gann eds. *Colonialism in Africa 1870–1960*, Vol. 4: *The Economics of Colonialism*, Cambridge University Press, Cambridge, 360–426.

Mitchell, J.C. (1951) 'A Note on the Urbanization of Africans on the Copperbelt', *The Rhodes-Livingstone Journal*, 12, 20–27.

Money, D. (2022) *White Mineworkers on Zambia's Copperbelt, 1926–1974: In a Class of Their Own*, Brill, Leiden and Boston, MA.

The National Archives of the UK (TNA), Kew, Colonial Office (CO); Dominions Office (DO); Foreign Office (FO); Prime Minister's Office (PREM); War Office (WO).

Parpart, J.L. (1983) *Labour and Capital on the African Copperbelt*, Temple University Press, Philadelphia, PA.

Pascual, P. and Nadal, J. (2008) *El coure*, Vol. I: *Producció i consum a l'era industrial*, Eumo Editorial and La Farga Group, Vic.

Perrings, C. (1979) *Black Mineworkers in Central African Industry: Industrial Strategies and the Evolution of the African Proletariat in the Copperbelt, 1911–1941*, Holmes & Meier, New York; Heinemann, London.

Rickard, T.A. (2 January1926) 'A Journey to South Africa – VI', *Engineering and Mining Journal*, 121:1, 13–21.

Rönnbäck, K. and Broberg, O. (2022) 'From Defensive to Transformative Business Diplomacy: The British South Africa Company and the End of Chartered Company Rule in Rhodesia, 1910–1925', *Business History Review*, 96:4, 777–803.

Société Générale Métallurgique de Hoboken (SGMH) (1958) L. Cuypers, Bruxelles.

Straube, C. (2021) *After Corporate Paternalism: Material Renovation and Social Change in Times of Ruination*, Berghahn, New York, Oxford.

Särkkä, T. (2021) *Paper and the British Empire: The Quest for Imperial Raw Materials, 1861–1960*, Routledge, London.

van Onselen, C. (1976) *Chibaro: African Mine Labour in Southern Rhodesia 1900–1933*, Pluto Press, London.

Varian, H.F. (1953) *Some African Milestones*. George Ronald, Wheatley, Oxford.

White, L. (2000) *Speaking with Vampires: Rumor and History in Colonial Africa*, University of California Press, Berkeley.

World Trade Information Service (1954) Part 4, Bureau of Foreign Commerce, U.S. Department of Commerce, Washington, DC.

Young, C. and Turner, T. (1985) *The Rise and Decline of the Zairean State*, The University of Wisconsin Press, Madison.

7 A post-colonial view of the Central African mining industry

This chapter focuses on the developments leading to the nationalisation of the *Union Minière du Haut-Katanga* (UMHK) and the birth of the new Congolese takeover company, the *Société Générale Congolaise des Minérais* (Gécomin), and the subsequent negotiations dealing with compensation for being nationalised. The literature dealing with the decolonisation in the Belgian Congo leading to its independence on 30 June 1960 and to the subsequent political, economic and military turmoil known as the 'Congo Crisis' is voluminous and comprehensive. Previous studies have revealed the roles played by the United Nations (UN), Belgium, the United States, Britain, the Soviet Union and the neighbouring Central African Federation and Angola in the crisis. Missing from this corpus, however, is an in-depth analysis of the pivotal role played by UMHK, the largest company in the Congo, and especially the preponderant role played by its parents, Tanganyika Concessions (Tanks) and the *Société Générale de Belgique* (SGB), with their significant and numerous subsidiary companies.

The birth of *Union Minière, Société Anonyme Belge*

> The only desire of the Union Miniére is to continue its operations undisturbed and in peace, in order to provide its contribution, in future as in the past, to the prosperity of the Congo and its people, at the same time ensuring a fair return of the savings which have been entrusted to it in the form of capital investment.[1]

The physical separation of the Copperbelt from Léopoldville, the administrative capital of the Congo, encouraged the growth of separate identities dating back to the early colonial epoch. Less than a week before Congolese independence on 30 June 1960, Katanga openly threatened to proclaim its secession, and then, a few days after independence, it did secede from the new Republic of the Congo-Léopoldville (altered in 1964 to the Democratic Republic of the Congo), in which it was not to be reintegrated for nearly three momentous years during which the Central Government exerted no real power whatever in Katanga.[2]

DOI: 10.4324/9781003247371-7

Only a few days prior to the granting of independence, the Belgian Government (very probably at UMHK's own instigation) introduced legislation by which companies operating in the Congo were granted permission to transfer their registered headquarters (*siège social*) to Belgium. By taking advantage of this, UMHK was able at the last moment to change its domicile to its former, 1931 registered address at 6 rue Montagne du Parc, Brussels and to remove a substantial part of its assets out of the reach of Congolese jurisdiction. At the same time UMHK declared that it had deleted *Haut-Katanga* (Upper-Katanga) from its name and reorganised itself as a Brussels-based listed company *Union Minière, Société Anonyme Belge* (UM, altered in 2001 to its present name, Umicore).[3]

The Central Government was thus deprived of its main source of foreign currency and of local revenue during the crucial period when, owing to widespread internal disorders, the economy of the country collapsed almost overnight. At the same time the new Brussels-based UM was obliged to submit to the secessionist provincial government (*i.e.* the Katanga Government), headed by President Moïse Tshombe (Tshombé) (1919–69), a fact which might have given the widely accepted impression that Belgian and British financial interests were backing his regime.[4] The measures which were imposed on UM by the Katanga Government applied especially to the methods of transfer of foreign exchange arising from the sale of the company's products on the world market. Under a Katangese decree of 12 September 1960, UM, in common with all exporters, was obliged to surrender the foreign exchange arising from the sale of its products on the world market to the Katanga Government, and foreign exchange earned by exports from Katanga had to be transferred solely to the *Banque Nationale du Katanga.* [5] In 1961 payments to the Katanga Government were £15 million in royalties, duties, taxes and dividends, while no payments were made to the Central Government. This meant that roughly 70% of the total yearly returns of UM (taxes, dividends, royalties and duties) went to the Tshombe Government, with private shareholders being allocated the rest.[6]

Whether this situation was legally or morally justifiable was a matter of debate throughout the world, and passions ran high on both sides. UM's stand was that the theoretical question of whether Tshombe's regime should exist should not be confused with the practical certainty that it did exist and had, moreover, demonstrated its capacity to enforce its will.[7] UM emphasised that it was not free to choose to whom it paid its taxes, given that its installations were entirely situated in Katanga and were controlled by the Katangese authorities, who were in a position to impose fiscal and other dispositions on all undertakings operating in their territory. Failure of UM to comply with local law would have been interpreted by the authorities as an act of insubordination against the Tshombe Government. Non-compliance would have resulted in serious penalties and could have caused a stoppage of work in the mines and the plants of the company as well as in enterprises whose activities were directly or indirectly connected with those of UM. Such a stoppage would have strangled the economic and social life of Katanga, depriving a large population of its means of subsistence, and schools, hospitals and other social welfare establishments, for which the mining sector had traditionally assumed responsibility, would have soon lost their means of support.[8]

While UM and Tanks were themselves not reluctant to accede to demands of Tshombe's regime, regarding its secession as the best means of safeguarding their investments in Katanga whatever happened to the rest of the Congo, world reaction was mixed. Importantly the United Nations (UN) opposed breaking up the Congo and was against recognising Katanga. To guarantee the occupation of Élisabethville the UN deployed heavily armed troops. The heavy fighting between UN troops and Katangese troops making up the Katangese Gendarmerie along with European mercenaries brought about various disturbances in the operations of UM. Installations in Élisabethville, Kolwezi, Luilu and the Le Marinel Power Station suffered bombardments from UN aircraft. The Lubumbashi Plant was shut down on 6 December 1961, and as soon as a ceasefire came into effect on 19 December the plant was occupied by UN troops who did not evacuate until 20 February 1962. In addition, all the high-tension lines in the neighbourhood of the Lubumbashi Plant were cut, with the consequence that operations at the Kipushi mine were stopped for about a month because of the lack of electrical power.[9]

The conflict did not have serious repercussions on the 1960–1 production, which in the cases of copper and zinc was superior to the 1957–9 production, and only for cobalt was production slightly lower (Table 7.1). Production then virtually ceased until March 1962 when it regained its normal level.

Although the fall of Tshombe's regime was followed by an agreement for the payment of UM's dues to the Central Government, this gesture was clearly insufficient to eliminate the long-standing hostility between the Central Government and Katanga on the one hand and between the Central Government and UM on the other. The Congolese authorities were determined to exercise strict control over UM in a way that the Colonial Government or Katanga Government had been neither able nor willing to exercise in the past. Strong Congolese participation in the direction and management of UM was to be expected as well.[10]

Table 7.1 Production of the principal products of UMHK/UM, 1957–61 (tons and kg)

	1957	*1958*	*1959*	*1960*	*1961*
Copper, tons	240,280	235,586	280,403	300,675	293,509
Cobalt, tons	8,115	6,501	8,431	8,222	8,326
Zinc concentrates, tons	188,183	200,017	117,778	193,004	183,050
Germanium, kg	9,065	16,255	13,643	25,101	13,549

Source: TNA, FO 371/161517, Background information concerning UMHK, 9 August 1962; UMHK, Reports of the Directors and Auditors Presented at the Annual General Meeting on May 24, 1962.

By virtue of a convention signed on 23 June 1960 in Brussels, the concessionary powers of the *Comité Spécial du Katanga* (CSK) were terminated by the Belgian Government and its assets were divided so that the *Compagnie du Katanga* (CK) got one-third of its shares in UM while the remaining two-thirds were to be held in trust by the Belgian Government pending the expiration of CSK's concession. CSK's portfolio was finally released to the Congo on 6 February 1965, officially dissolving CSK's parastatal organisation and transferring the responsibility of administering and policing Katanga to the Congolese Government, which thus became the owner of 17.95% of the shares and 23.8% of the voting rights of UM. This represented the biggest voting bloc controlled by any single interested party including Tanks (20.21%), CK (12.9%), the *Société Générale* group (6.94%) and the other interested parties (36.13% in total). Following the dissolution of CSK three Belgian directors, Messrs. A. Gillaume, E. Gordia and J.P. Paulus, as well as Captain Waterhouse, the Chairman of Tanks, tendered their resignation from the board of UM. These vacant directorships were filled by electing four Congolese directors, Chief Lumanga, Great Chief Mwenda Munongo, Monsieur B. Mwepu and Monsieur C. Nzau, signifying that the management structure based on the military ranking of the colonial-era 'pioneers' had finally been broken down. Yet no one suggested that the Congolese directors should actually try to manage the company – the Chair of the board was conferred upon Monsieur Edgar van der Straeten, a UM senior executive.[11]

When Commander-in-Chief Joseph Désiré Mobutu (1930–97) seized power in November 1965, two new ingredients were added to the brew. First was his personal antipathy to Katangese separatism, which had come to the fore when, as the leader of the country's armed forces, and with the Congolese troops at his disposal, he had failed to settle the Katanga secession, which had to be subjugated by the UN troops. Second, there was his personal antipathy towards UM, which he roundly accused of supporting the secession of Katanga and continuing to support Tshombe. Mobutu never forgave UM and the mining business for what he considered was a deliberate attempt to strangle the infant republic at birth. It showed him that Katanga still considered itself very much a separate entity and that UM continued to operate as a state within a state in the old colonial ways.[12]

Meanwhile, Mobutu found his plans to rebuild a new Congo dependent at every turn on increased supplies of foreign exchange. But mining interests in the Congo, of which UM was the cornerstone, hesitated to give him the help he needed. Determined to bring UM to its knees, he counted on the support of the other newly born African states – indeed, he would convince them of his own nationalistic spirit. If his attack failed, he could lay the blame on the hated *haute finance internationale* and Western colonialism; if he succeeded, he could take all the credit and could claim to have achieved the economic independence of his country. 'The day was not far off when the Congolese people would finally triumph against imperialism,' Brazzaville radio declared, praising the courage and nationalism of Mobutu.[13]

The nationalisation of Katanga copper

> UM refusal to consider the conditions of the Congolese is understandable, it would have amounted to forced labour.[14]

During the Congo Crisis the collapse of other sectors of the economy, especially agriculture, as opposed to the increase in production at the mines, magnified UM's importance in both relative and absolute terms. The gross operating results were positively influenced by the favourable conditions on the non-ferrous metal markets. The copper market was characterised by steeply rising prices. Demand for copper was brisk, stimulated in the United States by the Vietnam War effort, and in Europe by strong economic growth. The world copper output reached some 4,940,000 tons in 1965 against 4,760,000 in 1964, an increase of 3.8%. Nevertheless there was a shortage throughout the year. The political situation arising from the independence of Zambia (Northern Rhodesia) in 1964, and the political and social trouble which preceded the passing of legislation on 'Chileanization' of the copper industry in Chile in 1967, added to the consumer's fear for the copper supply. Prices on LME were characterised by very large increases. They were sometimes disordered fluctuations caused by speculative operations, which resulted in differences of up to £60 from one day to the next.[15] From 1963 to 1966 UM struggled with Southern African producers to maintain a profitable but steady copper price. When the Chileans announced their price increase, UM immediately consulted the Zambian and South African mining finance groups, and together they decided that the price of copper on the London market must be brought down to a more reasonable level, and if possible below £500 per ton. To do this it was necessary to break the price control arrangements and sell as much as possible on the open market. The result of these price-fixing measures was that the price on the London market did fall below £500 per ton.[16]

Meanwhile, UM was able to maintain a high level of investment (despite a good deal of difficulties with the Central Government regarding foreign exchange receipts) and was constantly in the financial news with announcements of increased production and dividends, and increased prices. They were investing three billion Belgian francs in 1966 (compared with 1.2 billion BEF in 1964 and somewhere between the two figures in 1965). UM did not declare a dividend in 1962 (for 1961). They were prevented from paying in 1962 and decided not to try in 1963, 1964 and 1965. In 1966 UM secured agreement with the Central Government to the payment from 7 June 1966 of the balance of the 1961 dividend (150 BEF per share) together with a small dividend of 200 Belgian francs per share for 1965 (the equivalent of only one-quarter of the dividend for 1961). Meanwhile, their gross sales in 1966 were expected to be about 16 billion Belgian francs (compared with about 15 billion BEF in 1965). The net profits for 1964 were 566,000,000 Belgian francs.[17] No wonder that the owners were getting nervous about their share of the profits.

Increases in copper prices together with the rise in the company's output meant substantially higher income in foreign currency for the Congo Government. UM's production for the year 1965 contributed 13,094 million Congolese francs to the state budget. The profits of UM attracted heavy deductions as a consequence of the dual taxation of a very complicated exchange mechanism, however. In 1965, the amount deducted was 54% (1,773 million BEF) of the operating profits after payment of taxes and export duties.[18] Though at the current high copper prices the company was still making a profit, despite all the deductions it now bore.

UM's strongest card in any bargaining with the Mobutu Government lay in the threat that any disruption of mineral production or sales would immediately reveal itself in the Congolese economy. The company also possessed two other important advantages. First, its integration with the *Société Générale Métallurgique de Hoboken* (SGMH) and the *Société Générale des Minerais* (SGM) for refining the mineral ores and marketing the copper and the cobalt it produced, and with its other affiliates for the purposes of research, recruitment of staff and the supply of machinery. Its second advantage was its hold over the vital skilled workforce in Katanga. For his part, Mobutu believed that UM needed the Congo at least as much as the Congo needed UM. And if European workers left, others could always be found. As far as the economy was concerned, since the Congo had done without the revenue of UM before, it could do so again.[19] But the Congolese actions were dictated far more by political and psychological considerations than by any rational calculation of what could in fact be achieved.

Relations between the Central Government and UM hit rock-bottom in early May 1966. The opening gambit of Mobutu's anti-colonial campaign came in a press interview on 3 May in which he criticised UM for behaving like a state within a state. This was a trumped-up affair to prepare the ground for the new tax and other measures he had in mind which were imposed on 6 May, comprising three (a–c) new decrees: (a) to raise the export tax of copper from 17% to 30%, (b) 10% of all strategic materials mined in the Congo should revert to the Congolese State, and (c) all firms established under Congolese Law had to transfer their Head Office to Kinshasa (Léopoldville) by midnight on 1 January 1967.[20] The government also announced their intention to close their railway link with the Benguela Railway and to cut off UM's communications between Lubumbashi (Élisabethville) and Brussels. There was no consultation with UM before these decisions were taken and announced. UM calculated that, taking account of the earnings of the Congolese authorities on the shares they held in the company, those authorities were already receiving 85% of the company's annual revenues. If the new measures were applied in full, they would receive nearly all (98%), so they would effectively be taking over control of the company.[21]

Politically the Mobutu Government grew more and more resentful of foreign influence in the Congo and did all it could to redirect Katanga's trade to government-controlled channels. Political pressure had always been brought to bear by the capital in favour of the Matadi route (*i.e. Voie Nationale*), a preference quite opposed to the interests of the industrial producers in Katanga. In 1966, roughly 42% of UM copper was transported to the world market by the Matadi route, with the remainder distributed via the Lobito (30%), Beira (21%) and Dar es Salaam routes (8%) (the *Compagnie du chemin de fer du Congo supérieur aux Grands Lacs africains*' railway to Albertville on Lake Tanganyika).[22] In May 1966 the Mobutu Government announced that exports of Katanga copper via the Lobito route would cease from midnight on 30 June, and all copper would thereafter be carried via the Matadi or Dar es Salaam routes – despite the fact that the Matadi route and the Dar es Salaam route were manifestly incapable of handling UM's copper and other mineral exports, let alone the whole of Katanga's requirements of imported goods (*e.g.* machinery, chemicals and gas oil).[23] Given the mood of the government at that time, it was no good telling them flatly, as UM may have wished to do, that it would be impossible to act on their decision successfully. The only thing for UM to do was to make a show of appearing to be helpful, while gently pointing out with facts and figures the real consequences of the closure of the Lobito route. Given the fact that the handling of Katanga's exports was a traditional and an important part of the Benguela Railway's business, any diminution of traffic, particularly the export of Katanga copper and other minerals, could have serious consequences for the Benguela Railway Company and consequently Tanks, which held a 90% interest in the company.[24] The primary aim of the government's boycott of the Lobito route, however, was said to be to build up a *Voie Nationale*, with curbing the influence of UM being secondary. But there was also the need to earn currency and revenue for the Congo and, of course, there was the question of providing employment for the Congolese people.

There was little doubt that Mobutu was fully committed to his anti-colonial campaign, aimed principally at UM, which with its affiliates had an interest that embraced the Congolese economy as a whole. The Mobutu Government accused UM of – amongst other things – having deliberately provoked the Katangese secessionist movement in order to repatriate from the Congo millions of francs which were then invested in other countries for their own profit. The campaign was not principally directed at UM (though fear and jealousy of the latter had a marked effect on Mobutu's thinking) but was part and parcel of Mobutu's determination to assert the economic independence of the Congo. Although Mobutu was himself a fervent nationalist, he was also an economic illiterate who therefore relied on a widely disparate group of personal advisers drawn largely from the ranks of young, inexperienced and recently graduated Congolese economists, whose only common denominator was resentment of foreign financial interests that were seen as an obstacle to the exercise of the Congo's economic sovereignty. The conflicting nature of the advice Mobutu received explains his repeated tendency to rush into promulgating decrees which it was impossible to implement. Furthermore he was headstrong and impulsive by nature and too inexperienced to grasp the magnitude of risk involved in executing his new decrees.[25]

With the threat of a new mining law in the wind as well, UM was in the dark about Mobutu's motives and intentions. The threat that Mobutu might one day unilaterally revise or cancel its concession altogether put the company's future on hold. What would happen next now seemed anyone's guess. There was considerable mistrust of Mobutu in UM following his frequent explosive anti-colonial talk and the political turmoil created in Katanga by his recent acts. But was he really a man to do a 'Mossadegh Act', to nationalise UM, just as Mohammad Mosaddegh, the Prime Minister of Iran, had done with the Anglo-Iranian Oil Company by revoking its concession in 1951? Or was it more likely that Mobutu was just seeking to bring UM to heel? Nothing so important and courageous as this had been undertaken by an African Head of State since President Nasser's nationalisation of the Suez Canal Company in 1956.[26]

The real blow came in the form of enforcement of the Bakajika law (*Loi Bakajika*) by virtue of which the Congo State appropriated to itself all the property and mining rights conceded before independence.[27] The law required the re-registration of all claims to cessions or concessions of land, thus implicitly cancelling UM's concession. UM stood to lose a great deal in the subsequent negotiations which took place in Kinsasha in October 1966. The UM delegation consisted of four members, two Belgian and two British. They were M. Louis Wallef, the President of the board of UM and the leading board member of the *Société Générale* group; Gérard S. Assoignon, the Managing Director of UM in Africa and also a director of SGB; Lord Colyton (Henry Hopkinson, 1st Baron Colyton, 1902–96), who had served under Winston Churchill as Secretary for Overseas Trade from 1951 to 1952 and as Minister of State for Colonial Affairs from 1952 to 1955 before he was appointed as a director of Tanks in June 1957 and then as Chairman in September 1966; and R.F. Medlicott, a director of Tanks and Barclays Bank among his other directorates. Colyton and Medlicott were also Tanks' representatives on the board of UM.

Colyton arrived in Kinshasa on 15 October and had audiences with President Mobutu and the Minister of Transport, Victor Nendaka, before the arrival of his colleagues on 18 October. He was very cordially received by both and was subsequently invited by the President to a private dinner party to celebrate the birth of his seventh child. Colyton had been impressed by Mobutu, who outlined with some moderation his external policy of aiming to strengthen relations with his African neighbours and his internal policy of economic independence. Mobutu stressed that it was not his intention to nationalise anything. Both he and Nendaka stressed to Colyton that they were not Communist-inclined and welcomed private investment and private enterprise in the Congo. Mobutu was however quite frank about expressing his suspicions that UM had links with the secessionist movement in Katanga, a suspicion which Colyton tried to disabuse him of.[28] Mobutu felt there was a conflict of generations between him and senior UM executives. Wallef, who belonged to the 'pioneers' of the early colonial years, adopted a very dictatorial and hectoring tone, saying that he, Wallef, had 'come to the Congo in 1924', to which Mobutu rejoined that he, Mobutu, 'had been born in 1930'.[29]

The other members of the Congolese negotiations team were Albert Ndele Bamu (1930–2023), the President of the National Bank of the Congo; Jean-Baptiste Kibwe (1924–2008), a director of UM; Justin-Marie Bomboko (1928–2014), the Foreign Minister; and Gérard Kamanda wa Kamanda (1940–2016), the President's Secretary General and a Marxist lawyer, who was intelligent, persuasive and passionately nationalist. During the discussions the Congolese made it clear that they considered the 1960 Belgian law under which UM had been enabled to transfer its domicile to Brussels to be illegal. At this point a long and involved argument followed as to whether the Bakajika law was nationalisation, or rather expropriation in the form of a purely national law intended to supersede international agreements reached between the former colonial government and UMHK. Another argument which the Congolese negotiations team tried to expound to UM was that 60% of installations and concessions belonged to the Congolese Government in any case (*fait du prince*).[30] The original charter of UMHK, dated 30 October 1906, stipulated that the concession would last for 90 years, and that on 11 March 1990 the Congo would acquire all the rights of the company and immediately acquire possession of the mines, their installations and equipment. Because in 1966 the period of the concession had already run almost two-thirds of its allotted time, two-thirds of the installations and property of UM therefore already belonged to the Congo. UM, therefore, could not properly speak of expropriation because the Congo could not expropriate something which already belonged to them (this is the reasoning the Congolese tried to expound to the UM directors).[31]

It was a very stormy meeting, during which all sorts of red herrings were brought into the negotiations and Ndele spent a large amount of time shouting and banging the table with his fist. The timing of the negotiations seemed to be entirely in favour of the Congolese. Mobutu had recovered a good deal of political power since July 1966. He had established a military government in Katanga, and, with the help of the Americans, broken the Kisangani Mutiny, during which the Katangese Gendarmerie and European mercenaries had mutinied against the Central Government. Meanwhile he had steadily reduced UM directors' morale down to the point where they were wondering whether it was even worth continuing to bargain.[32]

Whatever the outcome, Mobutu had already done his international reputation great harm. If he had signed the agreement, UM negotiators would have returned home saying that here at last was a Congolese government with which they could do business, and this confidence would be arriving at the moment when the Congo was desperately in need of foreign currency to meet its overseas commitments. There was a feeling among UM directors that Mobutu was motivated by a sort of love-hate for Belgium and UM, and that ultimately he would not dare to try to nationalise UM.[33] It was felt by the UM directors that the Congo was manifestly in a big enough mess already without adding the massive economic upheaval that would follow nationalisation. It was anticipated that UM nationalisation would lead to a massive exodus of European workers, the sole result of which would be to bring about a complete shutdown of production.

UM was deeply suspicious of the leftist training of the group of young nationalist intellectuals around Mobutu, his 'young Turks' as they were referred to by the UM negotiators, and their talk of re-establishing relations with the Soviet Union. On the other hand, UM was equally suspicious of the intentions of the French and the Americans, and also, to some extent, of Nippon Mining Co., which had been in the Congo for some months negotiating a concession in the Sakania area. The Japanese were interested not only in copper but also in cobalt, though they conducted themselves with such obvious caution that UM had no exaggerated fears in their direction. The Americans, who had no direct commercial interest in the negotiations, probably calculated that the more money the Congolese managed to squeeze out of UM, the less financial assistance they would be called upon to provide for the Congo in the long run.[34] UM was afraid that someone might stab them in the back in order to take over their assets and concession in Katanga. This was the main reason why UM was so anxious to bring in Colyton and Medlicott to the negotiations, their 'British friends', as the Belgian directors of UM liked to call them. They felt the need for an ally. Another reason was that the moderates in the company felt that the pragmatism and experience of their British partners in dealing with ex-colonies might give the negotiations a better chance of success than if the old inflexible UM diehards, Wallef and his colleagues, conducted negotiations alone. They had little patience to withstand what Wallef regarded as the 'distasteful treatment' by the former colony.[35]

On the morning of Thursday 1 December, the National Radio of the Congo broadcast a vitriolic attack on UM, saying that the negotiations had once again proved that UM had learned nothing from history, possessed a colonialist attitude and was a supreme example of colonial exploitation. On 8 December Mobutu decided to discontinue negotiations with UM and reissued his ultimatum that the company must transfer its Head Office back to Kinshasa by midnight on 1 January 1967 or he would permanently revoke all its concessions and issue a decree for their expropriation without compensation.[36] Mobutu justified his demands by stating that UM was not a Belgian company – it had been a Congolese company since its inception. The Congolese claim had been reinforced during the German occupation of Belgium in 1940–5 when the company headquarters had been evacuated to the Congo. During the war UMHK played a vital role in the Allied war effort, thus reinforcing its agency as a Congolese company. In 1960, however, just 13 days before Congolese independence, UMHK had suddenly decided without consulting the Congolese to move its domicile to Brussels on the basis of a juridical *manoeuvre* based on the view that the Congo and Belgium constituted at that time a unitary state governed by the King of the Belgians.

Are there any other considerations that might have contributed to the breakdown of the talks? In spite of the push for economic independence, it may seem surprising that the members of Mobutu's regime would actually want to deprive themselves at this stage of their convenient public enemy number one, UM, the great representative of *la haute finance internationale*, by coming to the endgame of nationalising the company. But instead of keeping UM as a scapegoat, how much more satisfactory for Mobutu it must have been to be able to declare to the Congolese populace that there was a conflict of generations here, and that he, Mobutu, had tired of trying to be reasonable with UM, and that henceforth UM would once again be a Congolese company conforming to Congolese laws whether UM liked it or not, and that a final financial compensation settlement would be left until the day when the senior and diehard UM military hierarchy had left the scene for good.[37]

UM also had good reason to complain about their treatment locally. Since the Kisangani Mutiny had been crushed in July 1966, searches of UM premises and interrogations and arrests of its personnel had become almost daily occurrences at Lubumbashi, Kipushi and Kolwezi. The government radio and press organs, *Le Progrès* among them, were endlessly pouring out against UM 'venomous ill-founded accusations', as Wallef regarded them. Amongst other things, the government accused UM of a deliberate policy of destroying the value of the Congolese franc, of trafficking foreign currency, of selling copper and other minerals clandestinely to Poland, Czechoslovakia and Romania, and of building up stockpiles of those minerals outside the Congo and refusing to repatriate the foreign currency earnings to the Congo. These and other accusations would then be used to justify the creation of a new Congolese company, to oust UM from the Katangese mining business once and for all and to undermine the financial power of SGB (which to the Congolese agitators was more or less synonymous with high finance).[38]

But besides threatening words, on 21 December 1966 two companies of the *Armée Nationale Congolaise*, the 2nd Paratrooper Battalion and an advance unit of the 12th Infantry Battalion, arrived from Kisangani and Kindu and were promptly organised into heavily armed joint patrols with the police in Lubumbashi, Jadotville and Kolwezi. On 22 December, on instructions from Kinshasa, the troops began house to house searches for arms and military clothing throughout the towns of Katanga.[39] They were roaming the streets and outskirts of these towns regularly and making periodic *actes de présence* at UM installations and offices to the extent that the government mouthpiece, *La Dépêche*, 'the eternal troublemaker', as UM directors regarded it, felt obliged on 23 December to announce in the headline of its special edition that fears of imminent civil war were unfounded.[40]

A day later Mobutu in a speech to the Parliament announced that in order to continue the activities of the most important sector of the Congolese economy (UM being legally unable to continue to exploit the mines in Katanga), the Congolese Government was transferring the rights of UM to a new Congolese company, the *Société Générale Congolaise des Minérais* (Gécomin). The company would be 60% owned by the Congolese Government, with the remainder available for international investment. At the same time, a wholly Congolese board of management with nine directors was appointed. The Congolese Government also announced that it would expropriate all the other assets and properties of UM in the Congo.[41]

The birth of Gécomin

On 1 January 1967 UM's concession and installations were unilaterally invalidated by the new Congolese mining law and were turned over to 'the sons of the country'. Nine Congolese directors were appointed to the board of UM, with Jean-Baptiste Kibwe as Chairman. The Mobutu Government also announced that they would expropriate all the other assets in the Congo owned by, controlled by or associated with UM. In total 13 such companies were seized, their boards sacked and replaced with Congolese directors.[42] The result was 'an obscene scramble for freebies' by the burgeoning Congolese elite as Wrong (2000) has put it.[43]

Before UM was relieved of all its property in Katanga and of the mining and other rights which were conceded to it under the Concession Agreement dated 30 October 1906, the company's principal object had been specified as the development and operation of mines situated in Katanga. So this expropriation deprived UM of its principal foundation, and any orientation of the company's activities towards Katanga was now deleted.[44] Gécomin Kinshasa had no further contact with UM Brussels. Contact with UM's purchasing, financial and research services and with the Hoboken Refinery in Belgium was lost as well. Telephone and telex communications with UM were completely blocked by the Congolese authorities, and so were UM bank accounts, so that no salaries or other payments could be made.[45]

The result was chaos in the affairs at both ends of the business. Imminent problems were as follows. (1) The payment of salaries in light of the blockage of UM bank accounts and the Central Government's lack of resources. (2) A shortage of labour. Normally there were 1,700 Europeans working, but following the exodus of Europeans after independence there were only 1,300 left to operate the installations. There was a worldwide shortage of skilled labour for copper mining and processing. If all Europeans left Katanga, the Congo would never be able to recruit a sufficient number of skilled replacements from anywhere in the world, either in the East or in the West, to keep operations going. (3) Low morale among the staff. Although the military sweeps had ceased temporarily, the Congo was very much a police state. Harassment had taken its toll on morale, and especially among migrant African employees. The Rwandans – who made up some 50% of the underground miners – were now a major target of the government's agitators. Besides the fact that the company was rapidly losing its workforce, another worry was that there could be demonstrations, leading to a flare-up, if food supplies (particularly the staple diet of mealy meal) dried up. (4) The run-down of equipment, refining materials etc. (5) The loss of UM recruiting, buying and research facilities in Brussels.[46]

There was a pervasive sense of uncertainty about the future of the mining industry around which the economy and society of Katanga revolved. Apart from the chaos it was creating in Gécomin, it added to the great economic uncertainty in the Congo as a whole. The mere fact that the board of management was to remain exclusively in Congolese hands led to innumerable difficulties. UM had to stop all local payments while their bank account was blocked. A Gécomin bank account was opened but the rule of the new company, dictated from Kinshasa, was that only the new self-styled *administrateur délégué*, the resident Managing Director, Emmanuel Kini, could sign decisions, however minor. If there was anything in the paperwork he hesitated to authorise he postponed action. Kini knew nothing whatever about mining or copper production. He was answerable to Kamanda, the President's Secretary General, who passed the presidential resolutions to the board. In consequence the board, either under instructions or on their own volition, were interfering grossly in the day-to-day working of the administration. They insisted on seeing and countersigning every paper, and even all cheques issued for minor expenditure. Soon there were 6,000 documents awaiting Kini's countersignature. The Congolese directors of UM were continually accusing the staff of European descent of attempting in some underhand way or another to diminish or delay production. Furthermore, inspections at one mining centre or another become almost weekly drills.[47] The Congolese directors were quite capable, by their own acts of interference, not only of bringing the administration to a standstill, but also of driving the personnel to such depths of frustration that they were often compelled to hand in their resignation. UM thought that the only way of ensuring satisfactory operation of the company was to allow personnel to get on with their job without vexatious interference and to have on board mining engineers and experts. UM personnel were out of the question and recruitment of outside mining technicians, with the necessary qualifications and language skills, proved difficult, however.[48]

Meanwhile, the economic situation in the Congo was precarious. Since 24 December 1966 UM's exports – which represented between 60% and 70% of all the exports of the Congo – had been halted.[49] The Congolese Exchequer depended on UM not only for between 60% and 70% of its foreign exchange, but also for some 30%–40% of its internal revenue from taxation. The Congo, therefore, found itself not only running out of foreign exchange but also running out of revenue from tax sources as well.[50] Foreign exchange reserves were exhausted and on top of this about 70,000 tons of Katangese copper valued at £70 million was awaiting shipment from the ports of Matadi and Dar es Salaam, but there were no purchasers in view of UM's threat to proceed legally against potential buyers. Gécomin's hard currency commitments included not only the salaries of the employees but also orders for the imported coal, petroleum products and expensive spare parts and machinery which were required to keep the installations going. The Congo was facing its greatest economic crisis since independence, and UM had no intention of bailing Mobutu's regime out. The President had shown himself irresponsible, immature and badly advised in embarking on a course that could bring great harm to the Congo and in particular to Katanga, without reflecting on the consequences. He had vanquished the Goliath but killed the economy. No investor, large or small, would ever again have the confidence to invest in the Congo.[51] The confidence in the future and in Congolese promises had gone with the wind.

This hasty, ill-prepared nationalisation left the Congolese with serious problems, with the issue of the 'pipeline' (*i.e.* copper and other products which had been exported from the Congo but had not yet been sold to outside customers) being the most important because of its considerable financial significance. In 1966, UM, in anticipation of a takeover, had been sending everything possible to the pipeline. In order to prevent UM from injecting any further minerals into it, all exports had been suspended from 23 December 1966 onwards, but in doing so the government had failed to make alternative arrangements for selling copper and other minerals and were thus denied the hard currency proceeds which were vital to them. The copper in the pipeline was estimated to be worth about £70 million, and was at the same time Gécomin's most easily realisable asset and a buffer stock to guard against contingencies and interruptions in production. Without it the company could not meet its various contractual obligations to its customers and employees. At this stage the US Government chose to intervene in the dispute by producing a set of proposals under which the Congolese would continue to make use of the personnel of the UM for the operation of the mines and of their installations in Belgium for refining the minerals, while the main financial points (*i.e.* the compensation for the loss of the installations and the pipeline question) would be submitted by both sides to arbitration.[52]

In previous studies the influence of the Americans in the whole episode has been regarded as puzzling, to say the least. While the Belgian and British governments could be discounted as being far from disinterested parties, the US Government, who had a heavy political stake in the prosperity of the Congo from their desire to stave off Soviet influence, constituted the only real outside force able to bring outside pressure to bear to achieve a rational solution to the dispute between the Congo Government and UM.[53] Originally there were several quite distinct American influences at work.[54] The main player was the US State Department, which was desperate to avoid involvement in a dispute which might injure the relationship with the Congo and which might lead the latter to turn again to the United States for financial aid if all else failed. The State Department had little sympathy with UM because it had all along been withdrawing foreign currency from the Congo for its own purposes (or, for that matter, with the principal Congolese politicians who were using UM assets for their own gain), while the United States had been required to pump in financial aid to maintain some sort of stability in the Congo. This was an old accusation. Even in colonial days, the colonial administration was convinced that UMHK was withholding considerable sums which were properly due to the government as taxes. The State Department placed a good deal of the blame on what they regarded as UM's colonialist attitude in the negotiations. The Americans feared that it would make the stabilisation programme of the Congolese economy (which US economic assistance to the Congo had been intended to implement) unworkable.[55] They calculated that without a rapid solution Congolese foreign exchange reserves could be exhausted within a month. To guarantee continued production the parties would have to work out a solution which would permit continued production of sales of copper and thus prevent the country from going bankrupt. The priority of the US Government was now to find some way out which would not involve Mobutu in a loss of face.

Eventually the US Government, having become alarmed by the economic instability of the Congo with this trend of events, instructed their *chargé d'affaires* in Kinshasa to propose a compromise whereby (a) UM would be allotted a continuing role in sales, refining and technical assistance in Katanga and (b) issues of compensation would be submitted to arbitration. The Congolese accepted but UM directors were tending to argue that the game was no longer worth the candle: Even if an agreement were reached, it would be torn up again by the Congolese, so that it would be better for their shareholders if they cut their losses in the Congo and carried on in business with their other resources – just as the Suez Canal Company had done so successfully.[56] UM was proceeding by applying a strict calculation of how to minimise its losses. To see their money now being transferred to a Congolese company without any guarantee of a dividend or compensation would surely be asking too much from the owners of UM. But it was only sensible to face the fact that their installations in the Congo were now lost. The most UM could hope for was the conclusion of an agreement for the continued purchase of copper produced by Gécomin.[57]

On 4 February 1967 UM came forward with a counterproposal to surrender its rights and properties in Katanga to the Congolese Government on condition in return that it would be invited to act as managing consultants for a fixed percentage fee. At first it seemed that the Congolese had no desire to budge. It did not cut much ice that Henry Fortemps, the former General Manager of UM, based in Lubumbashi until he was declared *persona non grata* in the summer of 1966, was acting as SGM's representative in the negotiations.[58] On 15 February 1967, however, the Mobutu Government was forced to come to terms with various UM subsidiaries engaged in refining and with the sale of products in Belgium in an agreement that would involve the production, transport and marketing of the minerals, but in order to save Mobutu's face the agreement was not directly with UM itself but with SGM. Finally on 17 February a convention was signed by Gécomin and SGM. According to this agreement SGM bought copper (f.o.b.) at the going daily world rate and for that particular quality of copper with a reduction of 4.5%. This was their remuneration from which they paid all their own expenses. The most important costs for SGM were the transport of the copper to Belgium and its refining, its share in the salary of the labour that was employed to work in Katanga and the costs of the management functions which it performed in Belgium for Gécomin. SGM itself did not make any profit but the net profit out of its 4.5% agency fee was transferred to UM.[59]

Why Gécomin relied on SGM for the commercialisation of its minerals and why no attempt had been made to sell the copper to countries of the Eastern Bloc were a matter of facing realities: the Hoboken Refinery was the only one with the right equipment and the spare capacity to accept Katangese minerals for processing.[60] Another explanation lies in Mobutu's aversion to the Russians: 'I didn't fight the Belgians to then have my country colonised a second time.'[61] Following the agreement, prohibitions of Europeans leaving the mining region were lifted and the 2nd Paratrooper Battalion, the biggest threat to the personal security of the Europeans and Africans alike, moved out of Lubumbashi to camp in the bush. In return, UM allowed its expatriate personnel to be reabsorbed by Gécomin.[62] The Congolese could still count on various technical services provided in Brussels and on the continuation of the refining and sale of minerals. UM would permit its board members nominated by the Congolese to serve on the new board of Gécomin, which was responsible for policy decisions related to the question of the government taxes, among other issues.

Concluding discussion

What then of the future? The close association with the hated 'high finance' remained transparently obvious in the Congo. Seven years after independence the Congo was still financially under colonial sway. Of the Congo's economy, 70% rested on Gécomin and remained dependent on foreign hands. The Congo National Bank was the first in the newly independent African countries to attempt a full analysis of the economic background. The financial reforms associated with the June 1967 devaluation had led to big cuts in public expenditure so that the budget was appreciably closer to being balanced.[63] Gécomin had managed to keep enough European technicians in the Congo to maintain and develop mining operations in Katanga. The current production of copper exceeded 300,000 tons per annum, more than was produced before independence. The dismissal of the former all-Congolese board of Gécomin (who had been quite incapable of fulfilling the functions of the board and had embezzled over £2.5 million) and their replacement by a mixed Belgian and Congolese board also augured well. The new board of Gécomin appeared now to be allowing more latitude to their senior ex-UM executives in Katanga in the handling of the day-to-day mining operations.[64] The Managing Director of Gécomin was now Robert Cayron, a young but highly competent mining expert. Next in the company's hierarchy came the Technical Managing Director, Jean Gonze, ex-UM senior executive. In 1968 Kolwezi emerged as the major mining centre of the Copperbelt which provided about one-half of Gécomin's entire production of copper and cobalt.

The operation was open-cast mining, though the company already had started to sink two shafts along the edge of the open quarries in order to get at the deeper ore deposits. The General Manager of the Kolwezi mine was Vladimir Apraxine, a Russian-born mining engineer, who had graduated at the Royal School of Mines in London.[65]

Relations between the Congolese Government and UM, soured by the expropriation, remained poor during 1967 and the first part of 1968, when all efforts were concentrated on keeping the mines in operation rather than attempting to achieve any financial settlement.[66] The situation remained generally static until Mobutu unexpectedly visited Belgium at the initiative of King Baudouin in June 1968. This was followed by an exchange of visits by leading personalities from both countries and led to sudden and far-reaching improvements in political relations. Mobutu, however, continued to be swayed by his emotions in the matter of UM, as exemplified by the intemperate outburst quoted in the journal *Le Soir*, the official Congolese bulletin, in November 1968.[67] The classic phrases about imperialism, neo-colonialism and racialism flew from his lips with such ease and familiarity that he was clearly no friend of the Western whites; he saw, however, that they could be cultivated for his own gain. UM, by contrast, lost some of its old military rigidity, though not all of its colonialist attitude, towards the Congolese. UM positively wanted Mobutu to proceed from folly to folly and only waited for the right moment to seek compensation.[68]

At the time of the nationalisation the book value of UM was estimated at £333 million but the company considered the market value to be close to £400 million. Brussels' valuations of UM are largely of academic interest, however. It is difficult to place a real value on UM shares, since many of them were held in large blocks and had an international political flavour. UM assets outside the Congo were standing at £116.6 million. Largely because of the exceptionally high price of copper in 1966 and 1967 and the substantial stockpiles the company held, it was able to write off the book value of its Congo assets (about £136 million net), establish a contingencies fund to begin the reconstruction of its reserves and offer its shareholders an increased dividend. In 1967 a Canadian subsidiary, the Union Minière Explorations and Mining Corporation, was set up with a capital of 10 million Canadian dollars and immediately signed exploration agreements with the Canada Nickel Company on the one hand and the *Société Québecoise d'Exploration Minière* on the other. In April 1968, UM subscribed to 90% of the capital of a new investment company – the Union Minière Canada. A month later the Union Minière Development and Mining Corporation and the Union Minière Australia were established in Australia, both with a capital of one million Australian dollars.[69]

In Belgium, UM was granted an extension of its term until 31 December 1997.[70] Under the guidance of SGB, UM increased its holdings in the technologically advanced non-ferrous sector, which accounted for 27.1% of the *Société Générale* group's portfolio – the biggest holding the group had in any sector. UM was SGB's fairy godchild who was clearly going to enjoy an increasingly important part in Belgium's non-ferrous metal industry. In 1967 it took important shareholdings in the *Société des Mines et Fonderies de Zinc de la Vieille-Montagne*, the world's largest zinc producer, in the *Compagnie Royale Asturienne des Mines*, and in Sidmar, Belgium's newest steelworks in Ghent. In addition UM already had a 47.6% holding in SGMH which operated the continent's largest smelter of non-ferrous metals.[71]

The claim of UM against the Congolese Government was brought to the notice of the World Bank, in the hope of gaining some leverage when loans to the government were being contemplated. Renewed hopes for a settlement of UM's claim against the Congo Government were spurred in November 1968, when Robert McNamara, the President of the World Bank, undertook to arbitrate in the dispute between the Congolese Government and UM over the compensation to be paid for the nationalisation and for the UM installations in Katanga. Similar international mediation duties had been performed in the past by presidents of the World Bank, with the most notable example being Eugene Black's assistance in handling claims arising out of the nationalisation of the Suez Canal Company.[72] The results of these negotiations were disappointing for UM, however. But from the point of view of the Congolese the result of the prolonged squabble was even more harmful: the remaining 40% of the capital of Gécomin which was on offer to non-Congolese interests had not been taken up. Mobutu saw the 40% offer chiefly as a means of drawing capital into the country and did not fully appreciate that investors would expect a return on it. UM on the other hand was completely fed up with Mobutu and had no desire to take up any share in Gécomin. UM was adamant in their wish to have nothing further to do with the Congo. UM's connection with the mining industry in Katanga was now at second hand and kept alive only through their holding in SGM.[73]

Long before the nationalisation, UM had been complaining that its increasing burden of Congolese taxation was absorbing the entire profit which they had been reaping hitherto. Gécomin for its part was also finding the burden of taxation crippling, but it had now also to provide the hard currency from the proceeds of the sale of the copper and other products to pay the 4.5% agency fee to SGM. Then again there was the 2% of the net proceeds of the sale which had to be set aside under the protocol of the agreement between Gécomin and SGM to constitute the guarantee fund for the latter to pay its expatriate employees. It was a fact that prior to nationalisation UM was only just breaking even and since the taxes had not been reduced, it followed that Gécomin, with the additional burden of the net tax 6.5% to meet, was very soon likely to be in the red, particularly if it wished to make good the arrears of expenditure on new and replacement equipment.[74]

The chief reason why the Congolese Government found itself in this humiliating predicament was the excessive reliance it had placed on the emergence of an international consortium, which first would provide financial cover to tide the country over the transitional difficulties resulting from the nationalisation, and second would arrange the marketing of the mineral products. As it transpired, however, the copper simply could not be refined or marketed without SGM, and no outside organisation was willing to lend the Congo money without an assured slice of the copper cake, though Mobutu had somehow convinced himself that Lord Colyton and Tanks would play his game and provide a convincing air of respectability. Further, Mobutu firmly believed that he could detach the younger generation of managers in Katanga from the old diehards like Wallef and his colleagues in Brussels. In the end, all these calculations had proved to be horribly wrong.[75]

As it turned out, Mobutu could not have picked a worse moment to deliver such a shock to the Congo economy. In 1974 the world copper price dropped nearly two-thirds as the Oil Shock of 1973–4 plunged the world into recession. Gécomin (in 1971 altered to *Générale des Carrières et des Mines*, or Gécamines) failed to produce for the Congolese their long-hoped-for economic independence. But instead, following the 'Zaireanisation' of the economy in 1974, the dwindling proceeds of the Congo Government-controlled mining sector were spent up on luxury items of the Zairean elite, with Mobutu's extravagant lifestyle as the most prominent example.[76]

Notes

1 TNA, FO 371/187758, Union Minière du Haut-Katanga, Communique to the Press, n.d.
2 TNA, FCO 25/118, End of an era – demise of Union Minière du Haut-Katanga, Mr J.R. Cotton to Mr Brown, Kinshasa, 12 April 1967. See also Kanza 1979; Gérard-Libois 1966; Cruise O'Brian 1962; O'Malley 2018; Young and Turner 1985, 48–49.
3 TNA, FCO 25/118, End of an era – demise of Union Minière du Haut-Katanga, Mr J.R. Cotton to Mr Brown, Kinshasa, 12 April 1967.
4 See, for instance, Kent 2013, 120, 122–123, 128–129.
5 TNA, FO 371/161517, UM, British Embassy, Brussels to Foreign Office, London, 8 August 1962.
6 TNA, FO 371/161517, Parliamentary Question, Mr Philip Noel-Baker to the Lord Privy Seal, 2 November 1962.
7 Kent 2013, 122–123.
8 TNA, FO 371/161517, Paul Gillet, the Chairman of the UM, Union Minière's policy in the Congo, 24 May 1962; Telegram, No. 762, British Consulate, Élisabethville to Foreign Office, London, 26 November 1962.
9 TNA, FO 371/161517, Union Minière du Haut-Katanga, Reports of the Directors and Auditors presented at the Annual General Meeting on May 24, 1962. See also *Revolt in the Congo 1960–64* 1965, 114–115.
10 TNA, FCO 25/118, End of an era – demise of Union Minière du Haut-Katanga, Mr J.R. Cotton to Mr Brown, Kinshasa, 12 April 1967.
11 TNA, FO 371/187757, The Annual General Meeting of the Union Minière du Haut-Katanga on May 26, 1966, Reports of the Board of Directors regarding 59th financial year 1965. See also Radmann 1978, 31–33; Hoskyns 1965, 53.
12 TNA, FCO 25/118, End of an era – demise of Union Minière du Haut-Katanga, Mr J.R. Cotton to Mr Brown, Kinshasa, 12 April 1967.
13 TNA, FCO 25/117, British Embassy, Kinshasa, 5 January 1967.

14 TNA, FCO 25/117, Telegram No. 18, British Embassy, Kinshasa to Foreign Office, London, 13 January 1967.
15 TNA, FO 371/187757, Union Minière du Haut-Katanga, Reports of the Board of Directors regarding 59th financial year 1965 presented at the Annual General Meeting on May 26, 1966; Soto and San Francisco 2022, 298–299.
16 TNA, FO 371/187757, J.R. Cotton, H.M. Ambassador, Léopoldville, 2 May 1966.
17 TNA, FO 371/187757, J.R. Cotton, H.M. Ambassador, Léopoldville, 2 May 1966.
18 TNA, FO 371/187757, Union Minière du Haut-Katanga, Reports of the Board of Directors regarding 59th financial year 1965 presented at the Annual General Meeting on May 26, 1966.
19 TNA, FCO 25/118, End of an era – demise of Union Minière du Haut-Katanga, Mr J.R. Cotton to Mr Brown, Kinshasa, 12 April 1967.
20 TNA, FCO 25/118, End of an era – demise of Union Minière du Haut-Katanga, Mr J.R. Cotton to Mr Brown, Kinshasa, 12 April 1967.
21 TNA, FO 371/187757, Telegram No. 75, British Consulate, Élisabethville to Foreign Office, London, 17 May 1966.
22 TNA, FO 371/187757, Telegram No. 136, British Embassy, Élisabethville to Foreign Office, London, 6 June 1966.
23 TNA, FO 371/187757, Telegram No. 158, Lusaka to Commonwealth Relations Office, 24 June 1966.
24 TNA, FO 371/187757, Telegram No. 4, British Consulate, Élisabethville to Foreign Office, London, 4 June 1966.
25 TNA, FO 371/187757, Telegram, No. 424, British Consulate, Élisabethville to Foreign Office, London, 11 June 1966.
26 For further information, see Kyle 2011.
27 Young and Turner 1985, 290–296.
28 TNA, FO 371/187758, Report on the talks between Union Minière delegation and Congolese authorities, British Embassy, Kinshasa, 27 October 1966.
29 TNA, FO 371/187758, Telegram No. 836, British Embassy, Kinshasa to Foreign Office, London, 8 December 1966.
30 TNA, FO 371/187758, Report on the talks between Union Minière delegation and Congolese authorities, British Embassy, Kinshasa, 27 October 1966.
31 TNA, FCO 25/117, British Embassy, Kinshasa, 5 January 1967.
32 TNA, FO 371/187758, Union Minière negotiations, British Embassy, Kinshasa, 5 December 1966.
33 TNA, FO 371/187758, Reflections on the negotiations now in progress between UMHK and Congolese Gov., British Consulate, Lubumbashi, 19 October 1966.
34 TNA, FO 371/187758, Reflections on the negotiations now in progress between UMHK and Congolese Gov., British Consulate, Lubumbashi, 19 October 1966; TNA, FO 371/187758, Views since the breakdown of negotiations, British Consulate, Lubumbashi, 12 December 1966; Telegram No. 378, British Embassy, Kinshasa to Foreign Office, London, 30 December 1966.
35 TNA, FO 371/187758, Reflections on the negotiations now in progress between UMHK and Congolese Gov., British Consulate, Lubumbashi, 19 October 1966.
36 TNA, FO 371/187758, Union Minière negotiations, British Embassy, Kinshasa, 5 December 1966.
37 TNA, FO 371/187758, Views since the breakdown of negotiations, British Consulate, Lubumbashi, 12 December 1966.
38 TNA, FO 371/187758, Report on a meeting with M. Wallef, British Embassy, Kinshasa, 15 December 1966; Telegram No. 882, British Embassy, Kinshasa to Foreign Office, London, 26 December 1966.
39 TNA, FO 371/187758, Deterioration in situation: army reinforced and patrolling the streets, British Consulate, Lubumbashi, 21 December 1966.

40 TNA, FO 371/187758, Telegram No. 364, British Embassy, Kinshasa to Foreign Office, London, 24 December 1966; FCO 25/122, Present Katangan discontents, British Consulate, Lubumbashi to Foreign Office, London, 25 January 1967.
41 TNA, FCO 25/118, End of an era – demise of Union Minière du Haut-Katanga, Mr J.R. Cotton to Mr Brown, Kinshasa, 12 April 1967.
42 TNA, FCO 25/117, British Consulate, Lubumbashi, 24 January 1967.
43 Wrong 2000, 92.
44 *La Libre Belgique* 4 January 1967.
45 TNA, FO 371/187758, Telegram No. 376, British Embassy, Kinshasa to Foreign Office, London, 30 December 1966.
46 TNA, FCO 25/117, Telegram No. 8, British Embassy, Kinshasa to Foreign Office, London, 3 January 1967; FCO 25/118, British Consulate, Lubumbashi, 21 June 1967.
47 TNA, FCO 25/120, Visit to Lubumbashi, British Embassy, Kinshasa, 21 February 1967; FCO 25/122, Present Katangan discontents, British Consulate, Lubumbashi, 25 January 1967.
48 TNA, FCO 25/120, Visit to Lubumbashi, British Embassy, Kinshasa, 21 February 1967.
49 TNA, FCO 25/117, Telegram No. 7, British Consulate, Lubumbashi to Foreign Office, London, 3 January 1967.
50 TNA, FCO 25/121, British Embassy, Kinshasa to Foreign Office, London, 17 January 1967.
51 Wrong 2000, 94.
52 TNA, FCO 25/120, Telegram No. 88, Union Minière, British Embassy, Kinshasa to Foreign Office, London, 19 and 31 January 1967; FCO 25/118, End of an era – demise of Union Minière du Haut-Katanga, Mr J.R. Cotton to Mr Brown, Kinshasa, 12 April 1967.
53 For further information, see Kent 2010; Helmreich 1998; Muschik 2022.
54 TNA, FCO 25/118, End of an era – demise of Union Minière du Haut-Katanga, Mr J.R. Cotton to Mr Brown, Kinshasa, 12 April 1967. See also Gibbs 1991; Gibbs 1997; O'Malley 2016; O'Malley 2018. The role of Mr Maurice Tempelsman of Leon Tempelsman and Son, New York as a key influencer behind Mobutu's decision-making has been discussed on a number of occasions. Refer, for instance, to Gibbs 1997.
55 Young and Turner 1985, 278.
56 TNA, FCO 25/120, Telegram No. 88, Union Minière, British Embassy, Kinshasa to Foreign Office, London, 19 and 31 January 1967.
57 TNA, FCO 25/118, Telegram No. 25, British Embassy, Brussels to Foreign Office, London, 4 and 5 January 1967; Wrong 2000, 93.
58 TNA, FCO 25/118, President Mobutu's press conference: Agreement between Gécomin and SGM, Kinshasa, 22 February 1967.
59 TNA, FCO 25/118, Agreement for technical co-operation, 15 February 1967.
60 TNA, FCO 25/118, President Mobutu's press conference: Agreement between Gécomin and SGM, Kinshasa, 22 February 1967.
61 Quoted in Wrong 2000, 67.
62 TNA, FCO 25/118, British Consulate, Lubumbashi, 8 March 1967.
63 Young and Turner 1985, 280–281; WBG, Folder 1771243: Contacts with member countries: Zaire – Correspondence 01, Recent economic and financial developments, n.d.
64 Gécomin Rapport Annuel 1969; *The Times* 8 January 1969.
65 TNA, FCO 25/120, Visit to Lubumbashi, British Embassy, Kinshasa, 21 February 1967.
66 *The Times* 27 April 1968.
67 *Le Soir* 3 et 4 novembre 1968; TNA, FCO 29/278, Union Minière: Compensation for Nationalisation, W. Peters, Central African Department, Foreign and Commonwealth Office, 7 November 1968.

68 TNA, FCO 29/278, W. Peters, Notes for HM Ambassador-Designate, Kinshasa, Union Minière/Congolese Government Dispute, 6 January 1969.
69 *The Economist* 31 August 1968.
70 *The Times* 25 January 1968.
71 *The Economist* 31 August 1968.
72 WBG, Folder 1771243: Contacts with member countries: Zaire – Correspondence 01, Memorandum of McNamara's meeting with Nendaka, 27 September 1968; 12 February 1969; *The Times* 1 November 1968; *Financial Times* 1 November 1968.
73 TNA, FCO 25/118, Report on a telephone conversation with Lord Colyton, 28 March 1967.
74 TNA, FCO 25/118, Convention between the Congolese Gécomin and the Belgian S.G.M., British Embassy, Kinshasa, 15 February 1967.
75 TNA, FCO 25/118, End of an era – demise of Union Minière du Haut-Katanga, Mr J.R. Cotton to Mr Brown, Kinshasa, 12 April 1967.
76 Wrong 2000, 92–94; Young and Turner 1985, 292.

References

Cruise O'Brian, C. (1962) *To Katanga and Back: A UN Case History*, Hutchinson, London.

The Economist (31 August 1968) 'Belgium and the Congo's New Dawn?'.

Financial Times (1 November 1968) 'McNamara Mediation for Congo Dispute'.

Gécomin Rapport Annuel (1969) Gécomin, Kinshasa.

Gérard-Libois, J. (1966) *Katanga Secession*, R. Young transl. The University of Wisconsin Press, Madison and London.

Gibbs, D.N. (1991) *The Political Economy of Third World Intervention: Mines, Money and U.S. Policy in the Congo Crisis*, The University of Chicago Press, Chicago, IL and London.

Gibbs, D. (1997) 'International Commercial Rivalries and the Zaïrian Copper Nationalisation of 1967', *Review of African Political Economy*, 72, 171–184.

Helmreich, J.E. (1998) *United States Relations with Belgium and the Congo, 1940–1960*, University of Delaware Press, Newark.

Hoskyns, C. (1965) *The Congo since the Independence: January 1960–December 1961*, Oxford University Press, London, Toronto, New York.

Kanza, T. (1979) *The Rise and Fall of Patrice Lumumba: Conflict in the Congo*, Schenkman, Cambridge, MA.

Kent, J. (2010) *America, the UN and Decolonisation: Cold War Conflict in the Congo*, Routledge, London.

Kent, J. (2013) 'Anglo-American Diplomacy and the Congo Crisis, 1960–1963: The Not So Special Relationship' in J.W. Young, E.G.H. Pedaliu and M.D. Kandiah eds. *Britain in Global Politics*, Vol. 2: *From Churchill to Blair*, Palgrave Macmillan, Houndmills, Basingstoke, 119–138.

Kyle, K. (2011) *Suez: Britain's End of Empire in the Middle East*, I.B. Tauris, London.

La Libre Belgique (4 January 1967) 'Les explications de l'U.M.H.K.'.

Muschik, E.-M. (2022) *Building States: The United Nations, Development, and Decolonization, 1945–1965*, Columbia University Press, New York.

The National Archives of the UK (TNA), Kew, Foreign and Commonwealth Office (FCO); Foreign Office (FO).

O'Malley, A. (2016) '"What an Awful Body the UN Have Become!" Anglo-American–UN Relations during the Congo Crisis, February–December 1961', *Journal of Transatlantic Studies*, 14:1, 26–46.

O'Malley, A. (2018) *The Diplomacy of Decolonisation: America, Britain and the United Nations during the Congo Crisis 1960–1964*, Manchester University Press, Manchester.

Radmann, W. (1978) 'The Nationalization of Zaire's Copper: From Union Minière to Gecamines', *Africa Today*, 25:4, 25–47.

Revolt in the Congo 1960–64 (1965) H.M. Epstein ed. Facts on File, New York.

Le Soir (3 et 4 novembre 1968) 238.

Soto, A. and San Francisco, A. (2022) 'Copper in Chile: From the New Deal to Full Concessions, 1955–81' in R. Declercq, D. Money and H.O. Frøland eds. *Born with a Copper Spoon: A Global History of Copper, 1830–1980*, The Chicago University Press, Chicago, IL, 292–312.

The Times (25 January 1968) 'The Extraordinary General Meeting of Union Minière du Haut-Katanga, 25 January 1968'; (27 April 1968) 'Congo Mines Deal Near'; (1 November 1968) 'McNamara's Congo Task'; (8 January 1969) 'Hopes Rise for Union Minière Settlement'.

World Bank Group (WBG) Archives, Washington D.C., Folder 1771243: Contacts with member countries: Zaire – Correspondence 01.

Wrong, M. (2000) *In the Footsteps of Mr Kurtz: Living on the Brink of Disaster in the Congo*, Fourth Estate Limited, London.

Young, C. and Turner, T. (1985) *The Rise and Decline of the Zairean State*, The University of Wisconsin Press, Madison.

8 Conclusions

Natural resource governance, finance and imperialism

This chapter focuses on the post-Second World War years of Tanganyika Concessions (Tanks) which were defined by the turbulence of the world copper markets brought about by the Second World War; the waning influence of the City as a financial centre; the collapse of the British-dominated copper empire in Northern Rhodesia (Zambia); and the expropriation, without compensation, of the installations and property of the *Union Minière* (UM). For more than 50 years Tanks was a London brass nameplate, headquartered in the City, and its directors felt that its independence as a free-standing company provided reliability and security for its shareholders in general, and in particular for its numerous small stockholders. Although Tanganyika Concessions was a London-based mining company, it requires a stretch of the imagination to regard it as a British industrial project. So far as ownership of Ordinary shares was concerned, Tanks of the post-Second World War era may be described as a multinational headquartered in the City (until 1952), then Salisbury, Southern Rhodesia (1952–65) and finally in Nassau, the Bahamas (from 1966 onwards). The chapter concludes that upheavals in the operational environment eroded Tanks' ability to play any important part in the development of the Central African Copperbelt. By 1970 Tanks had reorganised itself as a multi-branch holding company with interests dispersed from mining to the emerging travel and tourism sectors in Zambia and the Congo.

Not for Rider Haggard – the Tanks story

> His discovery of the fabulously rich minefields of Katanga, and his construction of two railways to connect them to the outside world, led to the opening of the vast and scarcely explored region of Central Africa stretching from the Zambezi to the Congo River and from Lake Tanganyika to the Atlantic, and it laid the foundations of the present prosperity of such countries as the Congo, Zambia and Angola. Among their populations are the descendants of those who worked for Williams and were proud to call themselves 'Bantu Robert' – 'Robert's People'.[1]

DOI: 10.4324/9781003247371-8

With these forewords Hutchinson and Martelli (1971) opened their biographical study *Robert's People* on the life of Sir Robert Williams, the long-time Managing Director of Tanks. Williams belonged to the late-nineteenth-century 'pioneers', the men on the spot who actively promoted mining and railway projects in South-Central Africa. The 'pioneers' have been considered as 'far too busy making history to find time to write it' and their lives and exacting times in Africa have frequently been subjected to a romanticised version of natural resource governance.[2] Yet the history of Tanks, the London brass nameplate which Williams steered for nearly 40 years with varied success, is hardly a subject for a modernised Rider Haggard romance. Tanks was rather the vanguard of an immaculate throng of gentlemen capitalists and the paradigm of a brass nameplate unlike any other.

Tanks was incorporated under the Companies Acts from 1862 to 1898 as a limited company. The objective for which the company was established was to acquire concessions, grants, leases, claims, mines and mineral properties in Northern Rhodesia, and in particular to enter into and implement an agreement between Tyndale White and The Zambesia Exploring Company (ZE), the 1891-established mining finance company, itself responsible for bringing Tanks into existence in 1899. The stock of ZE was held by private investors, rising to approximately 2,500 small shareholders by 1949, and there was no particular group controlling ZE.[3] As a finance company its purpose was to assist the numerous companies in the Tanks Group by dealing in their shares and providing finance when required. While the amount of Tanks stock held by ZE continually fluctuated, the interests of the two companies were always closely intertwined. The chairman of ZE was also the chairman of Tanks.

The aim of Tanks was a systematic exploitation of the mineral wealth of the area over which the *Compagnie du Katanga* (CK) had been granted a 99-year lease by King Léopold II in 1891. On 19 June 1900 the parastatal *Comité Spécial du Katanga* (CSK) was founded and acquired the concessionary powers from the Congo Free State (CFS), and those conceded earlier to CK, and subsequently allowed Williams prospecting rights over certain areas in Katanga for the next five years. From 1901 to 1906 Tanks was prospecting with the intention of opening, working, developing and maintaining gold, copper, tin, coal, iron and other minerals in its concession. The title of the company was therefore something of a misnomer since its interests in Tanganyika (or for that matter in any of the Colonial Office territories) were very small, with its geological surveys restricted to Katanga.

In 1906 Tanks subscribed, together with the *Société Générale de Belgique* (SGB) of Brussels, the share capital of the *Union Minière du Haut-Katanga* (UMHK), a Brussels-based mining company incorporated on 28 October 1906 by Royal Decree to exploit all the mines already discovered or to be discovered in Katanga. Of the founders' royalty, 40% was allotted to Tanks and 60% to CSK, which represented the interests of the state (initially CFS but later the Belgian State) and CK in the proportion two-thirds to one-third. The compensation for Tanks' successful work in the development of the mineral resources in Katanga was paid in this way, and when UMHK was constituted, provision was made for future compensation if the share capital of that company was increased. The royalty (or 'super-dividend', as it was described) from the profits of UMHK was a payment to which Tanks became entitled as the successor to Williams as further compensation for the latter's services.[4]

Henceforth Williams made his contribution to UMHK in the capacity of the Vice-President through the board meetings held at regular intervals at Brussels, except during the German invasion of Belgium (1914–18) when the company's day-to-day management was handled in London.[5] The rapid development of the Katangese mining industry during the war cast a positive reflection of UMHK's balance sheets, increasing its financial independence and reducing the scope for Tanks to wield its financial power. The direst year for Tanks was 1921, when the resources of the company were tied up in the construction of the Benguela Railway. Consequently Tanks' holding in UMHK equity was reduced to 15%.[6]

In 1925, 4.5% voting debentures were created with the declared object of assuring continued collaboration between CSK and Tanks in the management of UMHK. Tanks' interests in UMHK were therefore twofold: first, through direct shareholding, and second, through additional royalty and voting rights attached to debenture capital, which consisted of 61,384 (4.5%) voting debentures and 134,016 voting certificates. In the same year the capitalisation of UMHK was 264,000 capital shares of 100 francs each and 264,000 dividend shares of no par value. Besides the Ordinary shares there were 300,000 Privileged shares of which 100,000 were issued in 1925, with the rest having been issued previously.[7]

Tanks was now drawing a very appreciable annual revenue from its interests in UMHK which positively affected its balance sheets and share prices. Between 1922 and 1925 the value of Tanks' shares on the market trebled.[8] Average annual real return on investments remained at −13.2% until 1923, rising subsequently to a solid average profit of 5.3% per annum after 1924.[9] In 1936 UMHK had been in existence for 30 years and the time had come to pay for the extension of its concession until 1990 as had been agreed in its charter. This involved an increase in UMHK's capital by one-third and handing over to CSK the entire amount of voting rights attached to share capital represented by this increase by virtue of the agreement signed on 8 December 1900 between Williams and CSK. As a result, Tanks' holding in UMHK was reduced to 14.47%, though it still retained 20.21% of the voting rights along with two seats on the board.[10]

Williams' death in 1938 brought major changes in the management structure of the Tanks Group. The managerial responsibility was originally destined to Williams' son, Captain Gordon Williams, but in 1918, at an early age, he died in Élisabethville from influenza. Thereafter Williams increasingly relied on his two sons-in-law, Francis Follett and Godfrey Hutchinson, the latter of whom was nominated as the new Managing Director of Tanks. The vice-presidency of UMHK was entrusted to the Chairman of Tanks, Maurice Hely-Hutchinson (1887–1961), a Conservative Member of Parliament for Hastings from 1937 to 1945 and one of the biggest 'African mining men' in the City, who also occupied a seat on the board of BSAC among others.[11] The new board was no longer swayed by the mindset of the 'pioneers' but consisted of gentlemen capitalists who were bound to suffer as a result of their lack of management experience in such a multilayered mining finance group with significant holdings in Belgian and Portuguese companies.

The demise of City financial power

The Second World War brought significant changes to overseas British mining operations. Before the war, semi-speculative capital for mineral development overseas had been found in the City on the basis that subscribers knew that they were risking a substantial part of their money being tied up for a long period with little prospect of recovering it. Typically the investor ventured into such projects merely to develop a mine, intending to sell out as soon as it went into production. The flow of foreign capital that fell under the category of 'foreign direct investment' aimed at the establishment of manufacturing or some other industrial undertaking in the Colonial Office territories was blocked by law.[12] In the post-war economic reality, City dominance was on the wane, and it was getting increasingly difficult to find large sums for overseas investments from City sources. After the war American capital became a viable means to finance mining operations. In general, dollars were badly needed for railway and mining equipment in the Sterling Area, and particularly in Southern Africa, putting strain on the financial supremacy of the City.

Taxation was another obvious impediment to American investment in the Sterling Area, and underlined the impossibility of any mining, exploration or development company operating from a City address if there was to be any foreign participation in the enterprise. As a rule, British-controlled companies deriving income from overseas suffered a substantially greater tax burden than companies controlled abroad.[13] The significance of the place of management for taxation was that it determined where a company was resident for tax purposes. If a company was managed and controlled in Britain, it was resident in Britain (irrespective of where it was incorporated and irrespective of the residence of shareholders). In this case Income Tax was charged on the whole of its profits whether earned in Britain or abroad and whether remitted to Britain or not and whether distributed as dividends or not. If the company was not resident in Britain, its profits earned abroad were liable to Income Tax only to the extent that they were distributed as dividends to companies and individuals resident in Britain and Profits Tax only to the extent that they were distributed as dividends to companies resident in Britain.[14]

In the pre-1939 era, the place of management and control of a company where the board and directors met to decide on matters relating to the conduct of the business could be changed by the company. There were obvious non-revenue advantages in registering a mining company in the City where it had available financial facilities and the services of the shipping companies. The profits, products, contracts for new equipment, shipping and insurance services all tended to be dealt with through London. Once a company's headquarters was moved, however, the link with the City became progressively weaker and local feeling sometimes tended to turn against the absent owners. On the other hand, it was argued that greater efficiency could result from the proximity of management to the field of operation, and that the local capital market might be more easily induced to make its own contribution to the development of the country. This point, while of general importance, had particular significance in South Africa and in the Rhodesias, where there were well-developed capital markets for mining. In addition there was the consideration that the transfer of a company's headquarters to the country where its business was conducted, more particularly where that country was outside the Colonial Office territories, was sometimes (and was frequently alleged to be) an essential measure of self-protection against local political pressure of various kinds.[15]

The migration of companies was the subject of a report by the Board of Inland Revenue which had since 1915 kept a record of cases where the management and control of business had been transferred abroad. In the mid-1920s the topic was discussed at length by the Royal Commission and by the Colwyn Committee on National Debt and Taxation. On the outbreak of war in 1939, control over the migration of companies was imposed by Regulation 6A of Defence (Finance Regulations), which required a prior Treasury consent for any company migration. This control was introduced entirely for tax reasons, since it was felt at the time that the Exchequer could not afford in the circumstances of war to permit companies to migrate in order to avoid heavy wartime taxation. That control was removed after the war but after an interval a somewhat similar control was enacted in Section 30 of the Exchange Control Act of 1947, which required Treasury consent to be obtained for transactions involving the transfer of shareholding control abroad.[16] The control was primarily introduced to prevent foreign investors gaining a controlling interest in strategically important companies then primarily controlled by British residents, and to prevent corporate migration from Britain.[17] The case of Tanks, the first major British mining company making the case for legal grounds to enable their registration abroad after the reintroduction of exchange controls, had a considerable impact on the viability of the copper business in the imperial era.

Tanks calls it quits

On 29 April 1946 HM Treasury took over 2,100,000 Ordinary shares of 10s each in Tanks – together with a large volume of other securities – from the French Government.[18] These shares had previously belonged to French shareholders but had been requisitioned by the French Government shortly after the war and then handed over to the Bank of England in settlement of wartime debts. The Treasury became a major owner of Tanks quite fortuitously and saw no positive strategic interest in its holding. Liquidation proceeded very slowly, however. By 1948 the market had virtually dried up, and the shares lay at the Exchange Equalisation Account.

In the same year the capitalisation of Tanks was as follows. The share capital was divided into 6,279,356 Ordinary stock units, carrying one vote per 10s stock unit, and 2,305,783 Cumulative Participating Preference stock units, carrying one vote per £1 unit. The biggest owner of the Ordinary Bearer stock was the Treasury with 1,667,961 stock units which carried with them 19.5% of the voting power. The greater part of the Ordinary stock was held in Belgium, whereas nearly all the Preference stock was held in Britain. The biggest owner of Preference stock was ZE with its 21% interest. Most of the other institutional holders of Preference stock had acquired it for trading purposes and not for the purpose of gaining control.[19]

The board of Tanks considered itself charged with the obligation of preserving the balance between the relative rights of the Preference and Ordinary stockholders, which were somewhat unusual and extremely complicated in nature, and might, under certain circumstances, have given rise to a conflict of interest between the two classes of stock. The Ordinary stock shareholders did not have unfettered voting control because the Preference stockholders had voting rights as well.[20] However, only a very small proportion of the shareholders of the Preference stock was ever represented at the company's meetings, so the Treasury's holding of the Ordinary stock practically carried with it voting control at any Ordinary general meeting of the stockholders.

The post-war Tanks continued to be a goldmine for its owners but its managers were no longer very active in overseeing its interest in UMHK. It was also the case that Tanks' representatives on the board of UMHK were not exactly encouraged to contribute to the management. In 1948 Tanks' 14.47% holding of outstanding shares in UMHK (179,759 stock units) had a book selling value of £4,338,477. In the same year Tanks' royalty, based on profits, yielded £117,000 and dividends of about £522,000.[21] The real value of Tanks' interests in UMHK is not at all clear, however, even in terms of cash or voting strength, and quite apart from the political and strategic considerations involved. Tanks was after all a British company with a large public interest in its fortunes.

A further British interest in the prosperity of UMHK derived from the fact that Tanks also owned a 90% financial holding in the Benguela Railway Company (BRC), controlling a vast concession under which the company operated a freight-orientated 838-mile-long railway from Lobito Bay to the Congo border. Tanks' 90% (2,700,000 shares of £1 each) holding of the issued share capital of BRC and its outstanding debentures (£5,879,000 4% income debentures) were valued on its 1949 balance sheet at £490,000 and £980,050, respectively.[22] In 1949 dividend yield on the Ordinary was 10% per annum and the 10s shares were quoted on the Stock Exchange as high as 27s 9d.[23]

Tanks' holding of these two interests (*i.e.* UMHK and BRC) had remained substantially unchanged for many years and were connected since the Benguela Railway carried ore from the mines of Katanga and had the potential to be developed to carry minerals from Northern Rhodesia too. BRC had sustained very substantial losses in its history but after the war this slightly moribund railway had been doing very well. The company generated a modest profit for the first time after the war in 1948, rising already to about £1 million in 1949 and nearly £2 million in 1950. It was only in 1955, however, that BRC paid its first dividend, from which Tanks, as a holder of 90% of its shares, received £273,697.[24] Despite robust profits, the Benguela Railway put Tanks in a difficult financial position. It was expected that Tanks would be required to spend as much as £10 million in the near future to update the infrastructure and rolling stock. Another problem lay in the system of dual control in the management of BRC. While the company was financially controlled by Tanks in London its operations were directed from its Head Office in Lisbon. It must be borne in mind that there were certain hazards connected with additional investment in Portuguese territory. The British Government tended to be sceptical about Portugal's ultimate treatment of foreign investments, particularly concerning utilities, of which BRC was the prime example.[25] Thus far the policy of Tanks had been to put profits back into the business, but as the time was looming for the termination of the concession in 2001 it was likely to become increasingly difficult to convince the owners of the viability of this policy.[26]

In 1949 the Treasury was approached by a group of American financiers, headed by Ladenburg Thalmann & Co., a well-established New York merchant house with extensive experience of mining projects in various parts of the world, with a proposal to purchase its Tanks holding.[27] This investment proposal proved to be a test case of impediments to foreign investments in companies headquartered in the City and controlled by British residents. If the Treasury had accepted this investment proposal, it would have ignored its own ruling; if it had maintained a negative line, it would have turned down American capital which the British badly needed for the development of the Sterling Area. The question of the control or disposal of the Treasury's assets affected the national interests as well as interests of the large number of Ordinary stockholders of the company. The Treasury was also forced to consider the effect of rejecting the American investment proposal. If the Treasury had turned this kind of transaction down, the Americans would probably have accused the British of being unwilling in practice to cooperate in the aim to which they had been giving lip-service: the desirability of increasing American investments in the Commonwealth as the most effective means of making the Sterling Area a visible body.[28]

The Treasury's plan was to vitalise Tanks as an investment company and to bring in for this purpose Ladenburg Thalmann as an investor. This finance group would then act as a channel for the investment of American capital in the Sterling Area – not only in mining but also in longer-term infrastructure projects such as transport.[29] The plan also fitted in well with the object of the US Point Four Program which aimed at bringing American capital into 'underdeveloped' parts of the world and to counter exploitation for foreign profit of the colonial powers.[30] In the subsequent negotiations over details several interested parties were represented: the Treasury, the Bank of England, Tanks, Ladenburg Thalmann and the representatives of an Anglo-Belgian finance group comprising Anglo American Corporation of South Africa, Rio Tinto Company, Consolidated Mines Selection Company and Rhokana Corporation as well as SGB and ZE.

The American investors were mainly worried about the piling up of taxation. Tanks' assets were chargeable to British, Belgian and Portuguese taxes on profits from dealings in its primary investments (*i.e.* UMHK and BRC) and its income from those investments.[31] The Americans would have liked to move the domicile of Tanks somewhere else in the Commonwealth – to the Bahamas or, second best, Southern Rhodesia, in order to reduce the potential burden of triple taxation.[32] The mere administrative complication of trying to run a British company with investments and operations in the Belgian Congo and Angola, with American and Belgian participation through two mining finance groups, with part of its organisation in London and the seat of the company in the Bahamas, understandably raised a number of concerns. Ultimately any change to set up a brass nameplate address in the Bahamas was not regarded as acceptable by the Treasury.

Following proposals to alter the capital structure and transfer the management and seat of control of the company, the board of Tanks expressed a view that a reconstruction of share capital must precede any change of domicile to a place nearer to the properties in which the company had substantial investments – not only because of the need to vitalise the company's management but also because of the future development of its business. The operations of the Tanks Group being in and around Southern Rhodesia – a Crown Colony under white rule with well-established business connections to the City – the board considered Salisbury to be the most rational seat for the new Head Office.[33]

After very lengthy and involved negotiations the Treasury agreed to Tanks' proposal, and a relaxation of the law regarding foreign direct investments in British companies was brought into effect from 1 January 1950.[34] An agreement between Tanks and the Treasury, prior to the removal of the seat of management and control of the company to Salisbury, was subject to two important restrictions: (1) the UMHK holding could not be disposed of in under 10 years without consent of the Treasury and it would be given first refusal thereafter; (2) the disposal of the BRC holding would also require its consent.[35] Following this agreement the Treasury divested its holding of 1,667,961 Ordinary shares to the Anglo-Belgian group as follows: Anglo American Corporation of South Africa 561,182 stock units, Rio Tinto Company 478,785, SGB 300,000, Consolidated Mines Selection Company 113,997, ZE 113,997 and Rhokana Corporation 100,000.[36] At the same time, the Treasury gave consent to the group for the resale of 600,000 shares to Ladenburg Thalmann and its associates. This consent was given in the belief that this was one more step in the mobilisation of American capital in the development of mining resources in the Sterling Area.[37]

Negotiations had been conducted in great secrecy between a few of the highest officials of the Treasury and the Bank of England, so when the Communist *Daily Worker* journalist Derek Kartun published the full details of the deal on 26 April 1950 it caused a shock in the City. It was generally thought in the press that the deal jeopardised British strategic interests in Central Africa – UMHK being after all a major producer of uranium for Britain.[38] When the UK atomic energy programme began after the war, Shinkolobwe mine was the most important source of uranium available to Britain and it continued to use the ore in its atomic programme until 1953. Its entire output was covered by contracts between UMHK and the Combined Development Agency – the joint US–UK uranium procurement agency. These contracts were, in turn, covered by intergovernmental agreements between Belgium and the United States on one hand and the United States and Britain on the other.[39] The Treasury's stand was that Britain had secured its access to Congo uranium through these agreements and it saw no difficulty signing away its holding of Tanks.[40]

On 4 October 1950 the members of Tanks passed a resolution at an extraordinary general meeting agreeing to transfer the seat of control from London to a new registered address, 1 New Africa House, Union Avenue, Salisbury, Southern Rhodesia.[41] The transfer was finalised and came into effect on 11 March 1952 with some consequent relief from British taxation. As the board was now required to meet in Salisbury, Hely-Hutchinson took up residence in Salisbury and applied for Southern Rhodesian citizenship. In 1952 Sir Alexander Ulick (1889–1973) succeeded Hely-Hutchinson as Chairman (1952–7), and he also represented the company's interests on the boards of UMHK (1954–63) and BRC (1952–64). In the same year Sir Charles Geoffry Follows (1896–1983), the former Chief Secretary of Northern Rhodesia (1935–45) and the Financial Secretary of Hong Kong (1946–51), was nominated as Managing Director, and he also took up residence in Salisbury.

Stockholders of the Ordinary shares were the main beneficiaries of the changes in taxation resulting from the new domicile.[42] In Southern Rhodesia Income Tax extended only to income that was earned within the borders of the colony, with the sole exception of debenture interest received in Southern Rhodesia. Dividends from UMHK and BRC therefore could be passed through Tanks, without suffering a further tax charge, for ultimate distribution to shareholders.[43] No further relief was due to the stockholders under the unilateral relief provisions in the Finance Act of 1951 in respect of Belgian and Congolese taxes on the income from UMHK. The Act restricted relief in the case of foreign (as distinct from Dominion) taxes to taxes payable directly by the UK resident claiming the relief.[44]

The collapse of the Northern Rhodesian copper empire

That paragon of the late-nineteenth-century British imperialist, Cecil Rhodes, once argued that the British Empire is a 'bread and butter question'. The vast colonial empire that Britain had built since the late nineteenth century and the robust trade with the colonies that developed thereafter were first and foremost a source of national income that was manifested in improved economic performance in Britain. Did colonial trade then follow the flag? During the imperial era successive British governments encouraged the growth of British overseas trade.[45] The significance of the imperial-era trade for British economic performance has been intensely debated since the late nineteenth century. Most participants in the discussion, and particularly the most vocal critic of the British Empire, J.A. Hobson, opined that colonial trade did not provide the argued benefit but was in fact a vast waste of money that created wealth only for the likes of Rhodes – the rich capitalist class of financiers. Hobson calculated that despite the investment of a considerable amount of public interest, energy and money in seeking to secure colonial possessions and markets, not more than one-fortieth of British national income was derived from colonial trade. Besides, before pursuing a definite imperialist policy, Britain's foreign trade was advancing faster than its domestic trade, Hobson further argued. During the imperial era, Britain made its greatest advance in foreign trade with other industrial nations, in particular with France, Germany, Russia and the United States, and the colonial trade formed the smallest, the most uncertain and the least valuable part of her foreign trade.[46] The imperialist policy seemed to have no significant influence whatsoever on the volume and value of British foreign trade.

Imperial historians have also researched the topic extensively over the years and found that colonial trade did improve British economic performance when it came to certain colonial products. One notable example of successful colonial trade is the Northern Rhodesian copper trade. During the imperial era, the bulk of Northern Rhodesian copper imported into Britain was sold direct to consumers by producers' agents, at prices established at the LME. The Exchange provided a market where producers and consumers could sell their surpluses or made up deficiencies not covered by long-term contracts, and it also provided a market for buyers and sellers of copper who wished to hedge by means of forward sales and purchases. On certain occasions, copper producers, especially Northern Rhodesians, were even able to maintain the LME price for cash copper at a fixed level by buying up any cash copper that was directly offered for sale on the Exchange.

The smooth functioning of the imperial-era business system was facilitated by the fact that mining finance was directly linked to the City of London, the chief money market for mining and railways in Southern Africa, and also because the mining industry was controlled by a few gentlemen capitalists that built up a portfolio of investments, primarily in London-based mining and railway companies operating in the region. This business system also facilitated the supply of African labour at low wages and land for harvesting crops in the plantation economy that were geared towards supporting the mining industry. The system enabled the creation of a large copper mining industry in Northern Rhodesia and generated surplus profit for the industrialists and their financial sponsors, while providing a meagre subsistence for the rapidly urbanising working-class poor.[47]

It was in 1950 that an increasing interest on the part of mining companies to move their management and control abroad put the imperial-era business system in jeopardy and began to arouse official concern. Publicity about the tax advantages gained by company migration was greatly stimulated by the case of Tanks. Consequently there was much speculation in the press about which companies would be next to emigrate.[48] By the end of 1950 no fewer than 21 companies with a combined issued capital of £37 million had transferred their domicile abroad. The culmination point took place in October when Rhodesian Anglo American – a part of the Anglo American group and an important post-war copper producer for the British – announced that it wished to move its domicile to Northern Rhodesia.[49] On 1 January 1951 Rhokana Corporation and Nchanga Consolidated Copper Mines followed its lead and changed their domicile to Northern Rhodesia.[50]

Following this exodus, the Treasury decided to reintroduce full control of company migration. The first enactment in this direction was Section 36 of the Finance Act of 1951 which was followed by Section 468 of the Income Tax Act 1952. It was made unlawful for a company which was resident in Britain to remove its residence abroad; or transfer its business or part of its business abroad; or to permit certain transactions in shares or debentures of an overseas subsidiary without first getting a prior consent from the Treasury.[51] Restriction of freedom of movement within the Sterling Area was regarded by the Treasury as in principle a retrograde even if inescapable step. In 1951 when the relevant clause was drafted for the Finance Act, the Board of Trade and the Bank of England expressed their gravest misgivings. They both opposed the clause in principle, mainly on the grounds that it would in the long run strike at the root of London as a financial centre for international business, that it would provoke existing businesses which would otherwise have been content to remain there to seek permission to migrate before even worse befell them, and that it would discourage any new businesses which might have been thinking of locating their headquarters in London from doing so.

Neither the Bank of England nor the Board of Trade disputed the point that failure to enact a clause of the kind proposed might have led to some loss of revenue, but neither of them could suggest any alternative means of preventing this loss. They concluded that the prospect of permanent damage to the City as an international trading and financial centre outweighed the loss of revenue; it would indeed deter foreign interests from establishing new businesses in Britain; it would deter British companies from building up their business abroad by establishing overseas subsidiaries and by raising capital locally; and, finally, they concluded that it was in the interests of efficient management that the business of a company should be directed where the main operations were being carried out. The last point had less force in the post-war situation than in the past, however. The link between the central management in the City and the actual operations in Africa was now much closer than in the past because of the development of swift and frequent air transport. Besides, most of the mining companies in question had resided in the City for decades and they had capable and experienced managers on the spot.[52]

The Colonial Office, as guardians of the interests of the colonies, tended to assume that when a company operating in one of the dependent British territories desired to move its management and control to the place of its operations, the change of residence was beneficial to the colony concerned and ought therefore not to be obstructed by the government merely because it might have involved a loss of revenue to the Exchequer. Second, the Colonial Office argued that the control of company migration would probably have discouraged non-British private investments into the Colonial Office territories.[53]

The case of the Rhodesian Selection Trust (RST) group – comprising Rhodesian Selection Trust, Rhodesian Selection Trust (Services), Mufulira Copper Mines, Roan Antelope Copper Mines and Chibuluma Mines – which was seeking for legal grounds to enable their registration in Lusaka after the introduction of the Income Tax Act 1952, had considerable importance for the outcome of the debate because it involved a prospective loss of tax greater than any other case that had yet arisen.[54] The Board of Inland Revenue very strenuously opposed the migration of the RST group because it was unwilling to lose the revenue from the mining companies at a time when the Exchequer's receipts were causing anxiety.[55] The Treasury also deplored the tendency, and for many reasons besides the loss of revenue. Nevertheless, it was acknowledged that Northern Rhodesia was in a comparatively early period of its industrial development, and its copper mines were the most important part of its developing economy. RST and Rhodesian Anglo American were the chief employers of labour, and the two groups were also jointly responsible for Northern Rhodesia Power Corporation which supplied the necessary hydroelectric power to the copper mines. Rhodesian Anglo American was the biggest owner of the Wankie Colliery, and the supply of Wankie coal was of vital importance to the efficiency and development of their business and to the interest of Northern Rhodesia as well, and, no doubt, to the interests of the Commonwealth.[56]

RST and Rhodesian Anglo American were therefore the two most influential companies of Northern Rhodesia. The political future of the territory depended on the principle of partnership in the industrial relations of the Copperbelt and it was thought that the companies could not play their part properly until control was moved to Northern Rhodesia. The chief concern was therefore political. The Treasury estimated that there would be increasing criticism against 'absentee control' and that as trade unionism grew in Northern Rhodesia it would become more and more essential for the authority of the company to have efficient management on the spot.[57]

The Advisory Panel appointed by the Treasury recommended, mainly on political grounds, that permission should be given to the RST group to migrate to Lusaka. It was acknowledged that the transfer of registration probably meant some loss of profits from banking, insurance and possibly also the placing of contracts, though it was estimated that the general 'development advantages' probably outweighed those considerations, and that in the long run development of Northern Rhodesia should have a positive effect on the UK balance of payments from both old and new investments.[58]

In the post-war economic reality the capital for the development of the mines and of ancillary services was coming from the United States. In view of the American control of both groups, Rhodesian Anglo American and RST, and with investment markets in the City in the condition in which they were, it was in all likelihood going to be the American capital market that these groups would have to look to for fresh capital. Their capital needs were fulfilled more easily and cheaply if both groups were resident in Northern Rhodesia. It was therefore recommended by the Advisory Panel that when the desire to migrate genuinely arose from other causes than the weight of British taxation, it was probable that the least damage (ignoring the loss of revenue) would be done to the interests of Britain if companies were allowed to pursue their own best interests.

Ronald Prain, the Chairman and the Managing Director of the RST group and the leading figure of the British Overseas Mining Association, a lobby group concerned especially with questions of taxation,[59] assured the government that they had no intention of selling their copper to countries other than Britain, but bearing in mind the special relationship of the British with the Northern Rhodesian producers, Britain could not afford to take serious risks with its biggest source of supply providing two-thirds of all its copper. During the war the maximum production of copper had been vital to the British war effort, and the Copperbelt, taking Katangese and Northern Rhodesian production together, formed the most important single source of non-ferrous metals for the British Empire. Since 1946 the government had only a gentleman's agreement with the Northern Rhodesian copper producers that continued to supply to Britain virtually their whole output. On average 120,000 tons of Rhodesian copper per annum was shipped to Britain. This arrangement was very beneficial for Britain which was paying less than half the open market price for Rhodesian copper.[60]

The LME had been closed since the outbreak of war in 1939 but, with the possibility of its reopening now at the forefront of its agenda, the government could see that there might be an advantage in ensuring the maximum amount of copper and other mineral resources from the Copperbelt for the British markets through fixed long-term contracts. In 1952 two contracts for copper were made by the Ministry of Materials with the Rhokana Corporation and Nchanga Consolidated Copper Mines to sell their output to Britain. The two companies were expected to produce about 164,000 tons of copper, blister and refined, per annum, about 139,000 tons of which they would expect to sell for the Ministry. The copper was made available at Beira for shipment, and the price was based on the monthly quotation for copper in *The Engineering and Mining Journal* (c.i.f. British ports).[61]

In the pre-war era the LME was the only market on which surplus could be sold. In post-war years substantial quantities of surplus metals, which would otherwise have been sold on the LME, were absorbed in the US stockpile. Once the LME reopened for copper on 5 August 1953, the official turnover increased year on year and by 1958 (478,975 tons) the pre-war figures (475,000 tons in 1938) had been surpassed.[62] The number and volume of long-term contracts between producers and consumers increased, however, thereby reducing the quantity of metal sold through the Exchange.

Another factor that diminished City dominance over the copper trade was the fact that Britain's interest in Katanga copper was not normally very great. During the Second World War Katanga had been a vitally important source of copper. But by the time of the independence of the Congo in 1960, when some 280,000 tons of copper were imported to Britain, only about 3,000 tons of British imports came from Katanga. There were two factors which contributed to this situation. Much Katanga copper business was done outside the LME on long-term contracts between producers and consumers. UMHK normally sold its copper through Antwerp, some under fixed-price contracts, the remainder under *prix à fixé* contracts (*i.e.* the average market price of the past two months). About one-half of Katanga's production was exported in the form of blister, which could not be sold as such on the LME and which provided the staple raw material of the Belgian refiners. The other half of Katanga's production could have been offered for sale on the Exchange, however, but this would have imposed an intolerable strain on Northern Rhodesian producers. Instead of becoming an outlet for Katanga copper, the British Government tried to restore the pre-war stability of the copper trade by entering long-term contracts with the Northern Rhodesian producers and to guard its interests by relaxing its rulings over the desirability of foreign investments and the location of the seat of management.[63]

The long-term contracts with the Northern Rhodesian producers together with the booming economy temporarily managed to restore some of the former significance of the imperial-era copper trade. This turned out to be only a Pyrrhic victory, however. Ultimately several relaxations and exemptions to the law had to be made to appease the interests of the Northern Rhodesian copper producers. In May 1955 the RST group transferred their Head Office from Lusaka to Salisbury.[64] In 1961 Anglo American was lost completely due to the fact that South Africa became a republic and withdrew its close economic and other associations from the Commonwealth.[65] By the mid-1960s the British Empire had become an anachronism, and the former colonies were cutting their ties adrift from their former rulers one by one. In the Copperbelt the development began with the break-up of the Central African Federation and the independence of Zambia (Northern Rhodesia) in 1964 and culminated in the compulsory expropriation of a 51% holding of 25 British-owned mining and railway companies by the Zambian Government on 11 August 1969.[66]

The end of an era – Tanks' new dawn

> We respectfully request that in the forthcoming discussions with the Congolese Government, the special position of Tanks may be borne in mind and duly protected, particularly in view of the fact that approximately 40% of the issued Ordinary Share Capital of this company, which stood at present at £7,662,824, was owned by nationals of your country [Belgium].[67]
>
> But we have to recognise that the favoured foreign partner, Tanganyika Concessions, is regarded by Congolese and Belgians alike as a British Company and they are now in it above their necks.[68]

In June 1957 Captain Rt. Hon Charles Waterhouse, a Conservative party politician, former Member of Parliament and Junior Minister, was appointed to the board of Tanks as a director and he replaced Sir Alexander as Chairman in September of that year. Waterhouse's spell of nine years in the Chair saw the independence of the Congo, the Katanga secession, the break-up of the Central African Federation, the independence of Zambia and the Unilateral Declaration of Independence of Southern Rhodesia from Great Britain.[69] The other prominent Tanks directors of this turbulent era included Earl Grey (Charles Grey, 5th Earl Grey) who continued the long lineage of members of the Grey family in the company; the Earl of Selborne (Roundell Cecil Palmer, 3rd Earl of Selborne, 1887–1971), Conservative politician and a former government minister; and the Hon. Arthur Owen Crichton (1876–1970).

What was the impact of these decolonial upheavals on Tanks? The special position of Tanks in the Katangese mining industry was recognised during the Belgo-Congolese Economic, Financial and Social Conference in Brussels that took place in the course of April–June 1960. This conference was concerned with, amongst other issues, the probable dissolution of CSK. This dissolution would have left no agency for making the payments from UMHK to Tanks, so a specific agreement was signed on 23 June 1960 between UMHK and Tanks, whereby from that date onwards the former company was itself responsible for making payments directly to Tanks.[70]

During the Katanga secession (1960–3) Captain Waterhouse and Lord Selborne acted as key mediators between the British and American governments, whose differing interests in regards to the secession of Katanga might under certain circumstances have given rise to a conflict of interest. Whereas the Americans were primarily interested in staving off Soviet influence in the Congo and regarded it as an 'arena' of the Cold War, the British viewed the UN intervention in the 'internal' matters of the secessionist Katanga with scepticism and sought to minimise the possibility of disorder in the adjacent copper-producing Northern Rhodesia.[71] After Katanga broke away from the control of the Central Government, UM was able to mine more copper than ever under the benevolence of the Katanga Government and of President Tshombe, with the result that the royalty payable to Tanks amounted annually to several million pounds sterling. The Central Government was claiming that this money should have been paid to the Congo State as the legal heir of the Belgian Congo. President Tshombe on the other hand claimed that the Katanga Government should have some share of the royalty as all the copper was mined from Katanga. The board of Tanks wanted the Katanga Government to be awarded a share of the royalty. It took this view because the board felt that it was absurd to pay the royalty to Léopoldville, the capital 1,000 miles away from the mines, as opposed to Élisabethville, whose government had made it possible for the mining to continue.[72] After Tshombe rescinded all concession rights to foreign companies operating in Katanga in November 1964, Tanks wrote down the value of its investments by £1,600,000.[73]

On 18 November 1964, Tanks, a mining finance group with a book value of about £17 million, announced that it wished to move its headquarters from Salisbury to Nassau, in the Bahamas – an easy winner in the sterling leak competition due to its prominent location near the US capital market – to protect shareholders' interests from 'political risks' in Central Africa. 'The breakup of the [Central African] Federation and the lack of agreement on constitutional issues between the Governments of Great Britain and Rhodesia have introduced an element of doubt into the happy conditions under which the company has hitherto operated in Salisbury,' said the board's statement. With a large proportion of the company's shares being held by Belgian and French investors, the board felt it had a special responsibility to safeguard the interests of these shareholders from the said political risks. The statement emphasised, however, that the board had confidence in Southern Rhodesia's future and did not intend to dispose of its investments. It would 'continue to support and develop these holdings, which would be transferred to a subsidiary concern, Tanganyika Properties (Rhodesia)'.[74]

The British strategic interests in UM and the Benguela Railway had considerably diminished or even disappeared altogether over the years. The Shinkolobwe uranium mine had been all but worked out and had long ceased to be regarded as a future source of uranium for the British. Incidentally, the whole of the mineralised belt in Katanga and its extension into Zambia had been the subject of intensive uranium prospecting but the meagre results led the government to the conclusion that it was extremely unlikely that there would ever be a substantial uranium discovery. The Treasury felt that the future of mining and railway development in the Copperbelt would not be sufficient to justify continuing to insist on its rights under the agreement entered on 30 October 1950, whereby Tanks agreed not to dispose of certain interests in UMHK and BRC without first offering them to the Treasury. The Treasury therefore gave its consent to Tanks to transfer the whole of its interests to a new, wholly capitalised investment company, Tanganyika Holdings Limited, registered at Princes House, 95 Cresham Street in the heart of the City.[75] The change of Tanks' domicile to International Trust Building, Bank Lane, Nassau, Bahamas was finalised in June 1966. At the same juncture Lord Colyton replaced Captain Waterhouse as the Chairman of Tanks.[76] From then on Tanks was to exist as an offshore shell company, with the sole purpose of British tax-avoidance.

The decision to quit Salisbury and set up a new Head Office in the Bahamas affected a large number of Ordinary shareholders. So far as ownership of Ordinary shares is concerned Tanks was a 41.44% Belgian-, 32.71% British- and 20.78% French-owned company. The remaining roughly 5% of the Ordinary share capital was owned by shareholders representing diverse nationalities. Table 8.1 lists the owners of Tanks Ordinary stock by country in 1966.

Table 8.1 The owners of Tanganyika Concessions Ordinary stock by country, 1966 (*nominatiff* [N] and *au porteur* [P] stocks and %)

Great Britain	*N. and P. Stocks*	*% Share*
Kentan Gold Areas	N. 785,000	5.12
Anglo American Corporation	N. 444,614	2.90
Hambros Nominees	N. 92,274	0.60
Baring Nominees	N. 117,587	0.77
Rothschild Nominees	N. 27,385	0.18
Various	N. P. 3,546,627	23.14
Total	5,013,487	32.71
United States		
Depositary Nominees Inc.	N. 103,633	0.68
Various	N. P. 52,751	0.34
Total	156,384	1.02
Belgium		
SOFIGEN (The Albert Fisher Group)	N. 2,269,719	14.81
Banque Belge	N. 427,541	2.79
Cie du Katanga	N. 407,260	2.66
	P. 136,370	0.89
Société Générale de Belgique	N. 200,000	1.31
	P. 25,000	0.16
Société Minière du Bécéka	N. 200,000	1.31
	P. 50,000	0.32
Cie d'Afrique pour l'Industrie et la Finance	N. 100,000	0.65
Various	N. P. 2,534,357	16.54
Total	6,350,247	41.44
France		
SICOVAM	N. 3,029,972	19.77
Various	N. P. 155,371	1.01
Total	3,185,343	20.78
Diverse		
Various	N. P. 620,187	4.05
Grand total	15,325,648	100.00

Source: TNA, FCO 29/278, Tanks, Balance Sheet, n.d.

While Tanks was an offshore concern, it has sometimes been overlooked that it still held substantial assets in its equity. For nearly 60 years Tanks worked in close cooperation with SBG, CK and CSK with regard to the management of UMHK. Just prior to the dissolution of CSK in 1965 the situation was as follows. Tanks held 14.47% of shares in UM and 20.21% of voting rights. The other institutional owners were CK (1.49% of shares and 1% of votes) and SGB in Brussels (4.64% of shares and 6.94% of votes) and CSK (25.41% of shares and 35.73% of votes). Over half (53.99%) of the shares in UM were divided between 120,000 individual subscribers, mainly Belgian and French, who controlled 35.12% of the votes.[77] Each of the companies involved in or affiliated to UM had capital invested in some of the others, so that the interests of these companies were always heavily intertwined.[78] Amongst its many affiliations, Tanks was one of the owners of CK, which for its part owned one-third of CSK.

In June 1966 the Congo Government demanded that UM Brussels should transfer its domicile to Kinshasa and become a Congolese company by midnight on 1 January 1967. Subsequent negotiations took place in Kinshasa between UM and the Congo Government in which Lord Colyton played an important part. At the end of November 1966 the two parties reached a provisional agreement but last-minute demands from the Congolese, including a demand for control of the copper in the 'pipeline', were unacceptable to UM and negotiations were suspended on 4 December. On 15 December the Congolese announced that they would revoke all UM's concessions if it failed to move its headquarters to Kinshasa by midnight on 1 January 1967. Following its refusal all UM's assets in the Congo were expropriated by the Congo Government who announced that a new Congolese takeover-company Gécomin would be set up with a 60% holding by the Congolese Government. The remained 40% was allocated to international participation, with Tanks a prominent prospective candidate.[79]

Once the Congo Government expropriated UM's property, the Belgian Government was compelled to intervene, and Lord Colyton was in close touch with them and with the Americans. The British Government also kept in continuous contact with Lord Colyton who, as the Chairman of Tanks and a director of UM, played an important part in the negotiations in Kinshasa. In spite of his status as a UM director, the Congo Government appeared to place more trust in him than in the Belgian directors and seemed to have been prepared to some extent to accept him as a mediator.[80] Louis Wallef, the President of UM, was not noted for his negotiating skill, still less for understanding the mentality of the Congolese. In the good times UM had rarely acknowledged their British directors representing the interests of Tanks. Since bad times had hit them, it was noticeable how UM had rediscovered its British directors. On the other hand, Tanks may not have been directly involved in the compensation issue, but this did not make much of an impression on the Congolese. To their mind, Tanks, like UM, represented 'high finance', so it was to be distrusted and deplored.[81]

At a board meeting on 30 December 1966 Tanks decided that it could not accept the Congolese offer to subscribe for a share in the new government-held company which they were proposing to set up to take over the UM assets expropriated in the Congo. If it had done so it would have legalised the 'swag' and would have seriously jeopardised the relationship with UM.[82] The board was 'most anxious to preserve their long established and historical ties with the Congo together with their cordial relations with President Mobutu and the members of the Congolese Government'. But they found it impossible to accept participation in the new 'illegal' company – Gécomin. Quite apart from the moral issue involved in a unilateral act of confiscation without any proper compensation to other shareholders – who included many thousands of small private British, Belgian and French investors – it was felt by the board that to accept the Congolese offer to subscribe to shares of Gécomin would have done grave damage to the reputation of the company in financial and industrial circles throughout the world.[83]

There was an outstanding dispute over a compensation for the assets of Tanks in UM, which the Congo Government took over by a presidential decree on 1 January 1967. The owners of UM, acknowledging that it would probably prove almost impossible to secure compensation even by arbitration for themselves and their shareholders for their assets which had been expropriated by the Congolese, at the general meeting of shareholders held on 25 May 1967 declared as null and void the Congolese Government's shareholding and other rights in the company. At the same time, UM cancelled a number of historical but partly outmoded rights possessed by Tanks. These rights were:

1 A right to receive free dividend shares in any future increase of Ordinary share capital of UMHK
2 A right to a registered voting certificate, entitling Tanks to 134,016 votes at general meetings of UMHK
3 A right to preferential subscription in any future increase in share capital based on the above voting certificate
4 A right to receive 4% of any dividend distributed by UMHK in excess of 93,150,000 Frs.

The first three were clearly anomalies in the preconditions. The fourth right, however, since it was granted to Tanks in 1936, had produced substantial annual income. In 1967, when UM distributed a dividend of 200 Belgian francs per share, the sum Tanks received was £97,057. Tanks' directors, therefore, claimed some compensation for the cancellation of its prerogative. Compensation in the form of a cash lump sum of 198,151,000 Belgian francs was eventually agreed.[84]

Initially there were several cessations and a number of incidents during 1967 in Katanga copper traffic as a result of tensions between UM and the Congo Government. Tanks' consolidated account for the year showed a profit of £2,075,202, however, compared to £1,661,888 for the previous year. This increase was mainly attributable to the higher dividend declared by UM and to the devaluation of the pound sterling which took place in November 1967. The consolidated unappropriated profit amounted to £2,040,070 of which £199,734 was directly attributable to the owners of Tanks. The year 1967 showed a further increase in the net operating revenue of the Benguela Railway. The dividend for the year rose from 10% (Esc. 22$00) to 12.5% (Esc. 27$50).[85]

In 1969 the main assets of Tanks may be summarised as follows. Its assets included a 90% interest in BRC, a Lisbon-based company with an issued share capital of £3 million and debenture capital of £5.9 million, and a 17.4% holding in UM, a Brussels-based company operating mainly in refining and mining sectors in Belgium, Canada and Australia.[86] Besides this holding, Tanks had other relative minor investments in Britain, Rhodesia, Canada and Australia,[87] but insufficient liquid funds to play any important part in the development of the Central African region without selling part of its major holdings or raising additional capital.

Tanks, as a substantial shareholder of UM, was vitally interested in the compensation issue and certainly took the side of UM in its dispute with the Congolese Government. The company derived a very big annual income partly from its shareholding in UM, but also as a royalty on the copper sold, the greater part of which was liable to British taxation. We have no evidence that Tanks ever asked for the British Government's assistance over the compensation question. The government was not involved as a principal in the dispute regarding the appropriation of the assets of UM, and it wished to avoid any such involvement (*e.g.* by being associated with any *démarche* which the Belgian Government might have felt obliged to make at some stage).[88] The government's interest in this matter was indirect: first, Tanks' holding in UM meant that British business interests were indirectly involved in the dispute; second, the British were most concerned about the bearing they could have on British mining and railway interests in the Central African region and wanted to ensure that copper should continue to flow from the Copperbelt on to the world market; and finally, it was in the general Western interest that the Congolese economy should not collapse since a collapse would have inevitably led to further political instability in the Congo, and, by extension, possibly also in South-Central Africa as a whole.[89]

1970 was a year of reorientation for Tanks and its principal investment in BRC. Guerilla activities in Eastern Angola created security problems, while a lack of relations with the governments of the Congo and Zambia made a railway connection difficult. The Chinese were now about to begin construction of the Tanzania–Zambia Railway, linking eventually the port of Dar es Salaam in east Tanzania with the town of Kapiri Mposhi in Zambia, and Lord Colyton was worried about the effect this railway would have on the traffic on the Benguela Railway. There was already evidence that more Zambian as well as Congolese freight was travelling via the alternative and less expensive Dar es Salaam route.[90]

Tanks also had an interest in Rhodesian Anglo American, one of the 25 British mining and railway companies in which the Zambian Government had a 51% holding following a compulsory acquisition in 1969. In the face of losing everything and to nurture their cordial relations with the Zambian Government, Tanks was interested in seeking new investment opportunities in Zambia, especially in the emerging travel and tourism sectors, and to this end it formed a new subsidiary in Zambia – Zambesia Consolidated Finance – which absorbed the remaining interests of RHOKAT and ZE. Following this decision, local General Manager and Chief Executive Colonel Brooke-Fox, the former British military attaché in the Congo, opened an office in Lusaka on 4 June 1970. Tanks' Zambian connections were also assisted by an arrangement with Major Talmadge to act as a special messenger from London to Lusaka. It had been the original intention of Tanks to take over from Leopold Walford – a shipping company in which Tanks already held a 15% share – all its overseas travel and forwarding business. But following Lord Colyton's visit in London, which had aimed to improve Tanks' image in the City and to offer to act as an agent for Zambia, Colyton made some fairly disobliging remarks that British investors had lost their interest in Africa and 'didn't care a damn' about Zambia. At the same time the company was seeking a clearly visible investment in the tourism industry in the Congo, where it decided to take a 30% interest, the largest single interest (£250,000, of which £145,000 was in share capital and the rest in loan finance) being in Congo Safari, a firm being set up in Kinshasa with the participation of the Congolese Government (10%) and various foreign hotel and tourism interests. Tanks was also planning to build its own hotel chain in the Kivu Province and a hotel in Kinshasa to enhance its portfolio in the emerging safari and adventure travel business,[91] fuelled by the romance of gorgeous sunrises, sunsets and cloudless skies, and the pristine vast expanses of Central Africa – modernising the romance of Rider Haggard.[92]

Notes

1 Hutchinson and Martelli 1971, 9.
2 Brelsford 1950, 6.
3 TNA, T 236/2710, Considerations affecting a sale by the government, 2 February 1950.
4 TNA, T 317/624, Tanganyika Concessions Limited, Aide-mémoire à soumettre à Son Excellence M. le Ministre Spaak, 7 January 1965.
5 Hutchinson and Martelli 1971, 202–203.
6 Hutchinson and Martelli 1971, 225; Vellut 1983, 129–134.
7 *The Times* 18 December 1968; Rickard 1926, 13–21.
8 Hutchinson and Martelli 1971, 225.
9 Rönnbäck and Broberg 2019, 215, 217.
10 Hutchinson and Martelli 1971, 226, 124, 234.
11 Hutchinson and Martelli 1971, 208–209, 217, 235, 238, 241.
12 Mollan et al. 2022, 1603.
13 TNA, CO 537/4698, Tanganyika Concessions, Bank of England, 29 November 1949.
14 TNA, T 233/2162, Income Tax Act, 1952.

15 TNA, T 233/2162, Section 468, Income Tax Act, 1952.
16 Section 30 of the Exchange Control Act 1947.
17 Mollan et al. 2022, 1603, 1613–1614.
18 TNA, T 236/2710, The Bank of England, Tanganyika Concessions, 3 March 1949; T 236/2711, Extract from Hansard: 'Tanganyika Concessions, Ltd. (Shares Sale)', Written Answers, 27 April 1950, 118–119.
19 TNA, T 236/2710, Tanganyika Concessions, Balance Sheet, July 1948; Capitalisation of Tanks, 2 February 1950.
20 TNA, T 236/2710, Capitalisation of Tanks, 2 February 1950.
21 TNA, T 236/2710, Tanganyika Concessions Limited, 9 June 1949; 29 October 1949; Balance Sheet, July 1948.
22 TNA, T 236/2710, Tanganyika Concessions, Secretaries' Office, Inland Revenue, 9 December 1949.
23 *Financial Times* 20 December 1949; *Manchester Guardian* 27 April 1950.
24 Hutchinson and Martelli 1971, 241.
25 TNA, DO 35/3691, British Embassy, Lisbon, 25 March 1952; T 236/2710, Tanganyika Concessions, 3 November 1949.
26 TNA, DO 35/3691, a summary of a telephone conversation between Mr Hely-Hutchinson, the Chairman of the Tanks, and High Commissioner for the UK, Salisbury, Southern Rhodesia, 11 March 1952.
27 TNA, CO 537/4698, Tanganyika Concessions, Bank of England, 29 November 1949.
28 TNA, CO 537/4698, Tanganyika Concessions Ltd., Sale of shares, signed H.B., 28 October 1949; A.H. Poynton, 29 October 1949.
29 TNA, T 236/2710, Sir H. Wilson Smith, 11 June 1949.
30 TNA, T 236/2710, Colonial Office, 29 October 1949.
31 TNA, T 236/2710, Sir Henry Wilson Smith, Tanganyika Concessions, 30 January 1950.
32 TNA, T 233/2710, 'Tanganyika Concessions Limited', Bank of England, 29 November 1949; 'Tanganyika Concessions', Secretaries' Office, Inland Revenue, 9 December 1949.
33 *Financial Times* 4 August 1950. See also Hughes 2003, 594–596.
34 TNA, T 231/571, Minute sheet, 19 July 1950.
35 TNA, T 236/2712, Agreement between Tanganyika Concessions Limited and the Treasury, 30 October 1950.
36 TNA, T 236/2711, Agreement relating to Ordinary stock units of Tanganyika Concessions, Limited, 25 May 1950.
37 TNA, T 236/2711, Bank of England, A copy of an announcement released on 2 November 1950; DO, 35/3691, Mr Hely-Hutchinson to the Minister of Defence, 15 March 1952.
38 *Daily Worker* 26 April 1950; *Daily Mail* 28 April 1950; Hansard 9 May 1950.
39 TNA, T 236/2710, Bank of England, Tanganyika Concessions, 3 March 1949. See also Helmreich 1998, 29–61.
40 *Daily Mail* 28 April 1950.
41 *The Times* 5 October 1950.
42 *Financial Times* 4 August 1950.
43 TNA, T 236/2710, 'Tanganyika Concessions', Secretaries' Office, Board of Inland Revenue, 9 December 1949.
44 *The Times* 12 September 1950.
45 Hynes 1979, 9. See also Platt 1968.
46 Hobson 1901, 124–126.
47 Refer, for instance, to Butler 2007a; Butler 2007b.
48 *E.g. Financial Times* 2 March 1952.
49 TNA, T 233/2161, Chancellor of the Exchequer, Inland Revenue, 6 October 1952.
50 TNA, SUPP 14/29, Copper Agreement with Rhokana Corporation Ltd., Minute sheet 8/Non-F/301.

51 TNA, T 233, 2162, Board of Inland Revenue, Finance Bill, 1953.
52 TNA, T 233/2161, Chancellor of the Exchequer, Inland Revenue, 6 October 1952; Section 468, Income Tax Act, 1952. See also *Financial Times* 1 May 1950.
53 TNA, T 233/2161, Chancellor of the Exchequer, Inland Revenue, 6 October 1952; Section 468, Income Tax Act, 1952.
54 Mollan et al. 2022, 1612.
55 TNA, T 233/2162, Section 468, Income Tax Act, 1952.
56 TNA, FCO 25/117, Wankie Colliery Company Limited, n.d.
57 TNA, T 233/2161, Note of the reasons of the Advisory Panel's recommendation, 23 October 1952; Minute Sheet, Migration of copper companies, 31 October 1952.
58 TNA, T 233/2161, Note of the reasons of the Advisory Panel's recommendation, 23 October 1952; T 233/2162, Sir Leslie Rowan, Migration of companies from the U.K., 17 December 1952. See also Mollan et al. 2022.
59 Butler 2007a, 460.
60 TNA, SUPP 14/29, Minute Sheet A.S./M.3.; Mr. E.W. Jones, Payment for Rhokana and Nchanga Copper, 16 November 1951.
61 TNA, SUPP 14/29, Notes of a meeting between the representatives of the Ministry of Materials and the Rhokana/N'Changa copper companies, 30 October 1951; Standard Clauses, 30 November 1946.
62 It should be noted, however, that the official tonnages, published weekly by the Exchange and unofficially reported daily in some organs of the press, do not represent the whole of the business carried out by the Exchange members, since dealers could have merged orders (TNA, FO 371/161517, The London Metal Exchange, July 1961).
63 TNA, FO 371/161517, J.K.T. Frost, Board of Trade to G.E. Millard, Foreign Office, 3 and 10 August 1962; The London Metal Exchange, July 1961.
64 TNA, DO 35/3691, Mr A.W. Gaminara to Mr Morgan, Lusaka, 5 March 1955.
65 TNA, AB 16/3112, Anglo American Corporation of South Africa, Chairman's Statement, 1961.
66 TNA, FCO 29/278, T.J. O'Brien, Financial Policy and Aid Department, Countries in financial default to the UK, 3 March 1969. See also Ndulo 1974, 55–73; Libby and Woakes 1980, 33–50.
67 TNA, T 317/624, Aide-mémoire à soumettre à Son Excellence M. le Ministre Spaak, 7 January 1965.
68 TNA, FO 371/187758, Telegram No. 366, British Embassy, Kinshasa to Foreign Office, London, 24 December 1966.
69 TNA, FCO 29/278, Congo (Kinshasa): Manufacturing; Industries & Natural Resources: Union Minière, 6 March 1969.
70 TNA, T 317/624, Aide-mémoire à soumettre à Son Excellence M. le Ministre Spaak, 7 January 1965.
71 Kent 2013, 122, 128. See also James 2000, 152–168.
72 TNA, FO 371/155039, The Earl of Selborne to The Earl of Home, 9 December 1960. See also Kent 2010, 89–90, 101–104.
73 *Telegraph* 5 December 1964.
74 *The Times* 19 November 1964; TNA, T 317/624, Holmes, Son & Pott, Solicitors to the Treasury, 30 September 1964.
75 TNA, T 317/624, Holmes, Son & Pott, Solicitors to the Treasury, 30 September 1964; Treasury Chambers to Bank of England, 14 October 1964.
76 *The Times* 18 December 1968.
77 TNA, FO 371/176725, Lord Clitheroe and Captain Waterhouse, 27 February 1964; FO 371/187757, The Annual General Meeting of the Union Minière du Haut-Katanga on May 26, 1966, Reports of the Board of Directors Regarding 59th Financial Year 1965; *Essor du Katanga*, 26 May 1966; Radmann 1978, 28–29; Kent 2010, 81, 92, 101–102; Young and Turner 1985, 284.

78 For further information, see Ainslie 1962; Radmann 1978.
79 See Chapter 7.
80 TNA, FCO 25/120, Telegram 88, Union Minière, British Embassy, Kinshasa to Foreign Office, London, 19 and 31 January 1967.
81 TNA, FO 371/187757, Peter Mennell, British Consulate, Lubumbashi, 9 October 1966.
82 TNA, FCO 25/120, Telegram 88, Union Minière, British Embassy, Kinshasa to Foreign Office, London, 19 and 31 January 1967.
83 TNA, FO 371/187758, Telegram No. 502, Brussels to Foreign Office, London, Lord Colyton to President Mobutu, 30 December 1966; Telegram No. 1266, 31 December 1966.
84 *The Times* 18 December 1968.
85 *The Times* 18 December 1968.
86 TNA, FCO 29/278, Loans of Congo (Kinshasa), 7 March 1969.
87 *The Economist* 31 August 1968.
88 TNA, FO 371/187758, Reflections on the negotiations now in progress between UM and Congolese gov., British Consulate, Lubumbashi, 19 October 1966.
89 TNA, FCO 25/120, Telegram 88, Union Minière, British Embassy, Kinshasa to Foreign Office, London, 19 and 31 January 1967.
90 TNA, FCO 45/609, Tanganyika Concessions Ltd., British High Commission, Lusaka to Foreign Office, London, 30 May 1970.
91 TNA, FCO 45/609, Tanganyika Concessions Ltd., British High Commission, Lusaka to Foreign Office, London, 14 July 1970; 5 August 1970.
92 These new business ventures augmented well and in 1973 the dividend yield for Zambesia Consolidated Finance was £127,263 (*The London Gazette* 6 July 1973, 7853; *The Edinburg Gazette* 6 July 1973, 788).

References

Ainslie, R. (1962) *The Unholy Alliance: Salazar, Verwoed, Welensky*, Anti-Apartheid Movement, London.

Brelsford, W.V. (1950) 'Editorial', *The Northern Rhodesia Journal*, I, 5–6.

Butler, L.J. (2007a) 'Business and British Decolonisation: Sir Ronald Prain, the Mining Industry and the Central African Federation', *Journal of Imperial and Commonwealth History*, 35:3, 459–484.

Butler, L.J. (2007b) *Copper Empire: Mining and the Colonial State in Northern Rhodesia, c.1930–64*, Palgrave Macmillan, Houndmills, Basingstoke.

Daily Mail (28 April 1950) 'Cripps Confirms Scoop on Uranium'; (28 April 1950) 'Bongo, Bongo, Bongo. The Uranium in the Congo'.

Daily Worker (26 April 1950) 'Treasury Signs Away Uranium Mines to America'.

The Economist (31 August 1968) 'Belgium and the Congo's New Dawn?'.

The Edinburg Gazette (6 July 1973) 788.

Essor du Katanga (26 May 1966) 'L'Assemblée générale annuelle des actionnaires de l'U.M.H.K. (Exercice 1965)'.

Financial Times (20 December 1949) '"Tanks" Again Active'; (1 May 1950) 'Not for Rider Haggard'; (4 August 1950) 'Tanganyika Concessions' Reorganisation Plan'; (2 March 1952) 'Tax Threat to U.K. Metal Supplies'.

Hansard (9 May 1950) 'Tanganyika Concessions (Shares Sale)', vol. 475, col. 202–203.

Helmreich, J.E. (1998) *United States Relations with Belgium and the Congo, 1940–1960*, University of Delaware Press, Newark.

Hobson, J.A. (2 November1901) 'The Commercial Value of Imperialism', *Speaker*, V:109, 124–126.

Hughes, M. (2003) 'Fighting for White Rule in Africa: The Central African Federation, Katanga, and the Congo Crisis, 1958–1965', *The International History Review*, 25:3, 592–615.

Hutchinson, R. and Martelli, G. (1971) *Robert's People: The Life of Sir Robert Williams Bart. 1860–1938*, Chatto & Windus, London.

Hynes, W.G. (1979) *The Economics of Empire: Britain, Africa and New Imperialism 1870–95*, Longman, London.

James, A. (2000) 'Britain, the Cold War, and the Congo Crisis, 1960–63', *The Journal of Imperial and Commonwealth History*, 28:3, 152–168.

Kent, J. (2010) *America, the UN and Decolonisation: Cold War Conflict in the Congo*, Routledge, London.

Kent, J. (2013) 'Anglo-American Diplomacy and the Congo Crisis, 1960–1963: The Not So Special Relationship' in J.W. Young, E.G.H. Pedaliu and M.D. Kandiah eds. *Britain in Global Politics*, Vol. 2: *From Churchill to Blair*, Palgrave Macmillan, Houndmills, Basingstoke, 119–138.

Libby, R.T. and Woakes, M.E. (1980) 'Nationalization and the Displacement of Development Policy in Zambia', *African Studies Review*, 23:1, 33–50.

The London Gazette (6 July 1973) 46023, 7853.

Manchester Guardian (27 April 1950) 'The Tanganyika Story'.

Mollan, S., Frank, B. and Tennent, K. (2022) 'Changing Corporate Domicile: The Case of the Rhodesian Selection Trust Companies', *Business History*, 64:9, 1600–1622.

The National Archives of the UK (TNA), UK Atomic Energy Authority (AB); Colonial Office (CO); Dominions Office (DO); Foreign and Commonwealth Office (FCO); Foreign Office (FO); Ministry of Supply and successors (SUPP); Treasury (T).

Ndulo, M. (1974) 'The Nationalization of the Zambian Copper Industry', *Zambia Law Journal*, 6, 55–73.

Platt, D.C.M. (1968) *Finance, Trade and Politics in British Foreign Policy 1815–1914*, Clarendon Press, Oxford.

Radmann, W. (1978) 'The Nationalization of Zaire's Copper: From Union Minière to Gecamines', *Africa Today*, 25:4, 25–47.

Rickard, T.A. (2 January1926) 'A Journey to South Africa – VI', *Engineering and Mining Journal*, 121:1, 13–21.

Rönnbäck, K. and Broberg, O. (2019) *Capital and Colonialism: The Return on British Investments in Africa 1869–1969*, Palgrave Macmillan, Cham, Switzerland.

Section 30 of the Exchange Control Act (1947) Retrieved 8 May 2024 from https://www.legislation.gov.uk/ukpga/1947/14/pdfs/ukpga_19470014_en.pdf.

Telegraph (5 December 1964) 'Tshombe Seizes Mine Rights'.

The Times (12 September 1950) '"Tanks" Income and Taxation'; (5 October 1950) '"Tanks" Scheme Passed'; (19 November 1964) 'Investment Group Quits Rhodesia'; (18 December 1968) 'The Annual General Meeting of Tanganyika Concessions Limited, 23 January 1969'.

Vellut, J.-L. (1983) 'Mining in the Belgian Congo' in D. Birmingham and P.M. Martin eds. *History of Central Africa*, Vol. 2, Longman, London and New York, 126–162.

Young, C. and Turner, T. (1985) *The Rise and Decline of the Zairean State*, The University of Wisconsin Press, Madison.

Index

For Product Safety Concerns and Information please contact our EU
representative GPSR@taylorandfrancis.com
Taylor & Francis Verlag GmbH, Kaufingerstraße 24, 80331 München, Germany

www.ingramcontent.com/pod-product-compliance
Ingram Content Group UK Ltd.
Pitfield, Milton Keynes, MK11 3LW, UK
UKHW020006200926
475702UK00015B/2505
* 9 7 8 1 0 3 2 1 6 1 7 7 8 *